CUET

(UG) & Integrated PG

2022

Accountancy

DU | BHU | JNU | JMI | TISS & etc.

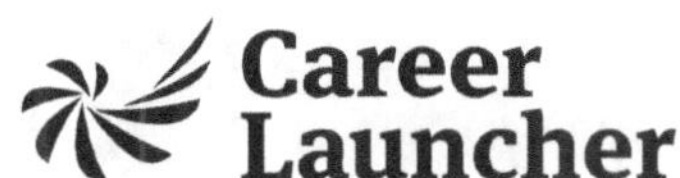

Title : CUET 2022 : Accountancy

Language : English

Editor's Name : Akshika Gupta

Copyright © : 2022 CLIP

Typeset & Published by :

Career Launcher Infrastructure (P) Ltd.

A-45, Mohan Cooperative Industrial Area, Near Mohan Estate Metro Station, New Delhi - 110044

Marketed by :

G.K. Publications (P) Ltd.

Plot No. 9A, Sector-27A, Mathura Road, Faridabad, Haryana-121003

ISBN : **978-93-95101-19-6**

Printer's Details: Printed in India, New Delhi.

CONTENTS

About CUET

A year ago, it would have been unimaginable that cut-offs in Delhi University would skyrocket to 100% for some of the undergraduate courses! While DU has always been known for its high cut-offs, there are several other universities where the story is no different.

However, the National Education Policy 2020 (NEP) aims to do away with the tyranny of the ever-rising cut-offs by introducing a Common Entrance Test for all the Central Universities in the country. NEP not only proposes a holistic approach in evaluating the students by giving them the option to select subjects based on their interest, but it also aims to simplify the process of admission to higher-education institutes.

To start with, there would be a Common Entrance Test for all the Central Universities, which would be conducted twice a year from 2022. While this might sound like a new concept to many, the fact is, there is already a CUET, which is conducted for the Central Universities established in or after 2009. As many as 14 of them already admit students based on their performance in the entrance test. The CUET scores are also accepted by four state universities of the country.

The proposed CUET aims to assess conceptual understanding and application of knowledge; and also, to lessen the burden of appearing in multiple tests.

CUET Eligibility

Getting into a premier University is every student's dream. The brand value of the University not only facilitates securing a seat in a master's program in a national/international institute, but also helps in getting job offers through campus placements.

Entry to a Central University, in most cases earlier, was based on merit, i.e., marks secured in Class XII Board exams. However, from the academic year 2021, all Central Universities will also consider the CUET score for admissions into their Undergraduate programs.

CUET 2022: Eligibility Criteria

While the official criteria will be learnt once the CUET 2021 notification is released, the stipulations are not expected to change much from those of previous years.

- A candidate must have passed Class XII (10+2) or equivalent from a recognized education Board.
- If the respective Board awards grades (or CGPA), the conversion factor given by the Board must be used to compute the percentage of marks.
- Candidates, who have completed their Class XII in 2021, and have passed the Board exams, will also be eligible to apply for CUET 2022.

Eligibility: Class XII Students

While CUET is for students who have passed the Class XII (or equivalent) Board exams, any student who is appearing for the Class XII Board exam in 2022 is also eligible to apply for CUET 2021. The candidate would be required to produce the marksheets and relevant certificates as mandated by the participating Central University, and follow the timelines provided for admissions.

Key Points

- Each participating Central University is free to decide its own eligibility criteria for admissions.
- The weightages for CUET and Class XII Board exam results(if, applicable) will be at the sole discretion of the Central University, to which admission is being sought.
- As of date, CUET does not have an age limit. However, Central Universities can fix minimum & maximum age limit for admissions to all (or any) of the programs on offer.

Reservation of Seats

As CUET is an entrance exam for admissions to Undergraduate courses at the Central Universities, which have been established under an Act of the Parliament, each Central University must follow the norms set by the Government of India, with respect to intake and reservation of seats.

Generally, the following break-up is followed:

Category	Reservation
Scheduled Castes	15%
Scheduled Tribes	7.5%
Other Backward Classes (Non-Creamy)	27%
Persons with Disability	5%

Some institutions might even have provisions for the Economically Weaker Sections, which can account for 10% of the total seats. These EWS seats are carved out from the Open Category.

To avail of the reservation benefit based on caste (or any other category as specified), a candidate must be able to produce valid documents/certificates to support such claims.

Conclusion

It is essential for every candidate to check the validity of their candidature for CUET, as well as the Central University he/she is applying to. The candidate should be aware of the documents that might be required while applying for the exam, or during the admissions.

CUET 2022 notification is expected in March 2022, and registration is also going to start then.

CUET: Exam Pattern

Examination Structure for CUET (UG) -2022:

CUET (UG) –2022 will consist of the following 4 Sections:

Section IA –13 Languages
Section IB –19 Languages
Section II –27 Domain specific Subjects
Section III –General Test

Choosing options from each Section is not mandatory. Choices should match the requirements of the desired University.

Broad features of CUET (UG) -2022 are as follows:

Section	Subjects/ Tests	Questions to be Attempted	Question Type	Duration
Section IA – Languages	There are 13* different languages. Any of these languages may be chosen.	40 questions to be attempted out of 50 in each language	Language to be tested through Reading Comprehension (based on different types of passages–Factual, Literary and Narrative, [Literary Aptitude and Vocabulary]	45 Minutes for each language
Section IB – Languages	There are 19** Languages. Any other language apart from those offered in Section I A may be chosen.			
Section II - Domain	There are 27*** Domains specific subjects being offered under this Section. A candidate may choose a maximum of Six (06) Domains as desired by the applicable University/Universities.	40 Questions to be attempted out of 50	• Input text can be used for MCQ Based Questions • MCQs based on NCERT Class XII syllabus only	
Section III-General Test	For any such undergraduate programme/ programmes being offered by Universities where a General Test is being used for admission.	60 Questions to be attempted out of 75	• Input text can be used for MCQ Based Questions • General Knowledge, Current Affairs, General Mental Ability, Numerical Ability, Quantitative Reasoning (Simple application of basic mathematical concepts arithmetic/algebra geometry/mensuration/s tat taught till Grade 8), Logical and Analytical Reasoning	

*** Languages (13):** Tamil, Telugu, Kannada, Malayalam, Marathi, Gujarati, Odiya, Bengali, Assamese, Punjabi, English, Hindi and Urdu
**** Languages (19):** *French, Spanish, German, Nepali, Persian, Italian, Arabic, Sindhi, Kashmiri, Konkani, Bodo, Dogri, Maithili, Manipuri, Santhali, Tibetan, Japanese, Russian, Chinese.*
***** Domain Specific Subjects (27):** 1. Accountancy/ Book Keeping 2. Biology/ Biological Studies/ Biotechnology/Biochemistry 3. Business Studies 4. Chemistry 5. Computer Science/ Informatics Practices 6. Economics/ Business Economics 7. Engineering Graphics 8.Entrepreneurship 9. Geography/Geology 10. History 11. Home Science 12.Knowledge Tradition and Practices of India 13. Legal Studies 14. Environmental Science 15. Mathematics 16. Physical Education/ NCC /Yoga 17.Physics 18.Political Science 19. Psychology 20. Sociology 21. Teaching Aptitude 22. Agriculture 23. Mass Media/ Mass Communication 24. Anthropology 25. Fine Arts/Visual Arts (Sculpture/ Painting)/Commercial Arts, 26. Performing Arts – (i) Dance (Kathak/ Bharatnatyam/Oddisi/ Kathakali/Kuchipudi/ Manipuri (ii) Drama- Theatre (iii) Music General (Hindustani/ Carnatic/ RabindraSangeet/ Percussion/ Non-Percussion), 27. Sanskrit *[For all Shastri (Shastri 3 years/ 4 years Honours) Equivalent to B.A./B.A. Honours courses i.e. Shastri in Veda, Paurohitya (Karmakand), Dharamshastra, Prachin Vyakarana, Navya Vyakarana, Phalit Jyotish, Siddhant Jyotish, Vastushastra, Sahitya,Puranetihas, Prakrit Bhasha,Prachin Nyaya Vaisheshik, Sankhya Yoga, Jain Darshan, Mimansa, AdvaitaVedanta, Vishihstadvaita Vedanta, Sarva Darshan, a candidate may choose Sanskrit as the Domain].*

- A Candidate can choose a maximum of **any 3 languages** from Section IA and Section IB taken together. (One of the languages chosen needs to be in lieu of Domain specific subjects)
- Section II offers 27 Subjects, out of which a candidate may choose a **maximum of 6 Subjects**.
- Section III comprises **General Test.**
- For choosing Languages (upto 3) from Section IA and IB and a maximum of 6 Subjects from Section II and General Test under Section III, the Candidate must refer to the requirements of his/her intended University.

Mode of the Test	Computer Based Test-CBT
Test Pattern	Objective type with Multiple Choice Questions
Medium	13 languages *(Tamil, Telugu, Kannada, Malayalam, Marathi, Gujarati, Odiya, Bengali, Assamese, Punjabi, English, Hindi and Urdu)*
Syllabus	**Section IA & IB:** Language to be tested through Reading Comprehension (based on different types of passages–Factual, Literary and Narrative [Literary Aptitude & Vocabulary]
	Section II : As per NCERT model syllabus as applicable to Class XII only
	Section III : General Knowledge, Current Affairs, General Mental Ability, Numerical Ability, Quantitative Reasoning (Simple application of basic mathematical concepts arithmetic/algebra geometry/mensuration/stat taught till Grade 8), Logical and Analytical Reasoning

Level of questions for CUET (UG) -2022:

All questions in various testing areas will be benchmarked at the level of Class XII only. Students having studied Class XII Board syllabus would be able to do well in CUET (UG) – 2022.

Number of attempts:

If any University permits students of previous years of class XII to take admission in the current year also, such students would also be eligible to appear in CUET (UG) – 2022.

Choice of Languages and Subjects:

Generally the languages/subjects chosen should be the ones that a student has opted in his latest Class XII Board examination. However, if any University permits any flexibility in this regards, the same can be exercised under CUET (UG) -2022 also. Candidates must carefully refer to the eligibility requirements of various Central Universities in this regard. Moreover, if the subject to be studied in the Undergraduate course is not available in the list of **27 Domain Specific Subject** being offered, the Candidate may choose the Subject closest to his choice for e.g. For Biochemistry the candidate may choose Biology.

Candidates are advised to visit the NTA CUET (UG)-2022 official website **https://cuet.samarth.ac.in/** for latest updates regarding the Examination.

CUET Syllabus

CUET Syllabus

Before you start your preparation for any entrance exam, it is important to understand the syllabus. Otherwise, your prep will be directionless, and you might be left wondering where things might have gone wrong!

With more than 1.68 lakh seats on offer for the undergraduate courses at the 54 Central Universities, CUET is one the most competitive examinations. For this very reason, while preparing for the exam, you will need to adopt a structured approach. And in doing that, understanding the syllabus is a critical step.

CUET 2022 Overview

CUET 2022 will be a Computer-Based Test (CBT), commonly referred to as an online exam. However, there is a difference between the two terms: CBT and online. In CBT, the questions are kept constant and simply presented in an online format; whereas in an Online Test, questions are stored as a bank, and the system decides which questions are to be presented to the candidate, based on a pre-defined logic.

CUET 2022 is likely to be a General Ability Test, with focus on English Language, Numerical Ability, Logical & Analytical Reasoning, along with General Awareness and Current Affairs.

CUET 2022 Syllabus

The CUET 2022 exam pattern gives a good idea about what is in store for the candidate and how one needs to prepare for the exam.

- **English Language:** The questions in this section will test one's proficiency in the language, based on comprehension passages, fundamentals of grammar, and vocabulary. In the Comprehension section, candidates will be evaluated on their understanding of a passage and its central theme, meanings of words used therein, etc. The Grammar section entails correcting grammatically incorrect sentences, filling of blanks in sentences with appropriate words, etc. Questions on synonyms & antonyms will check one's command over English vocabulary.
- **Numerical Ability:** Questions on Numerical Ability will test the candidate's knowledge of elementary mathematics. Areas like arithmetic, number system, basics of algebra, and modern maths will be central to these types of questions.
- **Logical & Analytical Reasoning:** This section tests the candidate's ability to identify patterns & logical links, and rectify illogical arguments. It can include a variety of Logical Reasoning questions, such as those on syllogisms, logical sequences, analogies, etc., along with Analytical Reasoning questions on series, directions, clocks & calendars, arrangements, and puzzles to name a few.
- **General Awareness and Current Affairs:** The General Awareness section includes static general knowledge, while questions on Current Affairs will gauge a candidate's knowledge of national & international current affairs.

CUET 2022 may or may not have a section on subject knowledge. Once the exam notification is out in March, there will be more clarity on this matter.

While there is no syllabus explicitly mentioned by CUET, the broad idea is always presented. One must look at the previous years' papers and solve the sample papers available to form a basic understanding.

About University of Delhi

University of Delhi (commonly known as DU) was established in 1922 and is one of the largest Universities in the country. With 16 faculties, 86 academic departments, 90 colleges and 540 programs on offer, Delhi University is no doubt one of the sought-after University in the country.

With 1, 96,000 students enrolled in UG programs, Delhi University is a valued university and constantly ranked among the top in the country. DU bagged 11th Rank in NIRF 2020 and ranked 6th in QS India Rankings 2020. The University has two Campuses: North and South.

DU UG Programs

Delhi University offers several programs at the undergraduate level. With more than 60 constituent colleges, the Delhi University offers many undergraduate courses.

Please refer to the table below for the important undergraduate courses offered by the DU and the intake across each program.

Program	Intake
B. A (Pass)	11249
B. A (Hons) Geography	788
B. A (Hons) Economics	2754
B. A (Hons) History	2791
B. A (Hons) Political Science	3657
B. A (Hons) Sociology	596
B. A (Hons) Psychology	670
B. A (Hons) Applied Psychology	252
B. A (Hons) Social Work	133
B. A (Hons) Philosophy	783
B. A (Hons) English	2886
B. A (Hons) Hindi	2829
B. A (Hons) Sanskrit	1407
B. A (Hons) Punjabi	214
B. A (Hons) Urdu	207
BA(Hons) French	49

BA(Hons) German	49
BA(Hons) Spanish	49
BA(Hons) Italian	49

B. Com (Hons)	7953
B.Com (Pass)	7854
Program	Intake
B.Sc. (H) Biomedical Science	162
B.Sc. (H) Botany	937
B.Sc. (H) Chemistry	1487
B.Sc. (H) Computer Science	1265
B.Sc. (H) Electronics	624
B.Sc. (H) Mathematics	2428
B.Sc. (H) Physics	1659
B.Sc. (H) Zoology	944
B.Sc. Life Sciences	1515
B.Sc. Physical Science with Chemistry	703
B.Sc. Physical Science with Computer Science	553
B.Sc. Physical Science with Electronics	247
B. Sc (Hons.) Statistics	476
B. Sc. (Prog.) Applied Physical Science Industrial Chemistry	96
B.Sc. (Hons.) Home Science	900
B. Sc. (Hons.) Psychology	57
B.Sc. (H) Food Technology	179
B.Sc. (H)Instrumentation	99
B.Sc. (H) Microbiology	238
B.Sc. (H) Polymer Science	59
B.SC. Mathematical Science	224
B.SC. (Hons.) Biochemistry	146
B.SC. Industrial Chemistry	78
B.Sc. (Prog.) Physical Science	940
B.SC. (Hons.) Geology	98

DU UG Programs Eligibility:

As the University offers multiple programs and separate intake for male and female candidates, it is important to check the university official website regularly to keep oneself updated about the eligibility for each program, which can change.

DU UG Admissions:

Until 2021, Delhi University admitted students on the basis of class XII marks. From the academic year 2022, admissions to UG programs offered Delhi University will be based on CUET. CUET will be a common entrance for admissions to UG programs offered by all the Central Universities in the country.

Delhi University UG Programs Reservation:

DU being a Central University offers reservations in admissions according to central government rules.

Schedule Caste (SC): 15% of the total seats are reserved for students who belong to SC category.

Schedule Tribe (ST): 7.5% of the total seats are reserved for students belonging to ST Category.

Other Backward Classes (OBC): 27% of the total intake is reserved for students from Other Backward Classes (OBC), excluding those from creamy layer.

Economically Weaker Section (EWS): The University has reserved 10% seats for EWS category, in accordance with the directive of Ministry of Education.

Persons with Disability (PWD): 5% of the seats are reserved on horizontal basis for students from PWD category.

About BHU

Banaras Hindu University (BHU), situated in the holy city of Varanasi, was founded by Pandit Madan Mohan Malviya in cooperation with Dr. Annie Besant, in 1916 under the act of Parliament-B.H.U Act, 1915. BHU, which is a Central University, comprises of 6 Institutes, 14 Faculties, 144 academic departments, and 4 Inter-disciplinary centers, spread over 1300 acres. The University consists of 15,000 students, 1700 teachers and 8000 non-teaching staff.

BHU was ranked 3rd among the Universities in India in 2020. According to university submissions for NIRF 2021, BHU has 10, 585 students pursuing UG programs, of which 236 students are foreign nationals.

BHU UG Programs

BHU offers a host of undergraduate programs including medical and engineering. Through its various faculties, BHU offers a range of programs which caters to students learning abilities. The University along with its main campus, also offers the undergraduate courses from the following colleges: Mahila Mahavidyalaya (MMV); Arya Mahila Post Graduate College (AMPGC), Vasant Kanya Mahavidyalaya (VKM); Vasanta College for Women (VCW); DAV Post Graduate College (DAVPGC) and Rajiv Gandhi South Campus (RGSC).

Please refer to the table below for the important undergraduate courses offered by BHU and the intake across each program/campuses.

Faculty of Arts				
Course	Campus	Intake	Status	Duration
B.A (Hons) Arts	Faculty of Arts	765	Co-Ed	3 Years
	Mahila Mahavidyalaya	286	Women	3 Years
	Arya Mahila Post Graduate College	383	Women	3 Years
	Vasant Kanya Mahavidyalaya	286	Women	3 Years
	Vasanta College for Women	412	Women	3 Years
	DAV Post Graduate College	309	Co-Ed	3 Years
Faculty of Social Sciences				
Course	Campus	Intake	Status	Duration
B.A (Hons) Social Sciences [incl. B. A (Hons) Economics]	Faculty of Social Sciences	573	Co-Ed	3 Years
	Mahila Mahavidyalaya	193	Women	3 Years
	Arya Mahila Post Graduate College	383	Women	3 Years
	Vasant Kanya Mahavidyalaya	249	Women	3 Years
	Vasanta College for Women	210	Women	3 Years
	DAV Post Graduate College	326	Co-Ed	3 Years

Faculty of Commerce				
Course	Campus	Intake	Status	Duration
B. Com (Hons)	Faculty of Commerce	286	Co-Ed	3 Years
	Vasant Kanya Mahavidyalaya	96	Women	3 Years
	Arya Mahila Post Graduate College	96	Women	3 Years
	DAV Post Graduate College	227	Co-Ed	3 Years
	Rajiv Gandhi South Campus, Mirzapur	114	Co-Ed	3 Years
B. Com (Hons) Financial Markets Management	Faculty of Commerce	62	Co-Ed	3 Years
	Rajiv Gandhi South Campus, Mirzapur	62	Co-Ed	3 Years
Institute of Science				
Course	Campus	Intake	Status	Duration
B.Sc (Hons) Maths Group	Faculty of Science	573	Co-Ed	3 Years
	Mahila Mahavidyalaya	96	Women	3 Years
B.Sc (Hons) Bio Group	Faculty of Science	383	Co-Ed	3 Years
	Mahila Mahavidyalaya	193	Women	3 Years

Faculty of Visual Arts				
Course	Campus	Intake	Status	Duration
B.F.A (Bachelor of Fine Arts)	Faculty of Visual Arts	96	Co-Ed	4 Years
Faculty of Arts				
Bachelor of Vocation (Retail and Logistics Management)	Rajiv Gandhi South Campus	62	Co-Ed	3 Years
Bachelor of Vocation (Hospitality & Tourism Management)	Rajiv Gandhi South Campus	62	Co-Ed	3 Years
Bachelor of Vocation (Fashion Designing anc Event Management)	Rajiv Gandhi South Campus	62	Co-Ed	3 Years
Bachelor of Vocation (Modern Office Management)	Rajiv Gandhi South Campus	62	Co-Ed	3 Years
Bachelor of Vocation (Food Processing & Management)	Rajiv Gandhi South Campus	62	Co-Ed	3 Years
Bachelor of Vocation (Medical Lab. & Technology)	Rajiv Gandhi South Campus	62	Co-Ed	3 Years

BHU UG Programs Eligibility:

Each of the courses have different eligibility for admissions. To be eligible for admissions, one must fulfil all the criteria as laid down by the respective faculties of the University.

B.A (Hons) Arts/ B.A (Hons) Social Sciences: Candidate must not be more than 22 years of age and must have passed class XII or equivalent with minimum 50% marks in aggregate.

B.A (Hons) Economics: Candidate must not be more than 22 years of age and must have passed class XII or equivalent with minimum 50% marks in aggregate along with mathematics as one of the papers.

B. Com (Hons)/B. Com (Hons) Financial Markets Management: Candidate must not be more than 22 years of age and must have passed class XII or equivalent with minimum 50% marks in aggregate with Commerce/ Economics/Maths/Computer Science/Finance/Financial Markets Management as one of the subjects.

B. Sc (Hons) Maths Group: Candidate must not be more than 22 years of age and must have passed class XII or equivalent with minimum 50% marks in aggregate in the subjects Physics, Maths plus any one of the following: Chemistry, Statistics, Geology, Computer Science, Information Technology and Geography and must have passed in each of the concerned three subjects.

B. Sc (Hons) Bio Group: Candidate must not be more than 22 years of age and must have passed class XII or equivalent with minimum 50% marks in aggregate in the subjects Physics, Chemistry plus any one of the following: Biology, Geology and Geography and must have passed in each of the concerned three subjects.

B. F. A (Bachelor of Fine Arts): Candidate must not be more than 22 years of age and must have passed class XII or equivalent with minimum 50% marks in aggregate.

Bachelor of Vocation: Candidate must have passed class XII or equivalent in any stream (Science for Food Processing and Medical Lab Technology) or level 4 NSQF certificate.

BHU UG Admissions:

Until 2021, admissions to BHU UG courses were based on Undergraduate Entrance Test (UET) conducted by the University. From the academic year 2022, admissions to UG programs offered by BHU will be based on CUET, which will replace the UET. CUET will be a common entrance for admissions to UG programs offered by all the Central Universities in the country.

BHU UG Programs Reservation:

BHU being a Central University offers reservations in admissions according to central government rules.

Schedule Caste (SC): 15% of the total seats are reserved for students who belong to SC category.

Schedule Tribe (ST): 7.5% of the total seats are reserved for students belonging to ST Category.

Other Backward Classes (OBC): 27% of the total intake is reserved for students from Other Backward Classes (OBC), excluding those from creamy layer.

Economically Weaker Section (EWS): The University has reserved 10% seats for EWS category, in accordance with the directive of Ministry of Education.

Persons with Disability (PWD): 5% of the seats are reserved on horizontal basis for students from PWD category.

About JNU

Ever wondered which University, the cadets from National Defence Academy (NDA) graduate from? Yes. It is Jawaharlal Nehru University (JNU). JNU started in the year 1969, three years after the act of Parliament in 1966. With several academic centres of JNU declared "Centres of Excellence" by the University Grants Commission, JNU has been ranked No. 1 by National Assessment and Accreditation Council (NAAC). JNU has been ranked No. 2 by National Institutional Ranking Framework (NIRF) 2020 and has been awarded the Best University Award by the President of India in 2017. The European Commission has awarded the Jean Monnet Centre of Excellence for European Union Studies in India (CEEUSI) to Jawaharlal Nehru University in 2018. This is one of the highest international recognition for any European Studies programme.

JNU was the first University to start integrated five-year Master of Arts in Language Courses. JNU actively collaborates with National and International Universities for student and faculty exchange programs.

According to university submissions for NIRF 2020, JNU has 1,048 students pursuing UG programs, of which 46 are foreign nationals.

JNU UG Programs

JNU offers a limited program at the undergraduate level, unlike other universities. The focus at undergraduate has been largely on language courses. In 2018, JNU started two programs in engineering and plans to add a few more specializations in future.

Please refer to the table below for the important undergraduate courses offered by JNU and the intake across each program.

School	Program	Intake	Duration
School of Language, Literature and Cultural Studies	B. A (Hons) Pashto	19	3 Years
	B. A (Hons) Persian	39	3 Years
	B. A (Hons) Arabic	39	3 Years
	B. A (Hons) Japanese	48	3 Years
	B. A (Hons) Korean	39	3 Years
	B. A (Hons) Chinese	44	3 Years
	B. A (Hons) French	48	3 Years
	B. A (Hons) German	48	3 Years
	B. A (Hons) Russian	68	3 Years
	B. A (Hons) Spanish	39	3 Years

School of Sanskrit and Indic Studies	B. Sc - M. Sc Integrated Program in Ayurveda Biology	20	5 Years
School of Engineering	B. Tech in Computer Science and Engineering & MS/M. Tech in Social Sciences/Humanities/Science/Technology	25	5 Years
	B. Tech in Electronics and Communication Engineering & MS/M. Tech in Social Sciences/Humanities/Science/Technology	25	5 Years

JNU UG Programs Eligibility:

Each of the courses have different eligibility for admissions. To be eligible for admissions, one must fulfil all the criteria as laid down by the respective faculties of the University.

B.A (Hons) Language Courses: Candidate must not be less than 17 years of age and must have passed Senior School Certificate (10+2) or equivalent examination with minimum of 45% marks.

B. Sc - M. Sc Integrated Program in Ayurveda Biology: Candidate must not be less than 17 years of age and must have passed Senior School Certificate (10+2) or equivalent examination with minimum of 45% marks.

B. Tech-M. Tech: Based on JEE Mains

JNU UG Admissions:

Until 2021, admissions to JNU UG courses were based on JNU Entrance Examination (JNUEE) conducted by the National Testing Agency (NTA). From the academic year 2022, admissions to UG programs offered by JNU will be based on CUET, which will replace the JNUEE. CUET will be a common entrance for admissions to UG programs offered by all the Central Universities in the country.

JNU UG Programs Reservation:

JNU being a Central University offers reservations in admissions according to central government rules.

Schedule Caste (SC): 15% of the total seats are reserved for students who belong to SC category.

Schedule Tribe (ST): 7.5% of the total seats are reserved for students belonging to ST Category.

Other Backward Classes (OBC): 27% of the total intake is reserved for students from Other Backward Classes (OBC), excluding those from creamy layer. Also, Central List of Caste to be followed.

Economically Weaker Section (EWS): The University has reserved 10% seats for EWS category, in accordance with the directive of Ministry of Education.

Persons with Disability (PWD): 5% of the seats are reserved on horizontal basis for students from PWD category.

About Jamia Milia Islamia

Jamia Milia Islamia (JMI) was founded in 1920 in Aligarh and became a Central University in 1988 by the act of Parliament. Jamia in Urdu stands for University and Milia means National, making Jamia Milia Islamia a National University. Jamia Milia Islamia moved to Delhi in 1925 and shifted to its present campus in Okhla in 1935.

Jamia Milia Islamia is a NAAC accredited University with grade "A" and was placed 10th in NIRF Rankings 2020. According to submissions made by University for NIRF 2021, Jamia Milia Islamia has a total of 5,911 students pursuing undergraduate courses at the University, of which 105 are foreign nationals. The University also manage to place a total of 681 UG students with an average salary ranging 4.2 Lacs-6.0 Lacs.

JMI UG Programs

Jamia Milia Islamia (JMI) offers a host of undergraduate programs for students. Through its various faculties, JMI offers a range of programs which caters to students learning abilities.

Please refer to the table below for the important undergraduate courses offered by Jamia Milia Islamia and the intake across each program.

Faculty	Course	Intake	Duration
Faculty of Humanities and Language	B. A (Hons) English	60	3 Years
	B. A (Hons) Hindi	40	3 Years
	B. A (Hons) Mass Media-Hindi	40	3 Years
	B. A (Hons) History	60	3 Years
	Bachelor of Hotel Management (BHM)	40	3 Years
	Bachelor of Tourism and Travel Management	40	3 Years
	B. Voc (Food Production)	40	3 Years
Faculty of Social Sciences	Bachelor of Arts (B. A)	68	3 Years
	B. Com (Hons)	55	3 Years
	BBA (Bachelor of Business Administration)	44	3 Years
	B. A (Hons) Economics	53	3 Years
	B. A (Hons) Sociology	42	3 Years
	B. A (Hons) Political Science	42	3 Years
	B. A (Hons) Psychology	42	3 Years
Faculty of Natural Sciences	B. Sc (Bachelor of Science)	50	3 Years
	B. Sc Biosciences	40	3 Years
	B. Sc Biotechnology	35	3 Years
	B. Sc (Hons) Chemistry	40	3 Years
	B. A/B. Sc (Hons) Geography	60	3 Years
	B. Sc (Hons) Mathematics	45	3 Years
	B. Sc (Hons) Applied Mathematics	45	3 Years
	B. Sc (Hons) Physics	45	3 Years
Faculty of Fine Arts	Bachelor of Fine Arts (Applied Art)	30	4 Years
	Bachelor of Fine Arts (Art Education)	20	4 Years
	Bachelor of Fine Arts (Painting)	20	4 Years
	Bachelor of Fine Arts (Sculpture)	10	4 Years

JMI UG Programs Eligibility:

Each of the courses have different eligibility for admissions. To be eligible for admissions, one must fulfil all the criteria as laid down by the respective faculties of the University.

B. Com (Hons) /BBA /B. A (Hons) Economics: Candidate must have passed class XII or equivalent with a minimum of 50% marks in five subjects.

BHM/BTTM/B. Voc (Food Production): Candidate must have passed class XII or equivalent with a minimum of 45% marks in five subjects.

B. A (Hons) Mass Media/B. A (Hons) Hindi: Candidate must have passed class XII or equivalent with a minimum of 45% marks in five subjects.

B. Sc/B. Sc (Hons): Candidate must have passed class XII or equivalent with minimum 50% marks in each of the science subjects i.e. Physics, Chemistry and Mathematics and 50% marks in aggregate of best 5-subjects.

JMI UG Admissions:

Until 2021, admissions to JMI UG courses were based on Entrance Test (JMI-ET) conducted by the University. From the academic year 2022, admissions to UG programs offered by JMI will be based on CUET, which will replace the JMI-ET. CUET will be a common entrance for admissions to UG programs offered by all the Central Universities in the country.

JMI UG Programs Reservation:

JMI is a minority reservation-based University and accordingly, seats are reserved for candidates as per the norms laid down by the University.

Muslim Minority: 30% of the total seats are reserved for Muslim applicants; 10% of the total seats are reserved for women applicants who are Muslim; 10% of the total intake is for OBC-NC candidates who are Muslims.

Persons with Disability (PWD): 5% of the seats are reserved for students from PWD category.

Jamia Students: 5% seats in all Undergraduate Programs shall be filled by internal students of Jamia who have passed their qualifying examination of the concerned programme (X or XII) from Jamia Schools as regular students.

In addition, Jamia Milia Islamia has supernumerary seats for Kashmiri Migrants and students from Jammu and Kashmir.

About Aligarh Muslim University

Aligarh Muslim University also referred as AMU was established by Sir Syed Ahmad Khan in 1875. The University started as Muhammadan Anglo-Oriental College and became a University (AMU) in 1920. The university has been ranked 801–1000 in the QS World University Rankings of 2021 and 17 in India by the National Institutional Ranking Framework in 2020.

Aligarh Muslim University is institution of national importance, under the seventh schedule of the Constitution of India.

AMU UG Programs

Aligarh Muslim University offers several programs at the undergraduate level. With 7 constituent colleges, the Aligarh Muslim University offers many undergraduate courses.

Please refer to the table below for the important undergraduate courses offered by the AMU and the intake across each program.

Course	Intake	Duration
B. Sc (Hons) Home Science	30*	3 Years
B.Sc (Hons) Agriculture	40	4 Years
B. A (Hons) Arabic	20+10*	3 Years
B. A (Hons) Communicative English	15+20*	3 Years
B. A (Hons) English	40+35*	3 Years
B. A (Hons) Hindi	40+25*	3 Years
B. A (Hons) Geography	50+20*	3 Years
B. A (Hons) Linguistics	20+25*	3 Years
B. A (Hons) Persian	15+25*	3 Years
B. A (Hons) Philosophy	20+10*	3 Years
B. A (Hons) Quaranic Studies	10+10*	3 Years
B. A (Hons) Sanskrit	15+10*	3 Years
B. A (Hons) Urdu	40+50*	3 Years
Bachelor of Fine Arts	15+15*	3 Years
B. Com (Hons)	180+100*	3 Years
B. Voc Production Technology	50	3 Years
B Voc Polymer and Coating Technology	50	3 Years
B. Voc Fashion Design and Garment Technology	50	3 Years
B. A (Hons) Chinese	20	3 Years
B. A (Hons) French	20	3 Years
B. A (Hons) German	20	3 Years

B. A (Hons) Russian	20	3 Years
B. A (Hons) Spanish	20	3 Years
B. Sc (Hons) Biochemistry	30+30*	3 Years
B. Sc (Hons) Botany	60+40*	3 Years
B. Sc (Hons) Zoology	60+45*	3 Years
B. Sc (Hons) Physics	120+35*	3 Years
B. Sc (Hons) Chemistry	120+65*	3 Years
B. Sc (Hons) Mathematics	120+40*	3 Years
B. Sc (Hons) Geography	45+30*	3 Years
B. Sc (Hons) Geology	100+30*	3 Years
B. Sc (Hons) Statistics	60+30*	3 Years
B. Sc (Hons) Industrial Chemistry	20+10*	3 Years
B. Sc (Hons) Computer Applications	40+20*	3 Years

AMU UG Programs Eligibility:

As the University offers multiple programs and separate intake for male and female candidates, it is important to check the university official website regularly to keep oneself updated about the eligibility for each program, which can change.

AMU UG Admissions:

Until 2021, AMU conducted its own entrance test to admit students for the UG programs. From the academic year 2022, admissions to UG programs offered by Aligarh Muslim University will be based on CUET. CUET will be a common entrance for admissions to UG programs offered by all the Central Universities in the country.

University of Allahabad UG Programs Reservation:

Allahabad University being a Central University offers reservations in admissions according to central government rules. Kindly check the university website for further details.

ACCOUNTANCY

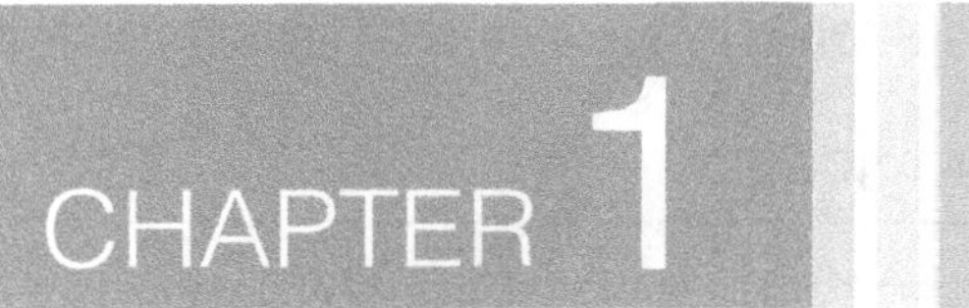

Accounting for Not-for-Profit Organisation

Summary

Meaning and Characteristics of Not-for Profit Organisation:_ Not-for -Profit Organisations refer to the organisations that are for used for the welfare of the society and are set up as charitable institutions which function without any profit motive. Their main aim is to provide service to a specific group or the public at large.

Characteristics or features of Not-For-Profit Organisation:

1. **Entity:** has a separate legal entity promoted by individuals
2. **Purpose:** is to further cultural, educational, religious, professional objectives and rendering service to people at large.
3. **Ownership:** it is set up as charitable society or trust. Thus owned by an individual or group of individuals
4. **Financial statements:** it prepares its financial statement every year which includes receipts and payments account, income and expenditure and balance sheet.
5. **Funds:** required for operations are given by its members and donors as entrance fee, membership fee, subscription and donations. It is supplemented by surplus from operations

Accounting Records of Not-For-Profit Organisations

As we know that Not-For-Profit Organisations are not engaged in any trading or business activity normally. Their main source of income is subscriptions/donations, financial assistance or grant from the government, etc. Most of their transactions are in form of cash or through the bank. These organizations are required by law to keep proper accounting records and keep proper control over the utilization of their funds.

For maintaining accounting records these organizations usually keep a cash book to record all receipts and payments and maintain ledger accounts of all income, expenses, assets, and liabilities. In addition, they maintain a stock register to keep records of all fixed assets and consumables.

Final Accounts or Financial Statements of Not-For-Profit Organisations

As they are non-profit making entities, so they are not required to make Trading and Profit and Loss Account but instead of these accounts to know whether the income during the year was enough to meet the expenses or not they prepare:

1. Receipts and Payment Account,
2. Income and Expenditure Account, and
3. Balance Sheet.

Receipts and ayment Account: is a summary of cash and bank transactions for a given period. It is prepared from the cash book at the end of financial year. All cash receipts are entered on the debit side and all the cash payments on the credit side. In 'other words, the Receipt and Payment Account simply is a summary of cash and bank transactions under various heads. On the debit side, it begins with an opening balance of cash and bank and records all the items of receipts irrespective of whether they are of capital or revenue nature or whether they pertain to the current or past or future accounting periods

FORMAT FOR RECEIPT AND PAYMENT ACCOUNT

Dr.			Cr.
Receipts	**Rs.**	**Payments**	**Rs.**
To opening balance (bal b/d)		By balance b/d(opening bal)	
Cash in hand		By salaries	
Cash at bank		By rent	
To capital receipts		By repairs	
(subscriptions)		By investment	
For previous year		By audit fee	
For present year		By miscellaneous payments	
For next year		By insurance	
To grant for specific purpose		By drawings	
To general grants		By bank overdraft	
To general donations		By building	
To rent received		By books	
To dividends		By loan	
To interest received		By Balance c/d (closing balance)	
To life membership fees		Cash in hand	
To sale of fixed assets		Cash at bank	
To balance c/d (bank overdraft)			
Total		Total	

Features:

- It is a summary of cash and bank transactions
- It can be inferred that the receipts and payment account is similar to a cash account
- No distinction is made between capital and revenue items, and excludes all non-cash items.
- It records all cash and bank transactions whether pertaining to the current period, previous period or succeeding period.

Non-cash items like depreciation, outstanding expenses, accrued income, etc. are not shown in this account.

Steps in the Preparation of Receipt and Payment Account

1. Take the opening balances of cash in hand and cash at bank and enter them on the debit side. In case there is bank overdraft at the beginning of the year, enter the same on the credit side of this account.
2. Show the total amounts of all receipts on its debit side irrespective of their nature (whether capital or revenue) and whether they pertain to past, current and future periods.
3. Show the total amounts of all payments on its credit side irrespective of their nature (whether capital or revenue) and whether they pertain to past, current and future periods.
4. None of the receivable income and payable expense is to be entered in this account as they do not involve inflow or outflow of cash.
5. Find out the difference between the total of debit side and the total of credit side of the account and enter the same on the credit side as the closing balance of cash/bank. In case, however, the total of the credit side is more than that of the total of the debit side, show the difference on the debit as bank overdraft and close the account.

Income and Expenditure Account

The surplus or deficit of a particular period for non-trading concern is determined by drawing up an income and expenditure account. It reveals the surplus or deficit arising out of the organization's activities during an accounting period. This account is prepared on an accrual basis and includes only items of revenue nature. All the revenue items relating to the current period are shown in this account, the expenses and losses on the expenditure side (debit side), and incomes and gains on the income side (credit side) of the account. It shows the net operating result in the form of surplus or deficit, which is transferred to the capital fund shown in the balance sheet.

Features:

- It is a revenue account prepared at the end of an accounting period to determine the surplus or deficit.
- The expenses and revenue of the period are matched in order to determine deficit or surplus
- Both cash and non-cash items are considered
- The surplus in this account is not distributed among members, but added to the capital fund.
- Excess of income over expenditure is a surplus and excess of expenditure over income is a deficit.

Steps in the Preparation of Income Expenditure Account:

1. From the Receipts and Payments, the Account excludes the opening and closing balance of cash and bank as they are not an income.
2. Exclude the items of capital nature as these are to be shown in the balance sheet.
3. Take out the revenue receipts only for the current year to be shown on the income side of the Income and Expenditure Account. These are adjusted by excluded the amounts relating to the preceding and the succeeding periods and including the amounts relating to the current year not yet received.
4. Take out the revenue payments only for the current year to be shown on the expenditure side of the Income and Expenditure Account. These are adjusted by excluded the amounts relating to the preceding and the succeeding periods and including the amounts relating to the current year not yet paid,
5. Make the adjustments of non-cash items like:
   (a) Depreciation on fixed assets.
   (b) Provision for doubtful debts, if required.
   (c) Profit or Loss on sale of fixed assets etc.

FORMAT FOR INCOME AND EXPENDITURE ACCOUNT

Expenditure	**Rs.**	**Income**	**Rs.**
To salaries		By subscriptions	
Add: outstanding at the end		By entrance fees	
Less: outstanding in the beginning		By sports fees	
To rent		By sale on old newspapers	
To insurance premium		By interest on investments	
To printing and stationary		By deficit (taken to bal. sheet)	
To sports expenses			
To electricity charges			
To loss on sale of furniture			
To sundry expenses			
To newspaper and periodicals			
To depreciation on			
Furniture			
Sports material			
To surplus taken to balance sheet			
Total		**Total**	

DISTINCTION BETWEEN INCOME AND EXPENDITURE ACCOUNT AND RECEIPT & PAYMENT ACCOUNT

Basis of distinction Account	Income and Expenditure	Receipt and Payment Account
Nature	It is like as profit and loss account.	It is the summary of the cash book.
Nature of Items	It records income and expenditure of revenue nature only.	It records receipts and payments of revenue as well as capital nature.
Period	Income and expenditure items relate only to the current period.	Receipts and payments may also relate to preceding and succeeding periods.
Debit side	Debit side of this account records expenses and losses.	Debit side of this account records the receipts.
Credit side	Credit side of this account records income and gains.	Credit side of this account records the payments.
Depreciation	Includes depreciation.	Does not includes depreciation.
Opening Balance	There is no opening balance.	Balance in the beginning represents cash in hand /cash at bank or overdraft at the beginning.
Closing Balance	Balance at the end represents excess of income over expenditure or vice-versa.	Balance at the end represents cash in hand at the end and bank balance (or bank overdraft).

Balance Sheet

The preparation of their Balance Sheet is on the same pattern as that of the business entities. It shows assets and liabilities as at the end of the year. Assets are shown on the right hand side and the liabilities on the left hand side. However, there will be a Capital Fund or General Fund in place of the Capital and the surplus or deficit as per Income and Expenditure Account which is either added to/deducted from the capital fund, as the case may be. It is also a common practice to add some of the capitalised items like legacies, entrance fees and life membership fees directly in the capital fund.

Steps in the Preparation of Balance Sheet:

1. Find out the Capital fund as per the Opening Balance Sheet and add surplus from the Income and Expenditure Account. Then, add capitalized items like legacies, entrance fees, and life membership fees, etc. received during the year.
2. Put all the fixed assets (from the opening balance sheet) with additions (from Receipts and Payments Account) after charging depreciation (as per Income and Expenditure Account), on the assets side of the balance sheet.
3. Compare items on the receipts side of the Receipts and Payments Account with the income side of the Income and Expenditure Account to find out the amounts of:
   (a) Subscription due but not yet received,
   (b) Income received in advance,
   (c) Sale of fixed assets made during the year,
   (d) Items to be capitalized etc.
4. Compare items on the payment side of the Receipts and Payments Account with the expenditure side of the Income and Expenditure Account to find out the amount of:
   (a) Outstanding Expenses,
   (b) Prepaid Expenses,
   (c) Purchases of a fixed asset during the year,
   (d) Depreciation on fixed assets,

(e) Stock of consumable items like stationery in hand,

(f) Closing balance of cash in hand and cash at bank etc

Balance Sheet of as on ....

Expenditure	Rs.	Income	Rs.
To salaries		By subscriptions	
Add: outstanding at the end		By entrance fees	
Less: outstanding in the beginning		By sports fees	
To rent		By sale on old newspapers	
To insurance premium		By interest on investments	
To printing and stationary		By deficit (taken to bal. sheet)	
To sports expenses			
To electricity charges			
To loss on sale of furniture			
To sundry expenses			
To newspaper and periodicals			
To depreciation on			
Furniture			
Sports material			
To surplus taken to balance sheet			
Total		**Total**	

Balance Sheet of as on ....

Liabilities	Amount (Rs.)	Assets	Amount (Rs.)
Capital fund:			
Opening Balance	....	Cash in hand and/or Cash at Bank	....
Add: Surplus			
OR		Outstanding income	....
Less: Deficit		Prepaid Expenses	....
Add: Capitalised Income of the	....	Stock of Consumbale items:	
Current Year on Account of		Previous Balance	
Legacies	....	Add: Purchases in the current period	....
Entrance Fees	....		
Life Membership Fees	....	Less: Value consumed during the period	....
Closing Balance	....		
Special Fund/Donations:		Previous Balance	....
Previous Balance (If any)		Add: Purchases in the current period	
Add: Receipts for the item during the period		Less: Book value of the Asset sold/disposed off	
Add: Income earned on fund/ Donations		Closing Balance	....
Investments			
Less: Expenses paid out of fund/Donations			
Net Balance	....		
Creditors for Purchases and/ or supplies	....		
Bank Overdraft	....		
Outstanding Expenses:	....		
Income received in Advance	....		....
	....		....

Some Important Terms

1. **Subscriptions:** Subscription is a membership fee paid by the member on annual basis. This is the main source of income of such orgnisations. Subscription paid by the members is shown as receipt in the Receipt and Payment Account and as income in the Income and Expenditure Account.

Particulars	Amount (Rs.)
Total Subscriptions Received during the current year	×××
Add: Subscription outstanding at the end of current year	×××
	×××
Less: Subscription outstanding in the beginning of the year	×××
	×××
Add: Subscription received in advance in the beginning of the year	×××
	×××
Less: Subscription received in advance at the end of the year	×××
Subscription to be shown in Income and Expenditure Account	×××

2. **Donations:** It is a type of gift in cash or in property received from some person, firm, or company. The donation can be for specific purposes or for general purposes. Both the donation received appears on the receipts side of the Receipts and Payments Account
3. **Legacies:** It is in the nature of a gift, received in cash or in the property as per the will of a deceased person. It is not treated as an income because it is not of recurring nature. Such receipts come very rarely and therefore it is of a capital nature and is shown on the liabilities side of the Balance §heet. It appears on the receipt side of the Receipts and Payments Account and is directly added to Capital Fund in the Balance Sheet.
4. **Life Membership Fees:** In order to become a member of an organization for the whole of the life, some members pay the fee in lump sum i.e. once in their lifetime. It is a receipt of non-recurring nature since the members will not be required to pay the fees regularly. It is shown on the receipt side of the Receipt and Payment Account and added to the Capital Fund in the Balance Sheet. It should not be credited to the Income and Expenditure Account.
5. **Entrance Fees:** Entrance fee also known as admission fee is paid only once by the member at the time of becoming a member. In case of organisations like clubs and some charitable institutions, is limited and the amount of entrance fees is quite high. Hence, it is treated as non-recurring item and credited directly to capital/general fund.
6. **Sale of old asset:** Receipts from the sale of an old asset appear in the Receipts and Payments Account of the year in which it is sold. But any gain or loss on the sale of asset is taken to the Income and Expenditure Account of the year
7. **Sale of Sports Materials:** Sale of sports materials (used materials like old balls, bats, nets, etc) is the regular feature with any Sports Club. It is usually shown as an income in the Income and Expenditure Account.
8. **Special Funds:** Not-For-Profit Organisation creates some special funds for a specific purpose such as 'prize funds', 'match fund' and 'sports fund' etc. The number of such hands is invested in securities and the income earned on such investment is added to the respective fund, not credited to the Income and Expenditure Account. Similarly, the expenses incurred on such a specific purpose are also deducted from the fund.

Exercise

1. Receipts and payments Account is a summary of
   (a) Journal
   (b) Contra entry
   (c) Sales book
   (d) Cash book
2. Out of the following items, which one is shown in the Receipts and Payments Account?
   (a) Outstanding Salary
   (b) Depreciation
   (c) Life Membership Fees
   (d) Accrued Subscription

For questions 3 to 5: Analyse the case given below and answer the questions that follows:

Dr. Rahul a qualified M.B.B.S. doctor got voluntary retirement at the age of 50 years from a renowned hospital. he was residing in a flat of a wide apartment which is surrounded by a slum which is inhabited by economically weaker strata of the society. As the people in that area were not aware about importance of health care, a widespread ailment had been persistently prevailing. Rahul met with some of the well-off people of apartment and decided to open a dispensary named as 'LOCAL Clinic' to provide them cost free medical assistance and make them aware about hygienic living, physical fitness, and economic balance diet. Many of the apartment members agreed to it. he approached health department of the town with his proposal which was accepted and an initial one time grant of Rs. 2,00,000 was sanctioned immediately for purchase of medical equipment and test kits for pathological tests. 10 members of the apartment contributed Rs. 20,000 each as lifetime subscription to the clinic. Rahul decided to charge Rs. 10 as one time registration fee from patients. Apart from above Rahul made following transactions for first year:

S.No.	Particulars	Amount in (Rs.)
1	Purchased Equipment	1,20,000
2	Purchased Medicines	95,000
3	Purchased Furniture	10,000
4	Rent paid	12,000
5	Fee received for medical tests	45,000
6	Honorarium paid to Yoga teacher	35,000
7	Honorarium paid to physiotherapist and sports teacher	38,000

Rahul informed that during the first year 10,500 patients were registered for treatment and for other services. Taking reference from the above, answer following questions.

3. Not for profit organization prepares
   (i) Income and Expenditure account
   (ii) Trading and Profit loss account
   (iii) Receipt and Payment account
   (iv) None of the above Options:
   (a) Only (ii)
   (b) Only (iii)
   (c) Both (i) and (ii)
   (d) Both (i) and (iii)
4. Honorarium paid to Physiotherapist and sports teacher Will be posted to
   (a) Debit side of Income and Expenditure Account
   (b) Debit side of Receipt and Payment Account
   (c) Debit side of Profit and Loss Account
   (d) Credit side of Income and Expenditure account

5. Lifetime subscription paid by 10 members will be posted in
   (a) Expenditure side of Income and Expenditure Account
   (b) Liability side of closing Balance Sheet
   (c) Income side of Income and Expenditure Account
   (d) Assets side of closing Balance Sheet
6. In case specific fund is maintained, the expenses exceeding the amount of the fluids, should be recorded on:
   (a) Liabilities side of the Balance Sheet
   (b) Debit side the Income and Expenditure Account
   (c) Credit side of the Income and Expenditure Account
   (d) Assets side of the Balance Sheet
7. If income is Rs. 14,000, and deficit debited to capital fund is Rs. 3,300, then expenditure is
   (a) Rs. 10,700 (b) Rs. 10,00
   (c) Rs. 17,300 (d) Rs. 20,000
8. Second hand machinery worth Rs. 7,000 was purchased. Rs. 400 was spend on its repair and Rs. 300 was paid for installation. The machinery should be capitalised for
   (a) Rs. 7,000 (b) Rs. 7,700
   (c) Rs. 7,400 (d) Rs. 6,600
9. Subscription received in advance during the current year is:
   (a) An income (b) An Asset
   (c) A liability (d) None of these
10. **Assertion (A):** The income and expenditure account is prepared on the accrual basis of accounting.
    Reasoning (R): The transactions related to the previous year are added and those related to the previous or followed year are to be subtracted.
    Codes:
    (a) Both Assertion and Reason are true and Reason (R) is the correct explanation of Assertion (A)
    (b) Both Assertion and Reason are true and Reason (R) is not the correct explanation of Assertion (A)
    (c) Assertion (A) is True but Reason (R) is False
    (d) Assertion (A) is False but Reason (R) is True
11. If debit side of receipt and payment account exceeds the credit side it represents
    (a) Cash at bank (b) Cash in hand
    (c) Bank overdraft (d) Surplus
12. The opening balance of Prize Fund was Rs. 28,800.During the year, donations reoeived towards this fund amounted to Rs. 13,400; amount spent on prizes was Rs.10,300 and interest received on prize fund investment was 3,000. State the closing balance of Prize Fund
    (a) Rs. 24,800 (b) Rs. 44,900
    (c) Rs. 34,900 (d) Rs. 30,000
13. Receipts and payment account is a summary of
    (a) All revenues and capital receipts/payments (b) Cash items
    (c) Only capital receipts (d) Only revenue receipts
14. Donation received for a special purpose:
    (a) Should be credited to Income and Expenditure A/c
    (b) Should be credited to a separate account and shown in the Balance Sheet
    (c) Should be shown on the Assets side of the Balance Sheet
    (d) None of these

15. Rv Verma Cricket club was inaugurated on 1st April, 2019. It had the following Receipts and Payments during the year ended 31st March, 2020:

Receipts: Entrance Fees Rs. 10,000; Subscriptions Rs. 60,000; Donations Rs. 10,000.

Payments: Rent Rs. 15,000; Postages Rs. 1,000; Newspapers and Magazines Rs. 8,000;

Investments Rs. 30,000; Stationery Rs. 4,000; Entertainment Expenses Rs. 3,000;

Miscellaneous Expenses Rs. 2,000.

Amount in the Receipts and Payments Account for the year ended 31st March, 2020

(a) Rs. 65,000 (b) Rs. 40,000

(c) Rs. 80,000 (d) Rs. 67,800

16. How are the following items shown in the accounts of a Not-for-Profit Organisation?

Tournament Fund	Rs. 50,000
Tournament Expenses	Rs. 15,000
Receipts from Tournament	Rs. 20,000

(a) Rs. 55,000 (b) Rs. 52,000

(c) Rs. 35,000 (d) Rs. 30,000

17. In the year ended 31st March, 2019, subscriptions received by the MG Literary Society were Rs. 4,20,000. These subscriptions include Rs. 14,000 received for the year ended 31st March, 2018. On 31st March, 2019, subscriptions due but not received were Rs. 10,000. What amount should be credited to Income and Expenditure Account for the year ended 31st March, 2019 as subscription?

(a) Rs. 4,10,000 (b) Rs. 4,16,000

(c) Rs. 4,00,000 (d) Rs. 3,80,000

18. A non-profit organization received Rs.10,000 as the entrance fee of a new member. If 20% of the fee has to be capitalized, what is the amount of fee needs to be shown in the income and expenditure account?

(a) Rs. 9,000 (b) Rs. 8,000

(c) Rs. 2,000 (d) Rs. 5,000

19. Subscription received during the year 40,000 Rs. Subscriptions outstanding at the end of the year 9,000 Rs. Subscription outstanding at the beginning of the year 7,000 Rs. Net Income from subscription will be :

(a) Rs. 48,000 (b) Rs. 44,000

(c) Rs. 42,000 (d) Rs. 36,000

20. Income and Expenditure Account is:

(a) Personal Account (b) Real Account

(c) Nominal Account (d) None of these

Topic Test – 1

1. Which should be considered as capital receipt of a club

(a) Donation (b) Sale of books

(c) Sale of bar items (d) Sale of furniture

2. Life Membership Fees received by a club is shown in:

(a) Income and Expenditure A/c

(b) Balance Sheet

(c) Receipts and Payments A/c

(d) None of these

3. Ella, a non governmental not-for-profit organization, received funds during its annual campaign that were specifically pledged by the donor to another non governmental not-for-profit health organization. How should Ella record these funds?
   (a) Increase in assets and increase in revenue
   (b) Increase in assets and increase in liabilities
   (c) Increase in assets and increase in deferred revenue.
   (d) Decrease in assets and decrease in fund balance.

4. From the following information, calculate amount of subscriptions to be credited to the Income and Expenditure Account for the year ended 31st March, 2019:

1st April, 2018	
Subscriptions in Arrears	Rs. 50,000
Subscriptions Received in Advance	Rs. 30,000
31st March, 2019	
Subscriptions in Arrears	Rs. 25,000
Subscriptions Received in Advance	Rs. 70,000
Subscriptions received during the year ended 31st March, 2019	Rs. 3,00,000
Subscription still in arrears for the year 2017 – 18	Rs. 10,000

   (a) Rs. 2,30,000 (b) Rs. 1,23,500
   (c) Rs. 2,35,000 (d) Rs. 1,35,000

5. Calculate amount of subscriptions which will be treated as income for the year ended 31st March, 2019

(i) Subscriptions collected during the year ended 31st March, 2019	Rs. 1,50,000
(ii) Subscriptions in arrears for the year ended 31st March, 2019	Rs. 6,000
(iii) Subscriptions received in advance for the year ended 31st March, 2020	Rs. 5,000

   (a) Rs. 1,51,000 (b) Rs. 1,50,000
   (c) Rs. 1,61,000 (d) Rs. 1,00,000

6. From the following information, calculate amount of subscriptions outstanding for the year ended 31st March, 2019:

   A club has 200 members each paying an annual subscription of Rs. 1,000. The Receipts and Payments Account for the year showed a sum of Rs. 2,05,000 received as subscriptions. The following additional information is provided :

Subscriptions Outstanding on 31st March, 2018	Rs. 30,000
Subscriptions Received in Advance on 31st March, 2019	Rs. 40,000
Subscriptions Received in Advance on 31st March, 2018	Rs. 14,000

   (a) Rs. 2,60,000 (b) Rs. 2,70,000
   (c) Rs. 2,00,000 (d) Rs. 1,00,000

7. Income and Expenditure account generally indicates
   (a) Net profit (b) Net loss
   (c) Capital (d) Capital/deficit

8. Amount received from the sale of old furniture is treated as
   (a) Loss (b) Liability
   (c) Earning (d) Capital receipt

9. Life membership fee received by a club is:
   (a) Revenue Receipt (b) Capital Receipt
   (c) Both (a) and (b) (d) None of these

10. What amount will be credited the Income and Expenditure Account for the year ending 31st March, 2019 on the basis of the following information:

	01-04-2018	31-03-2019
Advance Subscription	8,000	2,000

Subscriptions received during the year 2018-19 were 2,00,000.

(a) Rs. 2,06,000 (b) Rs. 2,00,000

(c) Rs. 2,08,000 (d) Rs. 2,02,000

Topic Test – 2

1. Sports Mania club New Delhi had received in 2020-21 Rs. 80,000 as subscription:-

I.	Subscription due but not received on 1-4-2020	5,200
II.	Subscription received in advance on 1-4-2000	2,400
III.	Subscription due but not received on 31-3-2021	4,800
IV.	Subscription received in advance on 31-3-2021	700

What amount should be credited Income and Expenditure Account as subscriptions?

(a) Rs. 80,000 (b) Rs. 81,000

(c) Rs. 76,000 (d) Rs. 81,300

2. **Assertion (A):** NGOs are charitable trusts or societies and subscribers to such organizations are called members.

Reasoning (R): Profits are distributed among its members

Codes:

(a) Both Assertion and Reason are true and Reason (R) is the correct explanation of Assertion (A)

(b) Both Assertion and Reason are true and Reason (R) is not the correct explanation of Assertion (A)

(c) Assertion (A) is True but Reason (R) is False

(d) Assertion (A) is False but Reason (R) is True

3. Calculate amount of subscriptions which will be treated as income for the year ended 31st March, 2019

(i) Subscriptions received during the year ended 31st March, 2019 Rs. 25,000

(ii) Subscriptions outstanding in the beginning of the year ended 31st March, 2019 Rs. 25,000

(iii) Subscriptions not yet collected for the year ended 31st March, 2019 Rs. 5,000

(a) Rs. 20,000 (b) Rs. 24,000

(c) Rs. 18,000 (d) Rs. 27,000

4. How much amount will be recorded in income and expenditure account if club has 300 members each playing an annual subscription of Rs.100. outstanding subscription on 31st March 2020 were 3,000

(a) Rs. 30,000 (b) Rs. 40,000

(c) Rs. 10,000 (d) Rs. 33,000

5. Subscription received in cash during the year amounted to Rs. 5,00,000; subscription outstanding at the end of previous year was Rs. 20,000 and outstanding at the end of current year was Rs. 25,000. Subscription received in advance for next year was Rs. 8,000 and received in advance during previous year was Rs. 7,000. The amount credited to Income & Expenditure Account will be:

(a) Rs. 5,04,000 (b) Rs. 5,06,000

(c) Rs. 4,96,000 (d) Rs. 4,94,000

6. Entrance fees received amounted to Rs. 50,000. In this 25% is to be capitalized. Mention the amount to be shown in income side of Income and Expenditure account:

(a) Rs. 12,500 (b) Rs. 13,200

(c) Rs. 50,000 (d) Rs. 37,500

7. No cash transaction will be excluded from:

(a) Balance Sheet (b) Profit & Loss A/c

(c) Receipts and Payments (d) Income and Expenditure A/c

8. The amount of 'Subscription received from members' by a Non-profit organisation is shown in which of the following?

(a) Debit side of Income and Expenditure Account

(b) Credit side of Income and Expenditure Account

(c) Liability side of Balance Sheet

(d) Assets side of Balance Sheet

9. Donation received for a special purpose :

(a) Should be credited to Income and Expenditure Account

(b) Should be credited to separate account and shown in the Balance Sheet

(c) Should be shown on the assets side

(d) Should not be recorded at all.

10. Not-for-profit organisations prepare :

(a) Trading Account

(b) Trading & Profit and Loss Account

(c) Income and Expenditure Account

(d) All of the above

Answer Keys

Exercise

1. (d)	2. (b)	3. (d)	4. (a)	5. (b)	6. (b)	7. (c)	8. (b)	9. (c)	10. (c)
11. (a)	12. (c)	13. (a)	14. (b)	15. (c)	16. (a)	17. (b)	18. (b)	19. (c)	20. (c)

Topic Test – 1

1. (d)	2. (b)	3. (b)	4. (c)	5. (a)	6. (b)	7. (d)	8. (d)	9. (b)	10. (a)

Topic Test – 2

1. (d)	2. (c)	3. (d)	4. (a)	5. (a)	6. (d)	7. (c)	8. (b)	9. (b)	10. (c)

CHAPTER 2

Accounting for Partnership Firms – Basic Concepts

Partnership is a separate business entity from the accounting viewpoint.

Partnership is a relationship between person who has agreed to share the profits of a business carried on by all or any of them acting for all.

Nature of Partnership

1. **Two or more persons:** There must be at least two persons to form a valid partnership. The maximum number of partners cannot exceed the number of partners prescribed by Companies Act, 2013 which is 50 in any business whether banking or non- banking.
2. **Agreement:** Partnership comes into existence by an agreement (either written or oral among the partners. The written agreement among the partners is called Partnership Deed.
3. **Existence of business and profit motive:** A partnership can be formed for the purpose of carrying on legal business with the intention of earning profits A joint ownership of some property by itself cannot be called a partnership.
4. **Sharing of Profits:** An agreement between the partners must be aimed at sharing the profits. If some persons join hands to run some charitable activity, it will not be called partnership. Futher, if a partner is deprived of his right to share the profits of the business, he cannot be called as partner.
5. **Business carried on by all or any of them acting for all:** It means that each partner can participate in the conduct of business and each partner is bound by the acts of other partners in respect to the business of the firm.
6. **Relationship of Principal and Agent:** Each partner is an agent ad well as a partner of the firm. An agent, because he can bind the other partners by his acts and principal, because he himself can be bound by the acts of the other partners.

Partnership Deed: The relationship between the partners may be expressed formally (oral or written) or implied by their conduct. A partnership agreement which is written and signed by all the partners and is duly stamped according to the stamp act.

Contents of the partnership Deed

The Partnership Deed usually contains the following details:

- Names and Addresses of the firm and its main business;
- Names and Addresses of all partners;
- Amount of capital to be contributed by each partner;
- The accounting period of the firm;
- The date of commencement of partnership;

- Rules regarding operation of Bank Accounts;
- Profit and loss sharing ratio;
- Rate of interest on capital, loan, drawings, etc;
- Mode of auditor's appointment, if any;
- Salaries, commission, etc, if payable to any partner;
- The rights, duties and liabilities of each partner;
- Treatment of loss arising out of insolvency of one or more partners;
- Settlement of accounts on dissolution of the firm;
- Method of settlement of disputes among the partners;
- Rules to be followed in case of admission, retirement, death of a partner; and
- Any other matter relating to the conduct of business.

Normally, the partnership deed covers all matters affecting relationship of partners amongst themselves. However, if there is no express agreement on certain matters, the provisions of the Indian Partnership Act, 1932 shall apply.

Benefits of Partnership Deed

(1) It regulates the rights, duties and liabilities of each partner.

(2) It helps to avoid any misunderstanding amongst the partners because all the terms and conditions of partnership have been laid down beforehand in the deed.

(3) Any dispute amongst the partners may be settled easily as the partnership deed may be readiy referred to.

Hence, it is always best course to have a written partnership deed duly signed by all the partners and registered under the Act.

Types of partners:

(a) Active partner: A partner who contributes capital and takes an active part in the management of the partnership

(b) Sleeping partner: A partner who merely contributes capital for the business but does not take part in the management of the partnership business.

Provisions of Partnership Act Relevant for Accounting:

The important provisions affecting partnership accounts are as follows:

(a) Profit Sharing Ratio: If the partnership deed is silent about the profit sharing ratio, the profits and losses of the firm are to be shared equally by partners, irrespective of their capital contribution in the firm.

(b) Interest on Capital: No partner is entitled to claim any interest on the amount of capital contributed by him in the firm as a matter of right. However, interest can be allowed when it is expressly agreed to by the partners. Thus, no interest on capital is payable if the partnership deed is silent on the issue.

(c) Interest on Drawings: No interest is to be charged on the drawings made by the partners, if there is no mention in the Deed.

(d) Interest on Loan: If any partner has advanced loan to the firm for the purpose of business, he/she shall be entitled to get an interest on the loan amount at the rate of 6 per cent per annum. (e) Remuneration for Firm's Work: No partner is entitled to get salary or other remuneration for taking part in the conduct of the business of the firm unless there is a provision for the same in the Partnership Deed.

Maintenance of Capital Accounts of Partners:

There are two methods by which the capital accounts of partners are maintained. They are the following:

(a) Fixed Capital Method

(b) Fluctuating Capital Method

(a) Fixed Capital Method: Under the fixed capital method, the capitals of the partner shall remain fixed or unaltered unless some additional capital is introduced or some amount of capital is withdrawn with the consent of all the partners.

In this method, two accounts for each partner are to be maintained:

1. Capital Account
2. Current Account.

1. **Capital Account:** This account is credited with the amount of capital introduced by the partner. This account will continue to show the same balance from year to year unless some amount of capital is introduced or withdrawn. This account always appears on the liabilities side in the balance sheet.
2. **Current Account:** All entries relating to drawings, interest on capital, interest on drawings, salary or commission, the share of profit or loss, etc. are made in this account. This account is debited with drawings, interest on drawings, the share of loss, etc. and credited with the interest on capital, salary, commission, the share of profit, etc. The balance of this account will fluctuate from year to year. If it has a credit balance then it will appear on the liabilities side of the Balance Sheet and if it has a debit balance then it will appear on the assets side of the Balance Sheet.

Partner's Capital Account

Dr. Cr.

Date	Particulars	J.F.	Amount (Rs.)	Date	Particulars	J.F.	Amount (Rs.)
	Bank (permanent withdrawal of capital)		×××		Balance b/d (opening balance)		×××
	Balance c/d (closing balance)		×××		Bank (fresh capital introduced)		×××
			×××				×××

Partner's Current Account

Dr. Cr.

Date	Particulars	J.F.	Amount (Rs.)	Date	Particulars	J.F.	Amount (Rs.)
	Balance b/d (in case of debit opening balance)		×××		Balance b/d (in case of credit opening balance)		×××
	Drawings		×××		Salary		×××
	Interest on drawings		×××		Commission		×××
	Profit & Loss a/c		×××		Interest on capital		
					Profit & Loss Appropriation (share of profit)		×××
	Balance c/d (in case of credit closing balance)		×××		Balance c/d (in case of debit closing balance)		×××
			×××				×××

Fig. 2.1: Proforma of Partner's Capital and Current Account under Fixed Capital Method.

(b) Fluctuating Capital Method: Under this method, only one account i.e. Capital Account is maintained for each partner. All the entries relating to the interest on capital, salary, commission to partners, the share of profit and loss, drawings, interest on drawings, etc. are directly recorded in the capital accounts of the partners. The balance of this account fluctuates from year to year. The format of Fluctuating Capital Account is as follows:

Partner's Capital Account

Dr. Cr.

Date	Particulars	J.F.	Amount (Rs.)	Date	Particulars	J.F.	Amount (Rs.)
	Balance b/d (in case of debit closing balance)		×××		Balance b/d (in case of credit opening balance)		×××
	Drawings				Bank (fresh capital introduced)		×××
	Interest on drawings		×××		Salaries		×××
	Profit and Loss A/c (for share of loss)		×××		Interest on capital		×××
	Balance c/d (in case of credit closing balance)		×××		Profit and Loss Appropriateion (for share of profit)		×××
					Balance b/d (in case of debit closing balance		×××
			×××				×××

Fig. 2.2: Proforma of Partner's Capital Account under Fluctuating capital Method.

Profit and Loss Appropriation Account:

In partnership, net profit after adjustment of partner's interest on capital, salary, and commission to partner's, interest on drawings, etc. is distributed among the partners in the agreed profit sharing ratio. For this purpose, a separate account is prepared called Profit and Loss Appropriation Account.

Journal Entries relating to Profit and Loss Appropriation Account:

1. Transfer of the balance of Profit and Loss Account to Profit and Loss Appropriation Account:

   (a) If Profit and Loss Account shows a credit balance (net profit):

   Profit and Loss A/c Dr.

   To Profit and Loss Appropriation A/c

   (b) If Profit and Loss Account shows a debit balance (net loss)

   Profit and Loss Appropriation A/c Dr.

   To Profit and Loss A/c

2. Interest on Capital:

   (a) For Allowing interest on capital:

   Interest on Capital A/c Dr.

   To Partner's Capital/Current A/c's (individually)

   (b) For transferring interest on capital to Profit and Loss Appropriation Account:

   Profit and Loss Appropriation A/c Dr.

   To Interest on Capital A/c

3. Interest on Drawings:

   (a) For charging interest on drawings to partners' capital accounts:

   Partners Capital/Current A/c's (individually) Dr.

   To Interest on Drawings A/c

   (b) For transferring interest on drawings to Profit and Loss Appropriation Account

   Interest on Drawings A/c Dr.

   To Profit and Loss Appropriation A/c

4. Salary to Partner(s):
   (a) For crediting partner's salary' to partner's Capital/Current A/c:
   Salary to Partner A/c Dr.
   To Partner's Capital /Current A/c (Individually)
   (b) For transferring partner's salary to Profit and Loss Appropriation A/c:
   Profit and Loss Appropriation A/c Dr.
   To Salary to Partner A/c
5. Commission to Partner(s):
   (a) For crediting partner's commission to partner's Capital/ Current A/c:
   Commission to Partner A/c Dr.
   To Partner's Capital/Current A/c (Individually)
   (b) For transferring partner's commission to Profit and Loss Appropriation A/c:
   Profit and Loss Appropriation A/c Dr.
   To Commission to Partner A/c
6. Share of Profit/Loss after adjustments:
   (a) If Profit
   Profit and Loss Appropriation A/c Dr.
   To partner's Capital/Current A/c (Individually)
   OR
   (b) If Loss:
   Partner's Capital/Current A/c (Individually) Dr.
   To Profit and Loss Appropriation A/c

Profit and Loss Appropriation Account

Dr. **Cr.**

Particulars	Amount (Rs.)	Particulars	Amount (Rs.)
Profit and Loss (if there is loss)	xxx	Profit and Loss (if there is profit)	xxx
Interest on Capital	xxx	Interest on Drawings	xxx
Salary to Partner	xxx	Partners Capital/Current Accounts (distribution of Loss)	xxx
Commission to Partner	xxx		
Partners Capital/Current Accounts (distribution of profit)	xxx		
	xxx		xxx

Interest on Capital:

Interest on Capital is generally provided for in two situations:

1. When the partners contribute unequal amounts of capital but share profits equally.
2. When the capital contribution is the same but profit sharing is unequal.

Interest on Capital = Amount of Capital × Rate / 100 × Time

Interest on Drawings:

(a) Drawings is the amount withdrawn, in cash or in-kind, for personal use by the partner(s). Interest on drawings is calculated with reference to the date of withdrawal.

The calculation of interest on drawings under different situations is shown as under:

When drawings are made:

1. At the beginning of each month of the financial year:

$$\text{Interest on Drawings} = \text{Interest on Drawings} = \text{Total Drawings} \times \frac{\text{Rate}}{100} \times \frac{6^{1/2}}{12}$$

Here, time period is $6\frac{1}{2}$ months.

2. At the middle of each month of the financial year

$$\text{Interest on Drawings} = \text{Total Drawings} \times \frac{\text{Rate}}{100} \times \frac{6}{12}$$

Here, time period is 6 months.

3. At the end of each month of the financial year:

$$\text{Interest on Drawings} = \text{Total Drawings} \times \frac{\text{Rate}}{100} \times \frac{5^{1/2}}{12}$$

Here, time period is $5\frac{1}{2}$ months.

4. At the beginning of the each quarter of the financial year:

$$\text{Interest on Drawings} = \text{Total Drawings} \times \frac{\text{Rate}}{100} \times \frac{7^{1/2}}{12}$$

Here, time period is $7\frac{1}{2}$ months.

5. At the end of each quarter of the financial year:

$$\text{Interest on Drawings} = \text{Total Drawings} \times \frac{\text{Rate}}{100} \times \frac{4^{1/2}}{12}$$

Here, time period is $4\frac{1}{2}$ months.

(b) **When Varying Amounts are Withdrawn at Different Intervals:** When the partners withdraw different amounts of money at different time intervals, the interest is calculated using the production method. In this method, each amount of drawing is multiplied by the number of days/months (from the date of drawings to the last date of the financial year) to find out the product and then all the products are totaled. Here, the total product and interest for 1 month at the given rate are calculated.

$$\text{Interest on Drawings} = \text{Total Drawings} \times \frac{\text{Rate}}{100} \times \frac{1}{12}$$

or

$$\frac{1}{365}$$

(c) When Dates of Withdrawal are Not Specified: When the total amount withdrawn is given but the dates of withdrawals are not specified, then it is assumed that the amount was withdrawn evenly throughout the year. Here, the time period is taken 6 months.

$$\text{Interest on Drawings} = \text{Total Drawings} \times \frac{\text{Rate}}{100} \times \frac{6}{12}$$

Guarantee of Profit to a Partner

Sometimes a partner may be guaranteed a minimum amount of profit by one or some or by all the partners in the existing profit sharing ratio or some other agreed ratio. The minimum guaranteed amount shall be paid to a partner when his share of profit as per the profit-sharing ratio is less than the guaranteed amount.

Past Adjustments:

Sometimes, after making of final accounts and the distribution of profits among the partners, a few omissions or errors in the recording of transactions or the preparation of summary statements are found. These errors or omissions need adjustments for correction of their impact.

This error or omissions may relate to:

1. Interest on capital may have omitted or have been wrongly treated.
2. Interest in drawings may have been omitted.
3. Salary or commission payable has been omitted in the capital account of the partner.
4. The profit-sharing ratio has been changed from the past.
5. Interest in the partner's loan has been omitted.

Instead of altering old accounts, necessary adjustments can be made either by:

(a) through 'Profit and Loss Adjustment Account'

Or

(b) directly in the capital account of the concerned partners.

(a) Profit and Loss Adjustment Account:

1. For omission of Interest on Capital, Salaries to partner(s), Commission to partner, etc.

   Profit and Loss Adjustment Account Dr.

   To Partner's Capital/Current A/c (Individually)

2. For omission of Interest on drawings etc

   Partner's Capital/Current A/c Dr.

   To Profit and Loss Adjustment Account

3. Calculate the difference or balance of the Profit and Loss Adjustment Account and transfer it to the Capital/ Current Accounts of partners in the profit-sharing ratio.

   (a) If Profit (Credit balance):

   Profit and Loss Adjustment A/c Dr.

   To Partner's Capital/Current A/c (Individually)

   OR

(b) If Loss (Debit balance):

Partner's Capital/Current A/c (Individually) Dr.

To Profit and Loss Adjustment A/c

(b) Adjustment through a single entry or directly in the capital account of the concerned partner(s):

In this case, the following steps should be taken:

1. Calculate amount which should have been credited to each partner's Capital/ Current Account by way of (Interest on Capital + Salaries to Partner(s) + Commission to Partner(s) – Interest on Drawings etc.)
2. Distribute the amount calculated in step (1) in the current profit sharing ratio.
3. Calculate the difference between the above two steps for each partner (1) – (2)

   (–) Excess or (+) Short

Exercise

1. Given below are two statements, one labelled as Assertion (A) and the other labelled as Reason (R)

Assertion (A): Transfer to reserves is shown in P & L Appropriation A/c.

Reasoning (R): Reserves are charge against the profits.

In the context of the above statements, which one of the following is correct?

Codes:

(a) (A) is correct, but (R) is wrong. (b) Both (A) and (R) are correct.

(c) (A) is wrong, but (R) is correct. (d) Both (A) and (R) are wrong

2. Profit will be divided in __________ in the absence of paertnership deed

(a) 2 : 1 (b) 1 : 2

(c) 3 : 1 (d) Equally

3. A, S and P are partners in a firm sharing profits and losses in the ratio of 2 : 2 : 1. On 1st April 2021, they decided to change their profit-sharing ratio to 5 : 3 : 2. On that date, debit balance of Profit & Loss A/c Rs. 30,000 appeared in the balance sheet and partners decided to pass an adjusting entry for it. Which of the undermentioned options reflect correct treatment for the above treatment?

(a) S's capital account will be debited by Rs. 3,000 and A's capital account credited by Rs. 3,000

(b) P's capital account will be credited by Rs. 3,000 and S's capital account will be credited by Rs. 3,000

(c) S's capital account will be debited by Rs. 30,000 and A's capital account credited by Rs. 30,000

(d) S's capital account will be debited by Rs. 3,000 and A's and P's capital account credited by Rs. 2,000 and Rs. 1,000 respectively.

4. A, B and C are partners, their partnership deed provides for interest on drawings at 8% per annum. B withdrew a fixed amount in the middle of every month and his interest on drawings amounted to Rs. 4,800 at the end of the year. What was the amount of his monthly drawings?

(a) Rs. 10,000 (b) Rs. 5,000

(c) Rs. 1,20,000 (d) Rs. 48,000

5. A and B are partners sharing profit in the ratio 3 : 1. On 31st March 2021, firm's net profit is Rs. 1,25,000. The partnership deed provided interest on capital to A and B Rs. 15,000 & Rs. 10,000 respectively and Interest on drawings for the year amounted to Rs. 6000 from A and Rs. 4000 from B. A is also entitled to commission @10% on net divisible profits. Calculate profit to be transferred to Partners Capital A/c's.

(a) Rs. 1,00,000 (b) Rs. 1,10,000

(c) Rs. 1,07,000 (d) Rs. 90,000

6. E, F and G are partners sharing profits in the ratio of 3 : 3 : 2. According to the partnership agreement, G is to get a minimum amount of Rs. 80,000 as his share of profits every year and any deficiency on this account is to be personally borne by E. The net profit for the year ended 31st March 2021 amounted to Rs. 3,12 ,000. Calculate the amount of deficiency to be borne by E?

(a) Rs. 1,000 (b) Rs. 4,000

(c) Rs. 8,000 (d) Rs. 2,000

7. In the absence of partnership deed, a partner is entitled to an interest on the amount of additional capital advanced by him to the firm at a rate of:

(a) entitled for 6% p.a. on their additional capital, only when there are profits.

(b) entitled for 10% p.a. on their additional capital

(c) entitled for 12% p.a. on their additional capital

(d) not entitled for any interest on their additional capitals.

8. A and V are partners in the ratio of 3 : 2. Their fixed Capital were Rs. 3,00,000 and Rs. 4,00,000 respectively. After the close of accounts for the year it was observed that the Interest on Capital which was agreed to be provided at 5% pa was erroneously provided at 10%p.a. By what amount will A's account be affected if partners decide to pass an adjustment entry for the same?

(a) A's Current A/c will be Debited by Rs. 15,000.

(b) A's Current A/c will be Credited by Rs. 6,000.

(c) A's Current A/c will be Credited by Rs. 35,000.

(d) A's Current A/c will be Debited by Rs. 20,000.

9. If no agreement is made by partner's then interest on loan will be given @ ________

(a) 4% (b) 6%

(c) 5% (d) None of the above

10. Salary to partners will be shown in ________.

(a) Manufacturing account (b) P/l adjustment A/c

(c) P/ L A/c (d) Expense A/c

11. In the absence of an agreement, partners are entitled to:

(a) Salary

(b) Profit share in capital ratio

(c) Interest on loan and advances

(d) Commission

12. Calculate interest on drawing @12% p.a. for B if he withdraw Rs. 2,000 once in month :

(a) Rs. 1,440 (b) Rs. 1,200

(c) Rs. 1,320 (d) Rs. 1,500

13. What should be the minimum number of persons to form a partnership

(a) 2 (b) 20

(c) 7 (d) 15

14. Liability of a partner is

(a) Limited

(b) Dertermined by partnership act

(c) Unlimited

(d) All of the above

15. A, B and C are partners sharing profits and losses equally. Their capital balances on March, 31, 2020 are Rs. 80,000, Rs. 60,000 and Rs. 40,000 respectively. Their personal assets are worth as follows : A — Rs. 20,000, B — Rs. 15,000 and C — Rs. 10,000. The extent of their liability in the firm would be :

(a) A — Rs. 80,000 : B — Rs. 60,000 : and C — Rs. 40,000

(b) A — Rs. 20,000 : B — Rs. 15,000 : and C — Rs. 10,000

(c) A — Rs. 1,00,000 : B — Rs. 75,000 : and C — Rs. 50,000

(d) Equal

16. Partnership Deed is also called

(a) Prospectus
(b) Articles of Association
(c) Principles of Partnership
(d) Articles of Partnership

17. X and Y are partners in partnership firm without any agreement. X has given a loan of Rs. 50,000 to the firm. At the end of year loss was incurred in the business. Following interest may be paid to X by the firm :

(a) @5% Per Annum
(b) @ 6% Per Annum
(c) @ 6% Per Month
(d) None of the above

18. Interest on capital will be paid to the partners if provided for in the partnership deed but only out of:

(a) Profits
(B) Reserves
(c) Accumulated Profits
(d) Goodwill

19. Sleeping partners are those who

(a) take active part in the conduct of the business but provide no capital. However, salary is paid to them.

(b) do not take any part in the conduct of the business but provide capital and share profits and losses in the agreed ratio

(c) take active part in the conduct of the business but provide no capital. However, share profits and losses in the agreed ratio.

(d) do not take any part in the conduct of the business and contribute no capital. However, share profits and losses in the agreed ratio.

20. What time would be taken into consideration if equal monthly amount is drawn as drawings at the beginning of each month ?

(a) 7 months
(b) 6 months
(c) 5 months
(d) 6.5 months

Topic Test – 1

1. A draws Rs. 1,000 per month on the last day of every month. If the rate of interest is 5% p.a., then the total interest on drawings will be :

(a) Rs. 125
(b) Rs. 275
(c) Rs. 400
(d) Rs. 50

For questions 2 to 4: Analyse the case given below and answer the questions that follows:

On 1-04-2021 A and B entered into a partnership for supplying water filters to government school situated in the outskirts of Delhi. They contributed Rs. 80,000 and Rs. 50,000 and agreed to share the profits in the ratio 3 : 2 . the partnership deed provided that interest on capital shall be allowed at 9% per annum. During the year the firm earned a profit of Rs. 7,800.

2. What should be the amount of B interest on capital?

(a) Rs. 3,500
(b) Rs. 4,000
(c) Rs. 3,000
(d) Rs. 2,500

3. What should be the amount of A's interest on capital?

(a) Rs. 4,500
(b) Rs. 3,000
(c) Rs. 2,500
(d) Rs. 4,800

4. Interest on capital will be calculated

(a) Opening capital
(b) Closing capital
(c) Both (a) and (b)
(d) None of the above

5. **Assertion (A):** Rent payable to a partner is transferred to the credit of Partner's Capital Account and not to Rent Payable Account.

Reasoning (R): Rent payable to a partner for letting the firm use his personal property for business is a transaction that is not related to him being a partner. Therefore, it is credited to Rent Payable Account.

Codes:

(a) Both Assertion (A) and Reason (R) are true and Reason (R) is the correct explanation of Assertion (A).
(b) Both Assertion (A) and Reason (R) are true and Reason (R) is not the correct explanation of Assertion (A).
(c) Assertion (A) is true but Reason (R) is False
(d) Assertion (A) is false but Reason (R) is true

6. Interest on drawings of the Partners is a :

(a) Loss to business
(b) Profit to business
(c) Profit to partners
(d) Loss to Bank

7. Partners' current accounts are opened when their capital is:

(a) Fluctuating
(b) Fixed
(c) Both (a) and (b)
(d) None of these

8. Which one is not the feature of partnership?

(a) Agreement
(b) Sharing of Profit
(c) Limited Liability
(d) Two or more than two persons

9. Which of the following is not incorporated in the Partnership Act?

(a) Profit and loss are to be shared equally
(b) No interest is to be charged on capital
(c) All loans are to be charged interest @6% p.a.
(d) All drawings are to be charged interest

10. In the absence of a partnership deed, the allowable rate of interest on partner's loan account will be :

(a) 6% Simple Interest
(b) 6% p.a. Simple Interest
(c) 12% Simple Interest
(d) None of the above

Topic Test – 2

1. X and Y are partners in partnership firm without any agreement. A has given a loan of Rs. 40,000 to the firm. At the end of year loss was incurred in the business. Following interest may be paid to X by the firm :

(a) @6% Per Annum
(b) @ 7% Per Annum
(c) @ 5% Per annum
(d) None of the above

2. Which one of the following items cannot be recorded in the profit and loss appropriation account?

(a) Interest on capital (b) Interest on drawings

(c) Rent paid to partners (d) Partner's salary

3. A and B were partners in a firm sharing profits and losses equally. A withdrew a fixed amount at the beginning of each quarter. Interest on drawings is charged @ 6% p.a. At the end of the year , interest on A's drawings amounted to Rs. 600. Choose the correct journal entry for the above case:-

(a)	A's capital A/c	- Dr	600
	To Interest on drawings		600
(b)	A's Capital A/c	- Dr.	600
	To B's capital A/c		600
(c)	B's capital A/c	- Dr.	600
	To Interest on drawings		600
(d)	Interest on drawings	- Dr.	600
	To A's A/c		600

4. X, Y and Z were Partners with capitals of Rs. 50,000; Rs. 40,000 and Rs. 30,000 respectively carrying on business in partnership. The firm's reported profit for the year was Rs. 80,000. As per provision of the Indian Partnership Act, 1932, find out the share of each partner in the above amount after taking into account that no interest has been provided on an advance by X of Rs. 20,000 in addition to his capital contribution.

(a) Rs. 26,267 for Partner Y and Z and Rs. 27,466 for Partner X.

(b) Rs. 26,667 each partner.

(c) Rs. 33,333 for X Rs. 26,667 for Y and Rs. 20,000 for Z.

(d) Rs. 30,000 each partner.

5. According to Profit and Loss Account, the net profit for the year is Rs. 4,20,000. Salary of a partner is Rs. 5,000 per month and the commission of another partner is Rs. 10,000. The interest on drawings of partners is Rs. 4,000. The net profit as per Profit and Loss Appropriation Account will be :

(a) Rs. 4,44,000 (b) Rs. 3,26,000

(c) Rs. 3,09,000 (d) Rs. 3,54,000

6. M and N are partners in a firm. M's capital is Rs. 70,000 and N's Capital is Rs. 50.000. Firm's profit is Rs. 60,000. N's share in profit will be :

(a) Rs. 15,000 (b) Rs. 3 0,000

(c) Rs. 25,000 (d) Rs. 20,000

7. Aman a partner in a firm withdrew Rs. 8000 at the beginning of each quarter. For how many months would the interest on drawings be charged.

(a) 6 months (b) 5 months

(c) 6½ months (d) 7 ½ months

8. Calculate interest on drawings @ 12% p.a. for Atul if he withdrew Rs. 72,000 once at the beginning of each month:

(a) Rs. 71,000 (b) Rs. 71,500

(c) Rs. 71,600 (d) Rs. 71,560

9. Which of the following statement is true?

(a) a minor cannot be admitted as a partner

(b) a minor can be admitted as a partner, only into the benefits of the partnership

(c) a minor can be admitted as a partner but his rights and liabilities are same of adult partner

(d) None of the above

10. On 31st Jul 2020 a partner introduced in the firm additional capital Rs. 30,000. In the absence of partnership deed, on 31st March 2021 he will receive interest :

(a) Rs. 2,000 (b) Zero

(c) Rs. 1,500 (d) Rs. 1,000

Answer Keys

Exercise

1. (a)	2. (d)	3. (a)	4. (a)	5. (a)	6. (d)	7. (d)	8. (b)	9. (b)	10. (b)
11. (c)	12. (a)	13. (a)	14. (c)	15. (b)	16. (d)	17. (b)	18. (a)	19. (b)	20. (d)

Topic Test – 1

1. (b)	2. (c)	3. (d)	4. (a)	5. (d)	6. (b)	7. (b)	8. (c)	9. (d)	10. (b)

Topic Test – 2

1. (a)	2. (c)	3. (a)	4. (a)	5. (d)	6. (b)	7. (d)	8. (d)	9. (b)	10. (b)

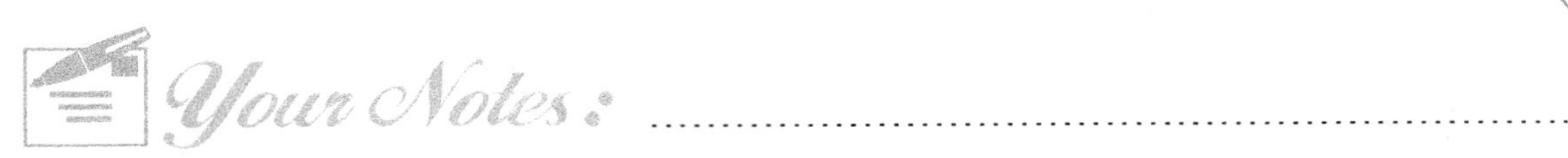
Your Notes :

CHAPTER 3

Reconstitution of A Partnership Firm– Admission of a Partner

Summary

Partnership is an agreement between two or more persons (called partners) for sharing the profits of a business carried on by all or any of them acting for all.

1. Admission of a New Partner: A new partner may be admitted when the firm needs additional capital or managerial help. According to the provisions of Partnership Act 1932 unless it is otherwise provided in the partnership deed a new partner can be admitted only when the existing partners unanimously agree for it.
2. Change in the profit sharing ratio among the existing partners: Sometimes the partners of a firm may decide to change their existing profit sharing ratio. This may happen an account of a change in the existing partners' role in the firm.
3. Retirement of an existing partner: It means withdrawal by a partner from the business of the firm which may be due to his bad health, old age or change in business interests.
4. Death of a partner: Partnership may also stand reconstituted on death of a partner, if the remaining partners decide to continue the business of the firm as usual.

Admission of a New Partner: When firm requires additional capital or managerial help or both for the expansion of its business a new partner may be admitted to supplement its existing resources. According to the Partnership Act 1932, a new partner can be admitted into the firm only with the consent of all the existing partners unless otherwise agreed upon. With the admission of a new partner, the partnership firm is reconstituted and a new agreement is entered into to carry on the business of the firm. A newly admitted partner acquires two main rights in the firm–

1. Right to share the assets of the partnership firm; and
2. Right to share the profits of the partnership firm.

Following are the other important points which require attention at the time of admission of a new partner:

1. New profit sharing ratio;
2. Sacrificing ratio;
3. Valuation and adjustment of goodwill;
4. Revaluation of assets and Reassessment of liabilities;
5. Distribution of accumulated profits (reserves); and
6. Adjustment of partners' capitals.

New Profit Sharing Ratio

The ratio in which all partners including new partner share the future profits is called the new profit sharing ratio. In other words, on the admission of a new partner, the old partners sacrifice a share of their profits in favour of the new partner. On admission of a new partner, the profit-sharing ratio among the old partners will change keeping in view their respective contribution to the profit-sharing ratio of the incoming partner. Hence, there is a need to ascertain the new profit sharing ratio among all the partners.

The new partner may acquire his share from the old partners in any of the following situations:

1. If only the ratio of the new partner is given, then in the absence of any other agreement or information, it is assumed that the old partners will continue to share the remaining profits in the old ratio.
2. If the new partner acquires his share of profit from the old partners equally. In that case, the new profit sharing ratio of the old partner will be calculated by deducting the sacrifice made by them from their existing share of profit.
3. In the new partner acquire his share of profit from the old partners in a particular ratio. In that case, the new profit sharing ratio of the old partners will be calculated by deducting the sacrifice made by them from their existing share of profit.
4. If the old partners surrender a particular fraction of their share in favour of the new partner. In that case, the new partner's share is calculated by adding the surrendered portion of the share by the old partners. Old partners' share is calculated by deducting the surrendered portion from their old ratio.
5. If the new partner acquires his share of profit from only one partner. In that case, the new profit sharing ratio of the old partner will be calculated by deducting the sacrifice made by one partner from his existing ratio.

Sacrificing Ratio

The ratio in which the old partners have agreed to sacrifice their shares in profit in favour of a new partner is called the sacrificing ratio. This ratio is calculated by taking out the difference between the old profit sharing ratio and the new profit sharing ratio.

Sacrificing Ratio = Old Ratio – New Ratio

Goodwill

Goodwill is the value of the reputation of a firm in respect of the profits expected in future over and above the normal profits earned by other similar firms belonging to the same industry. In other words, a well-established business develops an advantage of good name, reputation and wide business connections. This helps the business to earn more profits as compared to newly set-up business. This advantage in monetary terms called 'Goodwill'. It arises only if a firm is able to earn higher profits than normal.

Factors Affecting the Value of Goodwill: The main factors affecting the value of goodwill are as follows:

1. **Nature of business:** A firm that produces high value added products or having a stable demand is able to earn more profits and therefore has more goodwill.
2. **Location:** If the business is centrally located or is at a place having heavy customer traffic, the goodwill tends to be high.
3. **Efficiency of management:** A well-managed concern usually enjoys the advantage of high productivity and cost efficiency. This leads to higher profits and so the value of goodwill will also be high.
4. **Market situation:** The monopoly condition or limited competition enables the concern to earn high profits which leads to higher value of goodwill.
5. **Special advantages:** The firm that enjoys special advantages like import licences, low rate and assured supply of electricity, long-term contracts for supply of materials, well-known collaborators, patents, trademarks, etc. enjoy higher value of goodwill.

Need for Valuation of Goodwill

1. At the time of sale of a business;
2. Change in the profit-sharing ratio amongst the existing partners;

3. Admission of a new partner.
4. Retirement of a partner;
5. Death of a partner;
6. Dissolution of a firm;
7. The amalgamation of the partnership firm.

Methods of Valuation of Goodwill

Goodwill is an intangible asset, so it is very difficult to calculate its exact value. There are various methods for the valuation of goodwill in the partnership, but the value of goodwill may differ in different methods. The method by which the value of goodwill is to be calculated may be specifically decided among all the partners.

The methods followed for valuing goodwill are:

1. Average Profit Method
2. Super Profit Method
3. Capitalisation Method.

i. Average Profits: Goodwill is calculated on the basis of the number of past years profits. In this method, the goodwill is valued at an agreed number of 'years' purchase of the average profits of the past few years.

Steps:

1. Find the total profit of the past given years.
2. Add ail Abnormal Losses like loss from fire or theft etc. and any Normal Income if not added before to the total profit of past given year.
3. Then, subtract, Abnormal Income (income from speculation or lottery etc.), Normal Expenses (if not deducted), Income from investment (if not related to general activities of business) and remuneration of the proprietor (if not given), if any, from the total profit of past given years.
4. After this, calculate the actual average profit by dividing the total profit by a number of years.
5. Then multiply Average Profit by the numbers of year purchases to find out the value of goodwill.

ii. Super Profit Method:

Under this method, goodwill is valued on the basis of excess profits earned by a firm in comparison to average profits earned by other firms. When a similar type of firm gets a return as a certain percentage of the capital employed, it is called 'normal return'. The excess of actual profit over the normal profit is called 'Super Profits'

Steps:

1. Calculate Actual Average Profit i.e. [Total Profit / No. of Years]
2. Calculate Normal Profit i.e.

   = Capital Employed × NormalRate of Return / 100

   [Capital Employed = Total Assets – Outside Liabilities]
3. Find Out Super Profits

   Super Profits = Actual Average Profit – Normal Profit
4. Calculate the Value of Goodwill = Super profit × No. of years purchased

iii. Capitalisation method:

Under this method the goodwill can be calculated in two ways:

(a) by capitalizing the average profits, or

(b) by capitalising the super profits.

(a) Capitalisation of Average Profits: Under this method, the value of goodwill is ascertained by deducting the actual firm's capital in the business from the capitalized value of the average profits on the basis of normal rate of return. This involves the following steps:

   (i) Ascertain the average profits based on the past few years' performance.

   (ii) Capitalize the average profits on the basis of the normal rate of return to ascertain the capitalised value of average profits as follows: Average Profits × 100/Normal Rate of Return

   (iii) Ascertain the actual firm's capital (net assets) by deducting outside liabilities from the total assets (excluding goodwill and ficticious assets). Firms' Capital = Total Assets (excluding goodwill) – Outside Liabilities Where outside Liabilities include both long term and short term Liabilities.

   (iv) Compute the value of goodwill by deducting net assets from the capitalised value of average profits, i.e. (ii) – (iii).

Treatment of Goodwill

1. Goodwill (Premium) brought in cash through the firm

1. Cash A/c or Bank A/c Dr.
   To Goodwill A/c
   (For the amount of Goodwill brought by new partner)
   Goodwill A/c Dr.
   To Old Partner's Capital A/c
   (For the amount of Goodwill distributed among the old partners in their sacrificing ratio)

2. When goodwill already exists in books: If the goodwill already exists in the books of firms and the incoming partner brings his share of goodwill in cash, then the goodwill appearing in the books will have to be written off.

Old Partner's Capital A/c's Dr.
To Goodwill A/c
(For Goodwill written-off in old ratio)

After the admission of the partner, all partners may decide to maintain the Goodwill Account in the books of accounts.

Goodwill A/c Dr.
To All Partner's Capital A/c's
(For Goodwill raised in the new firm after admission of a new partner in new profit sharing ratio)

3. Goodwill does not exist in the books: When goodwill does not exist in the books, sacrificing partners are credited with their share of goodwill and new partner is debited by the amount of goodwill not brought by him.

The journal entry in this case is :

Incoming (New) Partners Current A/c Dr.
To Sacrificing Partners Capital A/c (individually)
(Account of goodwill not brought in by new partner)

4. No goodwill appears in the books:

Goodwill A/c Dr.
To Old Partner's Capital A/c's
(For Goodwill raised at full value in the old ratio)

5. When goodwill already exists in the books

1. When the value of goodwill appearing in books is equal to the agreed value:
   [No Entry is Required]
2. If the value of goodwill appearing in the books is less than the agreed value:
   Goodwill A/c Dr.
   To Old Partner's Capital A/c's
   (For Goodwill is raised to its agreed value)

3. If the value of goodwill appearing in the books is more than the agreed value:
   Old Partner's Capital A/c's Dr.
   To Goodwill A/c
   (For Goodwill brought down to its agreed value)

Hidden or Inferred Goodwill

1. To find out the total capital of the firm by new partner's capital and his share of profit.
2. To ascertain the existing total capital of the firm: We will have to ascertain the existing total capital of the new firm by adding the capital (of all partners, including new partner's capital after adjustments, if any excluding goodwill)
3. Goodwill = Capital from (1) – Capital from (2)

The journal entries recorded for revaluation of assets and reassessment of liabilities are following:

1. For increase in the value of an Assets
   Assets A/c Dr.
   To Revaluation A/c (Gain)
2. For decrease in the value of an Assets
   Revaluation A/c Dr.
   To Assets A/c (Loss)
3. For appreciation in the amount of Liability
   Revaluation A/c Dr.
   To Liability A/c (Loss)
4. For reduction in the amount of a Liability
   Liability A/c Dr.
   To Revaluation A/c (Gain)
5. For recording an unrecorded Assets
   Unrecorded Assets A/c Dr.
   To Revaluation A/c (Gain)
6. For recording an unrecorded Liability
   Revaluation A/c Dr.
   To Unrecorded Liability A/c (Loss)
7. For the sale of unrecorded Assets
   Cash A/c or Bank A/c Dr.
   To Revaluation A/c (Gain)
8. For payment of unrecorded Liability
   Revaluation A/c Dr.
   To Cash A/c or Bank A/c (Loss)
9. For transfer of gain on Revaluation if the credit balance
   Revaluation A/c Dr.
   To Old Partner's Capital A/c's (Old Ratio)
10. For transfer of loss on Revaluation if debit balance
    Old Partner's Capital A/c's Dr.
    To Revaluation A/c (Old Ratio)

Revaluation Account

Dr. **Cr.**

Particulars	Amount (Rs.)	Particulars	Amount (Rs.)
Decrease in value of Assets	××	Increase in value of Assets	××
Increase in value of Liabilities	××	Decrease in value of Liability	××
Unrecorded Liability	××	Unrecorded Assets	××
Payment of Liability (Cash A/c)	××	Sale of Unrecorded Assets (Bank A/c)	××
Profit tr. of Capital A/c of old partners (Old Ratio)	××	Loss tr. to Capital A/c of old partners A/c (Old Ratio)	××
	××		××

Adjustment of Capitals

1. When the new partner brings in proportionate capital OR On the basis of the old partner's capital.
   (a) Calculate the adjusted capital of old partners (after all adjustments)
   (b) Total capital of the firm
   = Combined Adjusted Capital × Reciprocal proportion of the share of old partners
   (c) New Partner's Capital = Total Capital × Proportion of share of a new partner.
2. On the basis of the new partner's capital:
   (a) Total Capital of the firm = New Partner's Capital × Reciprocal proportion of his share.
   (b) Distribute Total Capital in New Profit Sharing Ratio.
   (c) Calculate adjusted capital of old partners.
   (d) Calculate the difference between New Capital and Adjusted Capital.
1. If the debit side of the Capital Account is bigger then it means he has excess capital
   Partner's (capital Accounts) Dr.
   To Cash A /c or Bank A/c or Current A/c
2. If the credit side is bigger then it means that he has short capital
   Cash A/c or Bank A/c or Current A/c Dr.
   To Partner's Capital A/c's

Change in Profit Sharing Ratio among the Existing Partners

Sometimes the existing partners of the firm may decide to change their profit sharing ratio. In such a case, some partner will gain in future profits and some will lose. Here the gaining partners should compensate the losing partners unless otherwise agreed upon. In such a situation, first of all, the loss and gain in the value of goodwill (if any) will have to adjust.

1. Goodwill A/c Dr.
   To Partner's Capital A/c's (For raising the amount of Goodwill in old ratio)
2. Partner's Capital A/c's Dr.
   To Goodwill A/c
   (For writing off the amount of Goodwill in New Profit sharing ratio)

Exercise

1. Gain / loss on revaluation at the time of change in profit sharing ratio of existing partners is shared by ____(i)______ whereas in case of admission of a partner it is shared by_____(ii)______.
   (a) (i) Remaining Partners, (ii) All Partners.
   (b) (i) All Partners, (ii) Old partners.
   (c) (i) New Partner, (ii) All partner.
   (d) (i) Sacrificing Partner, (ii) Incoming partner.
2. At the time of admission of a partner, what will be the effect of the following information? Balance in Workmen compensation reserve Rs. 40,000. Claim for workmen compensation Rs. 45,000.
   (a) Rs. 45,000 Debited to the Partner's capital Accounts.
   (b) Rs. 40,000 Debited to Revaluation Account.
   (c) Rs. 5,000 Debited to Revaluation Account.
   (d) Rs. 5,000 Credited to Revaluation Account.
3. Revaluation of assets at the time of reconstitution is necessary because their present value may be different from their:
   (a) Market Value (b) Net Value
   (c) Cost of Asset (d) Book Value
4. If average capital employed in a firm is Rs. 8,00,000, average of actual profits is Rs. 1,80,000 and normal rate of return is10%, then value of goodwill as per capitalization of average profits is:
   (a) Rs. 10,00,000 (b) Rs. 18,00,000
   (c) Rs. 80,00,000 (d) Rs. 78,20,000
5. A and B were partners sharing profits and losses in the ratio of 5 : 3. On 1st April,2021 they admitted C as a new partner and new ratio was decided as 3 : 2 : 1. Goodwill of the firm was valued as Rs. 3,60,000. C couldn't bring any amount for goodwill. Amount of goodwill share to be credited to A and B Account's will be:
   (a) Rs. 37,500 and Rs. 22,500 respectively (b) Rs. 30,000 and Rs. 30,000 respectively
   (c) Rs. 36,000 and Rs. 24,000 respectively (d) Rs. 45,000 and Rs. 15,000 respectively
6. X , Y and Z are partners in the ratio of 5 : 3 : 2. If B's share of profit at the end of the year amounted to Rs. 1,50,000, what will be A's share of profits?
   (a) Rs. 5,00,000 (b) Rs. 1,50,000
   (c) Rs. 3,00,000 (d) Rs. 2,50,000
7. A and C ware partners in a firm. Their Balance Sheet showed Furniture at Rs. 2,00,000; Stock at Rs. 1,40,000; Debtors at Rs. 1,62,000 and Creditors at Rs. 60,000. S was admitted and new profit-sharing ratio was agreed at 2 : 3 : 5. Stock was revalued at Rs. 1,00,000, Creditors of Rs. 15,000 are not likely to be claimed, Debtors for Rs. 2,000 have become irrecoverable and Provision for doubtful debts to be provided @ 10%. A's share in loss on revaluation amounted to Rs. 30,000. Revalued value of Furniture will be:
   (a) Rs. 2,17,000 (b) Rs. 1,03,000
   (c) Rs. 3,03,000 (d) Rs. 1,83,000
8. A and N are partner's sharing profits in the ratio of 2 : 1. K was admitted for 1/4 share of which 1/8 was gifted by A. The remaining was contributed by N. Goodwill of the firm is valued at Rs. 40,000. How much amount for goodwill will be credited to N's Capital account?
   (a) Rs. 2,500 (b) Rs. 5,000
   (c) Rs. 20,000 (d) Rs. 40,000

9. Given below are two statements, one labelled as Assertion (A) and the other labelled as Reason (R):

   Assertion (A): Revaluation A/c is prepared at the time of Admission of a partner.

   Reasoning (R): It is required to adjust the values of assets and liabilities at the time of admission of a partner, so that the true financial position of the firm is reflected.

   In the context of the above two statements, which of the following is correct?

   Codes:

   (a) Both (A) and (R) are correct and (R) is the correct reason of (A).

   (b) Both (A) and (R) are correct but (R) is not the correct reason of (A).

   (c) Only (R) is correct.

   (d) Both (A) and (R) are wrong.

10. M, T and J were partners in the ratio of 5 : 3 : 2. On 31st March 2021, their books reflected a net profit of Rs. 2,10,000. As per the terms of the partnership deed they were entitled for interest on capital which amounted to Rs. 80,000, Rs. 60,000 and Rs. 40,000 respectively. Besides this a salary of Rs. 60,000 each was payable to M and T. Calculate the ratio in which the profits would be appropriated.

    (a) 1 : 1 : 1 (b) 5 : 3 : 2

    (c) 7 : 6 : 2 (d) 4 : 3 : 2

11. A and B are partners in the ratio of 3 : 2. C is admitted as a partner and he takes ¼th of his share from A. B gives 3/16 from his share to C. What is the share of C?

    (a) 1/4 (b) 1/16

    (c) 1/6 (d) 1/16

12. Goodwill is _________

    (a) Hidden asset (b) Tangible asset

    (c) Intangible asset (d) None of the above

13. Goodwill of the firm on the basis of 2 years purchase of average profit of the last 3 years is Rs. 25,000. Find the average profit.

    (a) Rs.30,000 (b) Rs. 20,000

    (c) Rs.2500 (d) Rs. 3000

14. When there is no Goodwill Account in the books and goodwill is raised, _______ account will be debited :

    (a) Partner's Capital (b) Goodwill

    (c) Cash (d) Reserve

15. X, Y and Z are three partners sharing profits and losses in the ratio of 4:3:2. W is admitted for 1/10 share, the new ratio will be :

    (a) 1 : 5 : 3 :4 (b) 3 : 3 : 4 : 1

    (c) 4 : 3 : 2 : 1 (d) 3 : 4 : 1 : 2

16. Find the goodwill of firm using capitalisation method, the total capital employed in the firm is Rs. 80,000. Rate of return is 15%. Profit of the year is Rs. 1,20,000.

    (a) Rs. 7,20,000 (b) Rs. 8,20,000

    (c) Rs. 5,60,000 (d) Rs. 7,15,000

17. General reserve at the time of admission of a partner is transferred to:

    (a) Revaluation account (b) Balance sheet

    (c) Old partner's capital account (d) Current account

18. Average profit of a business over the last five years ware Rs. 60,000. The normal yield on capital invested in such a business is estimated at 10% pa. Capital invested in the business is Rs. 5,00,000. Amount of goodwill, it is based on 3 year's purchase of last 5 years super profit will be

    (a) Rs. 1,00,000 (b) Rs. 1,80,000

    (c) Rs. 30,000 (d) Rs. 1,50,000

19. Average capital employed is considered while calculating average profit.

(a) True (b) False

(c) Partially true (d) Can't say

20. A and B are partners sharing profits and losses in the ratio of 5 : 4. C is admitted for 1/5th share. A and B decide to share equally in future. Sacrificing ratio will be :

(a) 5 : 4 (b) 2 : 7

(c) 7 : 2 (d) 1 : 1

Topic Test – 1

For questions 1 to 3: Analyse the case given below and answer the questions that follows:

A and M were partners in a fast-food corner sharing profits and losses in ratio 3 : 2. They sold fast food items across the counter and did home delivery too. Their initial fixed capital contribution was Rs. 1,20,000 and Rs. 80,000 respectively. At the end of first year their profit was Rs. 1,20,000 before allowing the remuneration of Rs. 3,000 per quarter to A and Rs. 2,000 per half year to M. Such a promising performance for first year was encouraging, therefore, they decided to expand the area of operations. For this purpose, they needed a delivery van, a few Scotties and an additional person to support. Six months into the accounting year they decided to admit S as a new partner and offered him 20% as a share of profits along with monthly remuneration of Rs. 2,500. S was asked to introduce Rs. 1,30,000 for capital and Rs. 70,000 for premium for goodwill. Besides this S was required to provide Rs. 1,00,000 as loan for two years. S readily accepted the offer. The terms of the offer were duly executed and he was admitted as a partner.

1. Upon the admission of S the sacrifice for providing his share of profits would be done:

(a) by A only. (b) by M only.

(c) by A and M equally. (d) by A and in the ratio of 3 : 2.

2. Remuneration will be transferred to ________ of A and M at the end of the accounting period.

(a) Capital account (b) Loan account

(c) Current account (d) None of the above

3. S will be entitled to a remuneration of ________ at the end of the year.

(a) Rs. 15,000 (b) Rs. 20,000

(c) Rs. 13,000 (d) Rs. 10,000

4. A and B are partners. They admit C for 13rd share. In future the ratio between A and B would be 2 : 1. Sacrificing ratio will be :

(a) 2 : 1 (b) 1 : 1

(c) 5 : 1 (d) 1 : 5

5. X and Y are partners sharing profits and losses as 2 : 1. Z is admitted and profit sharing ratio becomes 4 : 3 : 2. Goodwill is valued at Rs. 94,500. C brings required goodwill in cash. Goodwill amount will be Credited to :

(a) X Rs. 14,000 and Y Rs. 7,000 (b) X Rs. 12,000 and Y Rs. 9,000

(c) X Rs. 21,000 (d) Y Rs. 94,500

6. Net profits during the last three years of a firm are

1st Year – 18,000

2nd Year – 20,000

3rd Year – 22,000

The Capital investment of the firm is Rs. 60,000. The normal Rate of Return is 10%. Value of goodwill on the basis of three years purchase of the super profit for the last three years will be

(a) Rs. 21,000 (b) Rs. 42,000

(c) Rs. 84,000 (d) Rs. 20,000

7. A and B are partners sharing profits and losses in the ratio of 7 : 5. They agree to admit C, their manager, into partnership who is to get 1/6th share in the profits. He acquires this share as 1/24th from A and 1/8th from B, The new profit sharing ratio will be :
   (a) 13 : 7 : 4 (b) 7 : 13 : 4
   (c) 7 : 5 : 6 (d) 5 : 7 : 6
8. Which of the following assets is compulsorily revalued at the time of admission of a new partner :
   (a) stock (b) Fixed Assets
   (c) Investment (d) Goodwill
9. K is admitted in a firm for a 1/4 share in the profit for which he brings Rs. 7,30,000 for goodwill. It will be taken away by the old partners M and N in :
   (a) Old profit-sharing ratio (b) New profit-sharing ratio
   (c) Sacrificing ratio (d) Capital ratio
10. At the time of admission of a new partner, Undistributed Profits appearing in the Balance Sheet of the old firm is transferred to the Capital Account of:
   (a) Old partners is old profit-sharing ratio (b) Old partners in new profit-sharing ratio
   (c) All the partners in the new profit-sharing ratio (d) None of these

Topic Test – 2

1. The profit of the last three years are Rs. 42,000, Rs. 39,000 and Rs. 45,000. Value of goodwill at two years purchases of the average profits will be :
   (a) Rs. 42,000 (b) Rs. 84,000
   (c) Rs. 1,26,000 (d) Rs. 36,000
2. Under average profit basis goodwill is calculated by :
   (a) No. of years' purchased x Average profit
   (b) No. of years' purchased x Super profit
   (c) Super Profit -r Expected Rate of Return
   (d) None of these
3. Profits of the last three years were Rs. 6,000, Rs. 13,000 and Rs. 8,000 respectively. Goodwill at two years purchase of the average net profit will be :
   (a) Rs. 81,000 (b) Rs. 27,0000
   (c) Rs. 9,000 (d) Rs. 18,000
4. **Assertion (A):** Purchased goodwill means goodwill for which consideration has been paid.

   Reasoning (R): It is shown in the Balance Sheet as a liability.

   Codes:
   (a) Both Assertion (A) and Reason (R) are true and Reason (R) is the correct explanation of Assertion (A).
   (b) Both Assertion (A) and Reason (R) are true and Reason (R) is not the correct explanation of Assertion (A).
   (c) Assertion (A) is true but Reason (R) is False
   (d) Assertion (A) is False but Reason (R) is True
5. Super profits is calculated as ________-
   (a) Actual profit + normal profit (b) Actual profit – normal profit
   (c) Normal profit – actual profit (d) None of the above
6. X and Y are partners sharing profits and losses in the ratio of 7 : 5. They agree to admit Z, their manager, into partnership who is to get 1/6th share in the profits. He acquires this share as 1/24th from X and 1/8th from Y, The new profit sharing ratio will be :
   (a) 13 : 7 : 4 (b) 7 : 13 : 4
   (c) 7 : 5 : 6 (d) 5 : 7 : 6

7. A and B are partners sharing profit or loss in the ratio of 4 : 1. A surrenders 1/4 of his share and B surrenders 112 of his share in favour of C, a new partner. What will be the C's share?

(a) $\frac{3}{4}$ (b) $\frac{1}{5}$

(c) $\frac{1}{10}$ (d) $\frac{3}{10}$

8. A firm earned Rs. 60,000 as profit, the normal rate of return being 10%. Assets of the firm are Rs. 7,20,000 (excluding goodwill) and liabilities are Rs. 2 40,000. Find the value of goodwill by the capitalization of the Average Profit Method.

(a) Rs. 2,40,000 (b) Rs. 1,80,000

(c) Rs. 1,20,000 (d) Rs. 60,000

9. When the incoming partner brings his share of premium of goodwill in cash it is adjusted by crediting to :

(a) Sacrificing's partner's capital account (b) Premium goodwill

(c) Capital A/c (d) Current A/c

10. A and B are partners sharing profit and losses in ratio of 5 : 3. C is admitted for 1/4th share. On the date of reconstitution, the debtors stood at Rs. 40,000, bill receivable stood at Rs. 10,000 and the provision for doubtful debts appeared at Rs. 4000. A bill receivable, of Rs. 10,000 which was discounted from the bank, earlier has been reported to be dishonored. The firm has sold, the debtor so arising to a debt collection agency at a loss of 40%. If bad debts now have arisen for Rs. 6,000 and firm decides to maintain provisions at same rate as before then amount of Provision to be debited to Revaluation Account would be:

(a) Rs. 4,400 (b) Rs. 4,000

(c) Rs. 3,400 (d) None of these

Answer Keys

Exercise

1. (b)	2. (c)	3. (a)	4. (a)	5. (d)	6. (d)	7. (d)	8. (b)	9. (a)	10. (c)
11. (a)	12. (b)	13. (c)	14. (b)	15. (c)	16. (a)	17. (c)	18. (c)	19. (b)	20. (c)

Topic Test – 1

1. (d)	2. (c)	3. (a)	4. (d)	5. (c)	6. (b)	7. (a)	8. (d)	9. (c)	10. (a)

Topic Test – 2

1. (b)	2. (a)	3. (d)	4. (c)	5. (b)	6. (a)	7. (d)	8. (c)	9. (a)	10. (c)

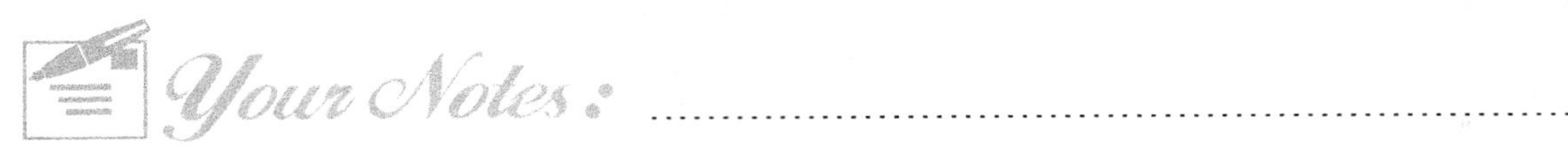
Your Notes :

CHAPTER 4

Retirement / Death of A Partner

Summary

Retirement of a Partner:

A partner may retire from the partnership firm:

1. with the consent of all other partners;

   or

2. in case of retirement at will i.e. (partnership at will);

   or

3. by giving notice in writing to all other partners by the retiring partner

   Ascertaining the Amount Due to Retiring/ Deceased Partner

   The sum due to the retiring partner (in case of retirement) and to the legal representatives/ executors (in case of death) includes:

   (i) credit balance of his capital account;

   (ii) (credit balance of his current account (if any);

   (iii) his share of goodwill;

   (iv) his share of accumulated profits (reserves);

   (v) his share in the gain of revaluation of assets and liabilities;

   (vi) his share of profits up to the date of retirement/death;

   (vii) interest on his capital, if involved, up to the date of retirement/death;

   (viii) salary/commission, if any, due to him up to the date of retirement/death.

   The following deductions, if any, may have to be made from his share:

   (i) debit balance of his current account (if any);

   (ii) his share of goodwill to be written off, if necessary;

   (iii) his share of accumulated losses;

   (iv) his share of loss on revaluation of assets and liabilities;

   (v) his share of loss up to the date of retirement/death;

   (vi) his drawings up to the date of retirement/death;

   (vii) interest on drawings, if involved, up to the date of retirement/death.

(b) Goodwill is raised at its full value and written off immediately:

If it is decided that the goodwill will not appear in the balance sheet of the reconstituted firm, then the following journal entries are required:

1. Goodwill A/c Dr.

   To All Partner's Capital A/c's (For raising of Goodwill and credited to all partners capital A/c's in their old profit sharing ratio)

2. Continuing Partner's Capital A/c's Dr.

   To Goodwill A/c

   (For written off goodwill between continuing partners in their new profit sharing ratio)

(c) Goodwill is raised to the extent of retired/deceased partner's share and written off immediately:

1. Goodwill A/c Dr.

   To Retiring/Deceased Partner's Capital A/c (For the goodwill raised by share of outgoing partner)

2. Continuing Partner's Capital AJc's Dr.

   To Goodwill A/c

   (For the goodwill written off between the continuing partners in their gaining ratio)

(d) No Goodwill account is raised at all in the firm's books:

If the outgoing partner's share of goodwill is adjusted in the capital accounts of the continuing partners without opening a goodwill account, the following entry will be required:

Continuing Partner's Capital A/c's Dr.

To Outgoing Partner's Capital A/c (For the share of outgoing partner in the goodwill adjusted through capital accounts in the gaining ratio)

Hidden Goodwill: If the firm has agreed to settle the retiring or deceased partner's account by paying him a lump sum amount, then the amount paid to him in excess of what is due to him, based on the balance in his capital account after making necessary adjustments in respect of accumulated profits and losses and revaluation of assets and liabilities, etc., shall be treated as his share of goodwill (known as hidden goodwill)

Revaluation of Assets and Liabilities

The retiring /deceased partner must be given a share of all profits that have arisen till his retirement/death and is made to bear his share of losses that have occurred till that period. This necessitates the revaluation of assets and liabilities. At the time of retirement/death of a partner, there may be some assets and liabilities which may not have been shown at their present values.

Journal Entries:

1. For increase in the value of assets:

   Asset(s) Alc (individually) Dr.

   To Revaluation A/c (For increase in the value of assets)

2. For decrease in the value of assets:

   Revaluation A/c Dr.

   To Assets A/c's (individually)

   (For decrease in the value of assets)

3. For increase in the number of liabilities:

   Revaluation A/c Dr.

   To Liabilities A/c's (individually)

   (for an increase in liabilities)

4. For decrease in the number of liabilities:
   Liabilities A/c's (individually) Dr.
   To Revaluation A/c (For decrease in the liabilities)
5. For an unrecorded asset:
   Assets A/c Dr.
   To Revaluation A/c
   (For unrecorded assets brought into books)
6. For an unrecorded liability:
   Revaluation A/c Dr.
   To Liability A/c
   (For an unrecorded liability brought into books)
7. For the sale of an unrecorded asset:
   Cash A/c Dr.
   To Revaluation A/c (For the sale of unrecorded assets)
8. For payment of an unrecorded liability:
   Revaluation A/c Dr.
   To Cash A/c
   (For the payment of an unrecorded*liability)
9. For-profit on revaluation:
   Revaluation A/c Dr.
   To All Partner's Capital A/c's (individually)
   (For the distribution of profit on revaluation to all partners in their old profit sharing ratio)
   Or
10. For Loss on revaluation:
    All Partner's Capital A/c's (individually) Dr.
    To Revaluation A/c
    (For the distribution of losses on revaluation to all partners in their old profit sharing ratio)

Reserves and Accumulated Profits and Losses:

The retiring/deceased partner is also entitled to his/her share in the accumulated profits, general reserve, workmen compensation fund 1 etc. and is also liable to share the accumulated losses.

For this purpose the following journal entries are required:

1. For Transferring accumulated profits, General Reserves etc.
   To All Partner's Capital A/c's (individually)
   (For accumulated profits are transferred to all partner's Capital A/c's in their old profit sharing ratio)
2. For transfer of accumulated losses:
   All Partner's Capital A/c's (individually) Dr.
   To Profit and Loss A/c To Any Accumulated Loss A/c (For accumulated losses transferred to all partner's Capital A/c's in their old profit sharing ratio)

Disposal of Amount Due to Retiring Partner:

The necessary journal entries recorded are as follows.

1. When retiring partner is paid cash in full.
   Retiring Partners' Capital A/c Dr.
   To Cash/Bank A/c
2. When retiring partners' whole amount is treated as loan.
   Retiring Partners' Capital A/c Dr.
   To Retiring Partners' Loan A/c
3. When retiring partner is partly paid in cash and the remaining amount treated as loan.
   Retiring Partners' Capital A/c Dr. (Total Amount due)
   To Cash/Bank A/c (Amount Paid)
   To Retiring Partners' Loan A/c (Amount of Loan)
4. When Loan account is settled by paying in instalment includes principal and interest.
   a) For interest on loan Interest A/c Dr.
      To Retiring Partner's Loan A/c
   b) For payment of instalment Retiring Partner's Loan A/c Dr.
      To Cash/Bank A/c

Adjustment of Partner's Capital:

At the time of retirement or death of a partner, the remaining partners may decide to adjust their capital contribution in their new profit sharing ratio. The adjustment of the remaining partner's capitals may involve any one of the following cases:

1. When the total capital of a new firm is specified.

   Steps:

   (a) Compute the new capitals of the remaining partners by dividing total capital in their new profit sharing ratio.

   (b) Calculate the amount of adjusted old capital of the remaining partners after all adjustments regarding goodwill, accumulated profit and losses, profit or loss on revaluation etc.

   (c) Find out the surplus or deficiency, as the case may be, in each of the remaining partner's capital account by comparing the new capital and the adjusted capital.'

   (d) Adjust the surplus by paying cash to the concerned partner or by crediting his Current Account as agreed. Adjust the deficiency by asking the concerned partner to pay cash or by debiting his current account.

Adjustment of Partners' Capitals

At the time of retirement or death of a partner, the remaining partners may decide to adjust their capital contributions in their profit sharing ratio. In such a situation, the sum of balances in the capitals of continuing partners may be treated as the total capital of the new firm, unless specified otherwise. Then, to ascertain the new capital of the continuing partners, the total capital of the firm is divided amongst the remaining partners as per the new profit sharing ratio, and the excess or deficiency of capital in the individual capital account's may be worked out. Such excess or shortage shall be adjusted by withdrawal of contribution in cash, as the case may be, for which the following journal entries will be recorded.

(i) For excess capital withdrawn by the partner :
   Partners' Capital A/c Dr.
   To Cash / Bank A/c

(ii) For amount of capital to be brought in by the partner:

Cash / Bank A/c Dr.

To Partners' Capital A/c

Death of a Partner:

The accounting treatment in the event of the death of a partner is the same as that in the case of the retirement of a partner. Here, his claim is transferred to his executor's account and settled in the same manner as that of the retired partner.

The only major difference between the retirement and death of a partner is that retirement normally takes place at the end of the accounting period whereas death may occur on any day. Therefore, in case of death, his claim shall also include his share of profit or loss, interest on capital, interest on drawings (if any), from the beginning of the year to the date of death.

Accounting Treatment of Outgoing Partner's Share in Profit:

1. Through Profit and Loss Suspense Account

   In case of Profit:

   Profit and Loss Suspense A/c Dr.

   To Deceased Partner's Capital A/c (Share of profit for the intervening period)

   In case of Loss:

   Deceased Partner's Capital A/c Dr.

   To Profit and Loss Suspense A/c (Share of loss for the intervening period)

2. Through Capital Transfer In case of Profit:

   Remaining Partner's Capital A/c's Dr.

   To Deceased Partner's Capital A/c In case of Loss:

   Deceased Partner's Capital A/c Dr.

To Remaining Partner's Capital A/c's The executors of deceased partner are entitled to the following:

1. The credit balance of deceased partner's capital account;
2. His share of goodwill;
3. His share of profit till the date of death;
4. His share of profit on revaluation of assets and liabilities;
5. His share of accumulated profits and reserves;
6. His interest on capital if partnership deed provides till the date of death;
7. His share of Joint Life Policy (if any);
8. His salary and commission due (if any);

The following deduction has to made from above.

1. His drawings, interest in drawings till the date of death;
2. His share of loss till the date of death;
3. His share of loss on revaluation of assets and liabilities. ,
4. His share of the reduction in the value of goodwill (if any).

Payment to the executors:

1. When payment is made in full Executor's A/c Dr.
   To Bank A/c.
2. When payment is made in instalment The executor's are entitled to interest when the payment is made in instalment. If the deed is silent about this, then 6% p.a. should be given as per Section 37 of the Indian Partnership Act, 1932.
   When interest is due
   Interest A/c Dr.
   To Executor's A/c
   When instalment paid along with interest
   Executor's A/c Dr.
   To Cash/Bank A/c

Exercise

1. Gaining Ratio' means :

(a) Old Ratio – New Ratio
(b) New Ratio – Old Ratio
(c) Old Ratio – Sacrificing Ratio
(d) New Ratio – Sacrificing Ratio

2. M, N and O are partners in 3 : 4 : 2. N wants to retire from the firm. The profit on revaluation on that date was Rs. 36,000. New ratio of M and O is 5 : 3. Profit on revaluation will be distributed as :

(a) M Rs. 14,000; N Rs. 10,000; O Rs. 6,000
(b) M Rs. 12,000; N Rs. 16,000; O Rs. 8,000
(c) M Rs. 20,500; O Rs. 12,500
(d) M Rs. 20,425; O Rs. 10,275

3. P, Q and R are partners sharing profits in the ratio of 5 : 4 : 3. Q retires and P and R decide to share future profits equally. Gaining Ratio will be :

(a) 5 : 3
(b) 1 : 1
(c) 1 : 3
(d) 3 : 1

4. A, B and C are partners sharing profit in the ratio of 2 : 2 : 1. C retires. The new profit sharing between A and B will be

(a) 3 : 1
(b) 2 : 1
(c) 5 : 3
(d) 1 : 1

5. Retirement or death of a partner will create a situation for the continuing partners, which is known as:

(a) Dissolution of Partnership
(b) Dissolution of partnership firm
(c) Winding up of business
(d) None of these

6. A, B and C were partners sharing profits and losses in the ratio of 4 : 3 : 1. B retires and gives her share of profit to A for Rs. 3,600 and to C for Rs. 3,000. The gaining ratio of A and C will be :

(a) 4 : 5
(b) 2 : 1
(c) 6 : 5
(d) 4 : 1

7. **Assertion (A):** On retirement, the old partnership agreement comes to an end and a new partnership agreement comes into existence between the remaining partners.

   Reasoning (R): Retirement of the partnership leads to the reconstitution of the firm.

   Codes:

   (a) Both (A) and (R) are correct and (R) is the correct reason of (A).

   (b) Both (A) and (R) are correct but (R) is not the correct reason of (A).

   (c) Only (R) is correct.

   (d) Both (A) and (R) are wrong

8. A, B and C are sharing profits and losses equally. C retires and the goodwill is appearing in the books at Rs. 30,000. Goodwill of the firm is valued at Rs. 1,50,000. Calculate the net amount to be credited to C's Capital A/c.

   (a) Rs. 60,000 (b) Rs. 50,000
   (c) Rs. 40,000 (d) Rs. 10,000

9. R, K and G were sharing profits and losses in the ratio of 5 : 3 : 2. R retires and K and G share the future profits and losses equally. Goodwill of the firm is valued at Rs. 1,00,000. Calculate the amount of goodwill to be debited to K and G Capital A/c.

   (a) Rs. 60,000 & Rs. 40,000 (b) Rs. 20,000 & Rs. 30,000
   (c) Rs. 40,000 & Rs. 60,000 (d) Rs. 30,000 & Rs. 20,000

10. X, Y and Z were partners in a firm sharing profits in the ratio of 3 : 2 : 1. X retired and the new profit sharing ratio between Yand Z will be 5 : 4. On Xs retirement the goodwill of the firm was valued at Rs. 54,000. Journal entry will be :

    (a) Y's Capital A/c Dr. 24,000 Z's Capital A/c Dr. 30,000 To X's Capital A/c 54,000

    (b) Y's Capital A/c Dr. 15,000 Z's Capital A/c Dr. 12,000 To X's Capital A/c 27,000

    (c) Y's Capital A/c Dr. 12,000 Z's Capital A/c Dr. 15,000 To X's Capital A/c 27,000

    (d) X's Capital A/c Dr. 27,000 To Y's Capital A/c 12,000 To Z's Capital A/c 15,000

11. P, Q and R were partners sharing profits and losses in the ratio of 2 : 2 : 1. Books are closed on 31st March every year. R dies on 5th November, 2020. Under the partnership deed, the executors of the deceased partner are entitled to his share of profit to the date of death, calculated on the basis of last year's profit. Profit for the year ended 31st March, 2020 was Rs. 2,40,000. R's share of profit will be :

    (a) Rs. 28,000 (b) Rs. 32,000
    (c) Rs. 28,800 (d) Rs. 48,000

12. Retiring partner's share of goodwill is debited to remaining partner's in their

    (a) New profit sharing ratio (b) Gaining ratio
    (c) Sacrificing ratio (d) Old ratio

13. P,Q and R are the partners sharing profits in the ratio of 5 : 3 : 1. If the new ratio on the retirement of P is 3 : 2. What will be the gaining ratio?

    (a) 14 : 11 (b) 11 : 14
    (c) 9 : 11 (d) 11 : 9

14. In case of death of a partner, the whole amount standing to the credit of his capital account is transferred to :

    (a) Capital Accounts of all partners (b) Capital Accounts of remaining partners
    (c) His Executor's Account (d) all of the above

15. What journal entry will be recorded for writing off the goodwill already existing in Balance Sheet at the time of retirement of a partner?

    (a) Retiring Partner's Capital A/c Dr. To Goodwill A/c

    (b) All Partner's Capital A/cs (including retiring) Dr. (in old ratio) To Goodwill A/c

    (c) Remaining Partner's Capital A/cs Dr. (in gaining ratio) To Goodwill A/c

    (d) Remaining Partner's Capital A/cs Dr. (in new ratio) To Goodwill A/c

16. Which of the following statement is correct?

(a) Goodwill at the time of retirement of a partner is credited to remaining Partners' Capital Accounts in sacrificing ratio.

(b) Goodwill at the time of retirement of a partner is credited to remaining Partners' Capital Accounts in gaining ratio.

(c) Goodwill at the time of retirement of a partner is debited to remaining Partners' Capital Accounts in sacrificing ratio.

(d) Goodwill at the time of retirement of a partner to the extent of retiring Partner's Share is debited to remaining Partners' Capital Accounts in gaining ratio.

17. The retiring/deceased partner must be compensated in the form of premium (goodwill) for the share of profit in favour of continued partners. .

(a) sacrificed (b) gained

(c) obtained (d) None of these

18. Partnership will be dissolved if

(a) profit sharing ratio changed (b) admission of a new partner

(c) retirement of a partner (d) All of these

19. Jusify the statement "Retiring partner is not liable for firm's act after his retirement".

(a) true (b) false

(c) partially true (d) partially false

20. Increase in the liability at the time of retirement of a partner is

(a) credited to revaluation A/c (b) debited to revaluation A/c

(c) debited to balance sheet (d) credited to realisation account

Topic Test – 1

For questions 1 to 3: Analyse the case given below and answer the questions that follow:

A, K and S were partners in a firm sharing profits in the ratio of 5 : 3 : 2. Goodwill appeared in their books at the value of Rs. 60,000. K decided to retire from the firm. On the date of his retirement, goodwill of the firm was valued at Rs. 2,40,000. The new profit sharing ratio decided among A and S was 2 : 3. Give the answers to the questions given below:

1. How much amount will be transferred to K's capital account of the existing goodwill?

(a) Rs. 3,000 (b) Rs. 12,000

(c) Rs. 20,000 (d) Rs. 18,000

2. What is A's gaining / sacrificing ratio?

(a) 1/10 gain (b) 3 /10 sacrifice

(c) 1/10 sacrifice (d) 4/10

3. What amount of goodwill will be transferred to k's capital Account?

(a) Rs. 18,000 (b) Rs. 36,000

(c) Rs. 86,000 (d) Rs. 72,000

4. **Assertion (A):** When goodwill is not appearing in the books, retiring or deceased partner's capital account is to be credited with his share of goodwill and gaining partners' capital accounts are to be debited in gaining ratio.

Reasoning (R): Goodwill needs to be compensated by the gaining partners in the gaining ratio.

Codes:

(a) Both (A) and (R) are correct and (R) is the correct reason of (A).

(b) Both (A) and (R) are correct but (R) is not the correct reason of (A).

(c) Only (R) is correct.

(d) Both (A) and (R) are wrong

5. A, B and C are partners in the ratio of 5 : 4 : 3. B retires and A and C decide to share profits equally. Gaining ratio will be:
   (a) 1 : 2 (b) 3 : 1
   (c) 1 : 3 (d) 4 : 3
6. A, B and C are partners sharing profits in the ratio of 1/2 : 1/4 : 1/4. New ratio on the retirement of B will be:
   (a) 2 : 4 (b) 1 : 2
   (c) 2 : 1 (d) 1 : 2
7. A , B and C share profits and losses of the firm equally. B retires from business and his share is purchased by A and C in the ratio of 2 : 3. New profit sharing ratio between A and C respectively would be :
   (a) 2 : 3 (b) 7 : 8
   (c) 1 : 3 (d) 3 : 1
8. The executors of deceased partner will be paid interest on the amount due from the date of death of the partner at:
   (a) 5% p.a. (b) 6% p.a.
   (c) 7% p.a. (d) 8% p.a.
9. B, C and D are partners sharing profit in the ratio 7 : 5 : 4. D died on 30th June, 2020 and profits for the year 2019-20 were Rs. 12,000. How much share in profits for the period 1st April, 2020 to 30th June, 2016 will be credited to D's Account:
   (a) Rs. 1,000 (b) Rs. 750
   (c) Rs. 825 (d) Rs. 2,000
10. Which account is prepared at the time retirement or death of a partner to show the changes in the value of assets and liabilities:
   (a) Revaluation A/c (b) Realisation A/c
   (c) Partner's Capital A/c (d) None of these

Topic Test – 2

1. On retirement of a partner, the retiring Partner's Capital Account will be credited with:
   (a) His/her share of goodwill (b) Goodwill of the firm
   (c) Share of goodwill of remaining partners (d) None of these
2. A, B and C are partners sharing profit equally. On C's retirement, his share is acquired by A and in the ratio of 3 : 2. The new profit-sharing ratio between A and B will be:
   (a) 8 : 7 (b) 4 : 5
   (c) 3 : 2 (d) 2 : 3
3. P, Q and R are sharing profits and losses equally. R retires and the goodwill is appearing in the books at Rs. 30,000. Goodwill of the firm is valued at Rs. 1,50,000. Calculate the net amount to be credited to R's Capital A/c.
   (a) Rs. 60,000 (b) Rs. 50,000
   (c) Rs. 40,000 (d) Rs. 10,000
4. A, B, C were partners sharing Profit and Losses in the ratio of 3 : 2 : 1 Books are closed on 31st March every year. C dies on 30th, Nov 2018. Under the partnership deed, the executors of deceased partner are entitled to his share of profit up to the date of death, Profit as on ended 31st Mar 2018 was Rs. 2,40,000. C's share of profit will be
   (a) Rs. 26,667 (b) Rs. 40,000
   (c) Rs. 30,000 (d) Rs. 53,333

5. A, B, C are partners sharing profit and losses in the ratio of 4 : 3 : 1. B retires and gives his share of profit to A Rs. 3,600 and C Rs. 4,500. What is the Gaining sharing ratio of A and C?
   (a) 4 : 5 (b) 2 : 1
   (c) 3 : 1 (d) 4 : 1
6. If three partners A, B, C are sharing profit as 5 : 3 : 2, then on the death of a partner A, how much B and C will pay to A executor on account of goodwill. Goodwill is to be calculated on the basic of 2 years purchase of last 3 years average profit, profits for the last 3 years are Rs. 3,28,000 Rs. 3,46,000 and Rs. 4,00,000.
   (a) Rs. 3,16,000 and Rs. 1,42,000 (b) Rs. 2,44,000 and Rs. 2,16,000
   (c) Rs. 4,29,600 and Rs. 2,86,400 (d) Rs. 2,16,000 and Rs. 1,44,000
7. A, B & C are partners sharing profits in ratio 3 : 2 : 1.C retired from the firm . The total capital of new firm is fixed at Rs. 60,000. What will be the new capital of A and B :
   (a) Rs. 30,000 and Rs. 30,000 (b) Rs. 24,000 and Rs. 36,000
   (c) Rs. 36,000 and Rs. 24,000 (d) Rs. 40,000 and Rs. 20,000
8. A, B and C were partners in a firm sharing profits and losses in the ratio of 2 : 2 : 1. The capital balance are Rs. 50,000 for A, Rs. 70,000 for B, Rs. 35,000 for C. B decided to retire from the firm and balance in. reserve on the date was Rs. 25,000. If goodwill of the firm was valued at Rs. 30,000 and profit on revaluation was Rs. 7,500 then, what amount will be payable to B?
   (a) Rs. 60,720 (b) Rs. 56,000
   (c) Rs. 75,000 (d) Rs. 95,000
9. After retirement of a partner, share of remaining partner will
   (a) increase (b) decrease
   (c) not change (d) None of the above
10. A, B and C sharing profit in ratio 3 : 2 : 1 C retires from the firm. Goodwill is to be valued at Rs. 60,000 find the amount payable to retiring on account of goodwill.
   (a) Rs. 30,000 (b) Rs. 20,000
   (c) Rs. 10,000 (d) Rs. 60,000

Answer Keys

Exercise

1. (b)	2. (b)	3. (c)	4. (d)	5. (a)	6. (c)	7. (a)	8. (c)	9. (b)	10. (b)
11. (c)	12. (b)	13. (a)	14. (c)	15. (b)	16. (d)	17. (a)	18. (d)	19. (b)	20. (b)

Topic Test – 1

1. (d)	2. (c)	3. (d)	4. (a)	5. (c)	6. (c)	7. (b)	8. (b)	9. (b)	10. (a)

Topic Test – 2

1. (a)	2. (a)	3. (c)	4. (a)	5. (a)	6. (c)	7. (c)	8. (d)	9. (a)	10. (b)

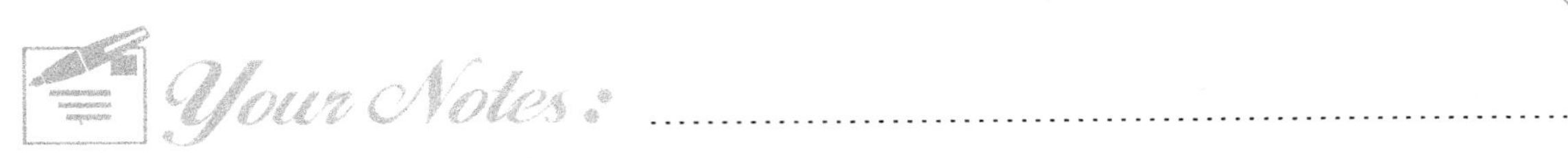
Your Notes :

CHAPTER 5

Dissolution of The Partnership Firm

Summary

Dissolution of partnership firm is a process in which relationship between partners of firm is dissolved or terminated. If a relationship between all the partners of firm is dissolved then it is known as dissolution of firm. In case of dissolution of partnership firm, the firm ceases to exist. According to Section 39 of the Indian Partnership Act, 1932, the dissolution of partnership between all the partners of a firm is called "Dissolution of the Firm". A firm may be dissolved with the consent of all the partners or in accordance with a contract between the partners

Dissolution of Partnership

(1) Change in existing profit sharing ratio among partners;

(2) Admission of a new partner;

(3) Retirement of a partner;

(4) Death of a partner;

(5) Insolvency of a partner;

(6) Completion of the venture, if partnership is formed for that; and

(7) Expiry of the period of partnership, if partnership is for a specific period of time.

Dissolution of a firm takes place in any of the following ways:

1. By Agreement (Section 40) According to Section 40 of the Indian Partnership Act, 1932, partners can dissolve the partnership by agreement and with the consent of all the partners. Partners can also dissolve the partnership based on a contract that has already been made.
2. Compulsory Dissolution (Section 41) An event can make it unlawful for the firm to carry on its business. In such cases, it is compulsory for the firm to dissolve. However, if a firm carries on more than one undertakings and one of them becomes illegal, then it is not compulsory for the firm to dissolve. It can continue carrying out the legal undertakings. Section 41 of the Indian Partnership Act, 1932, specifies this type of voluntary dissolution.
3. On the happening of certain contingencies (Section 42) According to Section 42 of the Indian Partnership Act, 1932, the happening of any of the following contingencies can lead to the dissolution of the firm:
   - Some firms are constituted for a fixed term. Such firms will dissolve on the expiry of that term.
   - Some firms are constituted to carry out one or more undertaking. Such firms are dissolved when the undertaking is completed.
   - Death of a partner.
   - Insolvency of a partner.

4. By notice of partnership at will (Section 43) According to Section 43 of the Indian Partnership Act, 1932, if the partnership is at will, then any partner can give notice in writing to all other partners informing them about his intention to dissolve the firm. In such cases, the firm is dissolved on the date mentioned in the notice. If no date is mentioned, then the date of dissolution of the firm is the date of communication of the notice.
5. Dissolution by Court: At the suit of a partner, the court may order a partnership firm to be dissolved on any of the following grounds:
   (a) when a partner becomes insane;
   (b) when a partner becomes permanently incapable of performing his duties as a partner;
   (c) when a partner is guilty of misconduct which is likely to adversely affect the business of the firm;
   (d) when a partner persistently commits breach of partnership agreement;
   (e) when a partner has transferred the whole of his interest in the firm to a third party;
   (f) when the business of the firm cannot be carried on except at a loss; or
   (g) when, on any ground, the court regards dissolution to be just and equitable.

Settlement of Accounts In Case Of Dissolution of Firm:

(a) Treatment of Losses Losses, including deficiencies of capital, shall be paid :
   (i) first out of profits,
   (ii) next out of capital of partners, and
   (iii) lastly, if necessary, by the partners individually in their profit sharing ratio.

(b) Application of Assets The assets of the firm, including any sum contributed by the partners to make up deficiencies of capital, shall be applied in the following manner and order:
   (i) In paying the debts of the firm to the third parties;
   (ii) In paying each partner proportionately what is due to him/her from the firm for advances as distinguished from capital (i.e. partner' loan);
   (iii) In paying to each partner proportionately what is due to him on account of capital; and
   (iv) the residue, if any, shall be divided among the partners in their profit sharing ratio.

Journal Entries on Dissolution of a Firm

1. For transfer of assets to Realization Account: (All assets excluding Cash/Bank, fictitious assets, accumulated losses are transferred to Realization Account)

   Realisation A/c Dr.

   To Assets (Individually) A/c

2. For transfer of liabilities to Realization Account: (All outside liabilities are transferred to Realization Account) Note:

   (i) Liabilities (individually) Dr.

   To Realisation A/c

3. For sale of assets Bank A/c Dr.

   To Realisation A/c

4. For an asset taken over by a partner

   Partner's Capital A/c Dr.

   To Realisation A/c

5. For payment of liabilities

   Realisation A/c Dr.

   To Bank A/c

6. For a liability which a partner takes responsibility to discharge

   Realisation A/c Dr.

   To Partner's Capital A/c

7. For payment of realisation expenses

   (a) When some expenses are incurred and paid by the firm in the process of realisation of assets and payment of liabilities:

   Realisation A/c Dr.

   To Bank A/c

   (b) When realisation expenses are paid by a partner on behalf of the firm:

   Realisation A/c Dr.

   To Partner's Capital A/c

   (c) When a partner has agreed to bear the realisation expenses:

   if payment of realisation expenses is made by the firm

   Partner's Capital A/c Dr.

   To Bank A/c

8. For agreed remuneration to such partner who agrees to undertake the dissolution work. Realisation A/c Dr.

   To Partner's Capital A/c

9. For realisation of any unrecorded assets including goodwill, if any

   Bank A/c Dr.

   To Realisation A/c

10. For settlement of any unrecorded liability

    Realisation A/c Dr.

    To Bank A/c

11. For transfer of profit and loss on realisation (Cr. Blance)

    (a) In case of profit on realisation

    Realisation A/c Dr.

    To Partners' Capital A/c (individually) A/c

    (b) In case of loss on realisation

    Partners' Capital A/c (individually) Dr. (Dr. Blance)

    To Realisation A/c

12. For settlement of loan by a firm to a partner:

    Bank A/c Dr.

    To loan to partners A/c

13. For transfer of accumulated profits in the form of general reserve to partners' capital accounts in their profit sharing ratio:

    General Reserve A/c Dr.

    To Partners' Capital A/c (individually)

14. For transfer of fictitious assets, if any, to partners' capital accounts in their profit sharing ratio:

    Partners' Capital A/c (individually) Dr.

    To Fictitious Asset A/c

15. For payment of loans due to partners

    Partner's Loan A/c Dr.

    To Bank A/c

FORMAT FOR REALISATION ACCOUNT

Particulars	Amount	Particulars	Amount
To Sundry Assets (Excluding Cash, Bank, fictitious assets, accumulated losses, debit balance of Partner's capital A/c and Loan to Partners)		By Sundry Liabilities A/c (Excluding Parner's Capital A/c, loan from Partners Reserves and Accumulated Profit etc.)	
To Provision (on liability)		By specific Reserves (if required)	
To Bank/Cash A/c (Payment of liabilities)		By Provision (on assets)	
To Bank/Cash A/c (Payment of unrecorded liabilities)		By Bank/Cash A/c (Assets realized)	
To Bank/Cash A/c(Payment of Realization Exp.)		By Bank/Cash A/c (Unrecorded Assets realized)	
To partner's Capital/Current A/c (For discharge of liability)		By Partner's Capital/Current A/c (Assets taken over)	
To Partner's capital/current A/c		By Partner's Capital/Current A/c (For distribution of Realization Loss)	

FORMAT FOR PARTNER'S CAPITAL ACCOUNT

Particulars	A	B	Particulars	A	B
To Balance b/d			To Balance b/d		
To Profit and Loss			By Reserves		
To Advertisement Suspense A/c			By Profit and Loss		
			By WCR/IFF		
To Realization A/c (Assets taken over)			By Realization A/c (Liabilities taken)		
To Realization (Loss on Realization)			By Realization A/c (Profit on Realization)		
To Bank/Cash A/c (Excess cash paid			By Bank/Cash A/c (Cash brought in)		

BANK/CASH ACCOUNT

Particulars	Amount	Particulars	Amount
To Balance b/d (opening balance)		By Realization A/c (Payment of liabilities)	
To Realization A/c (Assets Realized)		By Realization A/c (Payment of realization Exp.)	
To Partner's Capital A/c (Cash brought in)		By Partner's Loan A/c (Amount of loan paid to the Partner)	
		By Partner's Capital A/c (Final cash paid to the partner)	

Exercise

1. Unrecorded liability when paid on dissolution of a firm is related to
   (a) Bank account (b) Partner's capital account
   (c) Revaluation account (d) Realisation account
2. At the time of dissolution goodwill is transferred to
   (a) Partner's capital account (b) Partner's current account
   (c) On the debit side of realisation account (d) On the credit side of realisation account
3. Realisation expenses Rs. 10,000 were paid by the firm on the behalf of a partner. Choose the correct journal entry for :-

(a) Realisation A/c	Dr.	10,000
To cash A/c		10,000
(b) Cash/bank A/c	Dr.	10,000
To Realisation A/c		10,000
(c) Realisation A/c	Dr.	10,000
To concerned partner's A/c		10,000
(d) Concerned partner's A/c	Dr.	10,000
To Cash/Bank A/c		10,000

4. R, M and S were partners sharing profits ecually. At the time of dissolution of the partnership firm, R's loan amount to the firm will be
   (a) Credited to Bank Account (b) Debited to realisation account
   (c) Credited to realisation account (d) Credited to partner's capital account
5. There was an Unrecorded asset of Rs. 10.000 which was taken over by a partner at Rs. 8,500. Partner's Capital Account will be debited by.......
   (a) Rs. 10,000 (b) Rs. 18,500
   (c) Rs. 8,500 (d) Rs. 2,500
6. Which of the following is correct profit or loss in case the amount received from the sale of assets is Rs. 50,000, total assets is Rs. 60,000, total liabilities Rs. 20,000 and realisation expenses Rs. 2,000?
   (a) Rs. 12,000 Loss (b) Rs. 32,000 Profit
   (c) Rs. 30,000 Loss (d) Rs. 12,000 Profit
7. If the total assets are Rs. 1,25,000 and the total outside liabilities Rs. 5,000 then the amount of all partner's capital will be:
   (a) Rs. 1,70,000 (b) Rs. 1,30,000
   (c) Rs. 1,20,000 (d) None of these
8. On dissolution of a partnership firm, profit or loss on realisation is distributed among the partners
   (a) In capital ratio (b) In Profit sharing ratio
   (c) Equally (d) None of the above
9. On firm's dissolution, when a partner voluntarily gives his personal asset to firms' creditor as payment, the account credited will be :
   (a) Realisation A/c (b) Partner's Capital A/c
   (c) Cash A/c (d) None of the A/c
10. Pick the odd one out:-
   (a) Debtors (b) Payment of liabilities
   (c) Provision for doubtful debts (d) Fixed assets

11. **Assertion (A):** Dissolution of partnership is different from the dissolution of the partnership firm.

    Reasoning (R): Dissolution of the partnership doesn't dissolve the firm but the firm is dissolved in the partnership.

    Codes:

    (a) Both Assertion (A) and Reason (R) are true, and Reason (R) is the correct explanation of Assertion (A).

    (b) Both Assertion (A) and Reason (R) are true, but Reason (R) is not the correct explanation of Assertion (A).

    (c) Assertion (A) is true, but Reason (R) is false.

    (d) Assertion (A) is false, but Reason (R) is true.

12. In case of dissolution, assets are transferred to Realisation Account:

    (a) At Book Value (b) At Market Value

    (c) Cost or Market Value, whichever is lower (d) None of the Above

13. On dissolution, the balance of a partner's capital account appearing on the assets side of a balance sheet is transferred to :

    (a) On the Debit of Realisation Account (b) On the Credit of Realisation Account

    (c) On the Debit of Partner's Capital Account (d) On the Credit of Cash Account

14. Sundry Creditors amounted to Rs.6,000. These were paid at a discount of 5%. Realisation account will be debited by

    (a) Rs. 6,000 (b) Rs. 6,600

    (c) Rs. 5,700 (d) Rs. 6,300

15. On dissolution of a firm, an unrecorded furniture of the value of Rs. 5,000 was taken up by a partner for Rs. 4,300. Which Account will be credited and by how much amount?

    (a) Cash Account by Rs. 4,300 (b) Realisation Account by Rs. 700

    (c) Partner's Capital Account by Rs. 5,000 (d) Realisation Account by Rs. 4,300

16. If total assets are Rs. 2,00,000; total liabilities are Rs. 40,000; amount realised on sale of assets is Rs. 1,75,000 and realisation expenses are Rs. 3,000, the profit or loss on realisation will be :

    (a) Profit Rs. 12,000 (b) Loss Rs. 68,000

    (c) Loss Rs. 28,000 (d) Loss Rs. 25,000

17. On the basis of the following data, how much final payment will be made to a partner on firm's dissolution? Credit balance of Capital Account of the partner was Rs. 50,000. Share of loss on realisation amounted to Rs. 10,000. Firm's liability taken over by him was for Rs. 8,000.

    (a) Rs. 32,000 (b) Rs. 48,000

    (c) Rs. 40,000 (d) Rs. 52,000

18. Investments of Rs. 2,00,000 were not shown in the boooks. One of the creditors tool these investments in settlement of his debt of Rs. 2,20,000. How much amount will be payable to that creditor?

    (a) Rs. 20,000 (b) Rs. 2,20,000

    (c) Rs. 4,20,000 (d) Nil

19. On dissolution of a firm , its Balance sheet revealed total creditors Rs.50,000 , Total Capital Rs. 48,000 , Cash Balance Rs. 3,000. Its assets were realised at 12% less. Loss on realisation will be:

    (a) 4,000 (b) 10,000

    (c) 11,400 (d) 12,400

20. When realisation expenses are to be borne by a partner actual realisation expense is credited to

    (a) Partner's capital account (b) Realisation account

    (c) Cash A/c (d) None of the above

Topic Test – 1

For questions 1 to 3: Analyse the case given below and answer the questions that follows:

Vani , Tanu and Hiten were partners in a partnership firm sharing profits and losses in their capital ratio, i.e., 1 : 2 : 3. On 31st March 2020, they decided to dissolve the partnership firm. The following information is given to you on the dissolution of the firm: The firm had total assets of Rs. 12,00,000 that realized Rs. 10,80,000. The creditors were settled at 90% by paying them Rs. 54,000.There was an unrecorded asset in the books of the firm which was taken by Vani for Rs. 12,000. Realisation expenses amounted to Rs. 2,000 and were paid by Tanu on behalf of the firm. There was general reserve in the books of the company of Rs. 21,000. The capitals of the partners were in the, proportion of their profit sharing ratio. Their balance sheet also showed a cash balance of Rs. 81,000.

1. What was the capital of Tanu before the dissolution of the firm?

   (a) Rs. 8,00,000 (b) Rs. 4,00,000
   (c) Rs. 3,00,000 (d) Rs. 6,00,000

2. What was the loss on realization?

   (a) Rs. 2,00,000 (b) Rs. 1,47,000
   (c) Rs. 1,37,000 (d) Rs. 1,16,000

3. What will be the final amount to be paid to Hiten?

   (a) Rs. 6,05,000 (b) Rs. 52,000
   (c) Rs. 5,52,500 (d) Rs. 6,08,500

4. An unrecorded asset was valued at Rs. 1,00,000. On firm's dissolution, it was sold for 52%. Realisation account will be credited with :

   (a) Rs. 42,000 (b) Rs. 18,000
   (c) Rs. 2,00,000 (d) Rs. 52,000

5. At the time of dissolution of firm, at what stage the balances of partner's Capital Accounts are paid?

   (a) After payment of outsider's liabilities
   (b) Before payment of loan by partner
   (c) After payment of outsiders liabilities and Partners loan
   (d) Before payment of outside liabilities

6. On the basis of the following data, how much final payment will be made to a partner on firm's dissolution?

   Credit balance of Capital Account of the partner was Rs. 50,000. Share of loss on realisation amounted to Rs. 10,000.

   Firm's liability taken over by him was for Rs. 8,000.

   (a) Rs. 48,000 (b) Rs. 32,000
   (c) Rs. 56,000 (d) Rs. 72,000

7. Choose the correct journal entry for the following case:

   Dissolution expenses were Rs. 8000. Out of the said expenses Rs. 3000 were to be borne by the firm and the balance by R, a partner. Rs. 8000 are paid by the firm.

   (a) Cash A/c Dr. 8,000
       To Realisation A/c 5,000
       To R's Capital A/c 3,000
   (b) Realisation A/c Dr. 3,000
       R's capital A/c Dr. 5,000
       To cash/ bank A/c 8,000
   (c) Cash A/c Dr. 3,000
       Realisation A/c Dr. 5,000
       To R's Capital A/c 8,000

(d) Realisation A/c Dr. 5,000
R's capital A/c Dr. 3,000
To cash/ bank A/c 8,000

8. Debit balance of capital Account Rs. 14000. Share of his profit on realisation Rs. 43,000. Firms asset taken over by him for Rs. 17,000. On the basis of the above data the final payment to a partner on firm's dissolution will be
(a) Rs. 30,000
(b) Rs. 12,000
(c) Rs. 14,000
(d) Rs. 20,000

9. On dissolution of a firm, firm's Balance Sheet total is Rs. 77,000. On the assets side of the Balance Sheet items were shown preliminary expenses Rs. 2,000; Profit & Loss Account (Debit) Balance Rs. 4,000 and Cash Balance Rs. 1,800. Loss on realisation was Rs. 6,300. Total assets (including cash balance) realised will be:
(a) Rs. 62,900
(b) Rs. 70,000
(c) Rs. 64,700
(d) Rs. 66,700

10. P, Q and R are partners in a firm. The firm had given a loan of Rs. 15,000 to Q. They decided to dissolve the firm. The loan will be settled by
(a) Dr. side of Q's capital Account
(b) Cr. Side of Q's capital Account
(c) Cr. Side of realisation Account
(d) Dr. side of Realisation Account

Topic Test – 2

1. **Assertion (A):** Realisation account is prepared in the dissolution of the firm.
Reasoning (R): Dissolution of partnership involves the partners selling the assets and settling the liabilities. Thus, various amounts are recovered or paid to partners.
(a) Both Assertion (A) and Reason (R) are true, and Reason (R) is the correct explanation of Assertion (A).
(b) Both Assertion (A) and Reason (R) are true, but Reason (R) is not the correct explanation of Assertion (A).
(c) Assertion (A) is true, but Reason (R) is false.
(d) Assertion (A) is false, but Reason (R) is true.

2. General Reserve appearing in the Balance Sheet is transferred to:
(a) Realisation Account
(b) Partners' Capital Accounts in profit sharing ratio
(c) Partners' Capital Accounts in capital ratio
(d) None of the above

3. On firm's dissolution, which one of the following account should be prepared at the last?
(a) Realisation Account
(b) Partner's Capital Accounts
(c) Cash Account
(d) Partner's Loan Account

4. On dissolution of a firm, an unrecorded furniture of the value of Rs. 5,000 was taken up by a partner for Rs. 4,300. Which Account will be credited and by how much amount?
(a) Cash Account by Rs. 4,300
(b) Realisation Account by Rs. 700
(c) Partner's Capital Account by Rs. 5,000
(d) Realisation Account by Rs. 4,300

5. While transferring assets to realisation account is omitted to be transferred:
(a) Patents
(b) Goodwill
(c) Cash
(d) Investments

6. On the basis of following data, final payment to a partner on firm's dissolution 'will be made : Debit balance of Capital Account Rs. 14,000; Share of his profit on realisation Rs. 43,000; Firm's asset taken over by him for Rs. 17,000.

(a) Rs. 31,000
(b) Rs. 29,000
(c) Rs. 12,000
(d) Rs. 60,000

7. If total assets are Rs. 2,00,000; total liabilities are Rs. 40,000; amount realised on sale of assets is Rs. 1,75,000 and realisation expenses are Rs. 3,000, the profit or loss on realisation will be :

(a) Profit Rs. 12,000
(b) Loss Rs. 68,000
(c) Loss Rs. 28,000
(d) Loss Rs. 25,000

8. Aman, a partner, is to bear all expenses of realisation for which he is to be paid Rs. 2,000. Aman had to pay realisation expenses of Rs. 2,500. How much amount will be debited to Realisation Account?

(a) Rs. 1,500
(b) Rs. 3,500
(c) Rs. 4,500
(d) Rs. 2,000

9. How much amount will be paid to Robert, if his opening capital is Rs. 2,00,000 and his share of realisation profit amounts to Rs. 10,000 and he has taken over assets valuing Rs. 25,000 from the firm?

(a) Rs. 1,35,000
(b) Rs. 2,65,000
(c) Rs. 1,85,000
(d) Rs. 2,80,000

10. On dissolution of a firm, a partner took over Rs. 17,000 investments for Rs. 14,000. Which one of the following account will be debited/credited with how much amount?

(a) Partner's Capital Account Debit with Rs. 14,000
(b) Partner's Capital Account Credit with Rs. 17,000
(c) Realisation Account Credit with Rs. 17,000
(d) Realisation Account Credit with Rs. 3,000

Answer Keys

Exercise

1. (d)	2. (c)	3. (d)	4. (a)	5. (c)	6. (a)	7. (c)	8. (b)	9. (b)	10. (c)
11. (a)	12. (a)	13. (c)	14. (c)	15. (d)	16. (c)	17. (b)	18. (d)	19. (c)	20. (d)

Topic Test – 1

1. (b)	2. (d)	3. (c)	4. (d)	5. (c)	6. (a)	7. (b)	8. (b)	9. (c)	10. (a)

Topic Test – 2

1. (a)	2. (b)	3. (c)	4. (d)	5. (c)	6. (c)	7. (c)	8. (d)	9. (c)	10. (a)

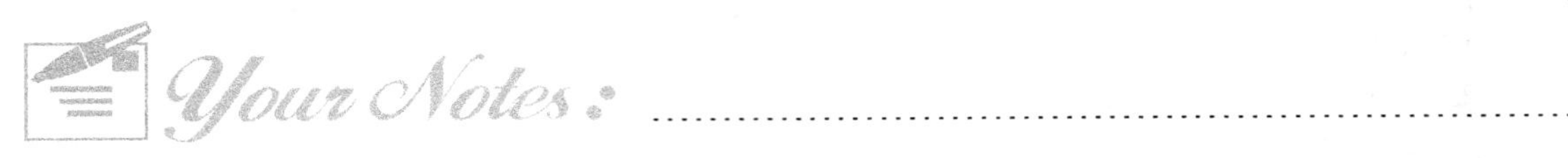
Your Notes :

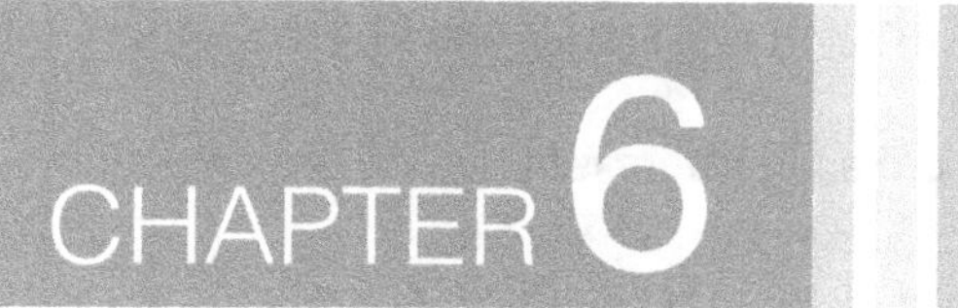

Accounting for Share Capital

Summary

A company form of organisation is the third stage in the evolution of forms of organisation. Its capital is contributed by a large number of persons called shareholders who are the real owners of the company. A company usually raises its capital in the form of shares (called share capital) and debentures (debt capital.)

Features of a company:

1. **Body Corporate:** A company is formed according to the provisions of Law enforced from time to time.
2. **Separate Legal Entity:** A company has a separate legal entity which is distinct and separate from its members. It can hold and deal with any type of property. It can enter into contracts and even open a bank account in its own name.
3. **Limited Liability:** The liability of the members of the company is limited to the extent of unpaid amount of the shares held by them. In the case of the companies limited by guarantee, the liability of its members is limited to the extent of the guarantee given by them in the event of the company being wound up.
4. **Perpetual Succession:** The company being an artificial person created by law continues to exist irrespective of the changes in its membership. A company can be terminated only through law
5. **Common Seal:** The company being an artificial person, cannot sign its name by itself. Therefore, every company is required to have its own seal which acts as official signatures of the company. Any document which does not carry the common seal of the company is not binding on the company.
6. **Transferability of Shares:** The shares of a public limited company are freely transferable. The permission of the company or the consent of any member of the company is not necessary for the transfer of shares.

Types of Companies:

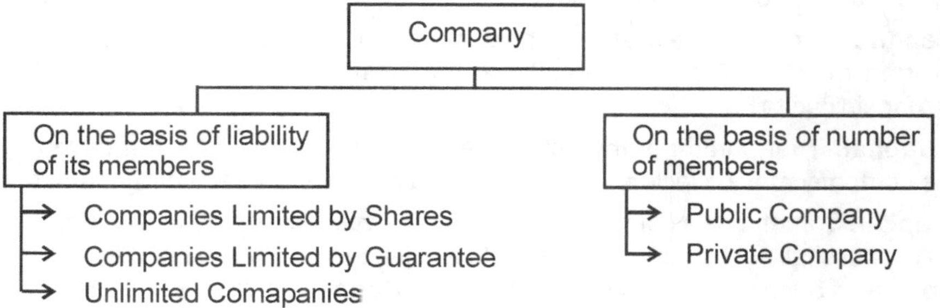

1. **Companies Limited by Shares:** In this case, the liability of the members is limited to the extent of the nominal value of shares held by them.
2. **Companies Limited by Guarantee:** In this case, the liability of its members is limited to the extent of the guarantee given by them in the event of the company being wound up.
3. **Unlimited Companies:** When there is no limit on the liability of its members, such Companies are called unlimited companies.
4. **Public Company:** A Public Company means a company that is not a Private Company.
5. **Private Company:** A Private Company is one which by its Articles of Association:
    1. Restricts the right to transfer its shares;
    2. Limits the number of its members to fifty;
    3. Prohibits any invitation to the public to subscribe for any shares in or debentures of the company.

Share Capital of a Company

Every company should have capital in order to finance its activities. The company raises this capital by issue of share because it does not have capital of its own being an artificial person. Thus, the total capital of the company is divided into shares, therefore, it is called share capital.

Categories of Share Capital:

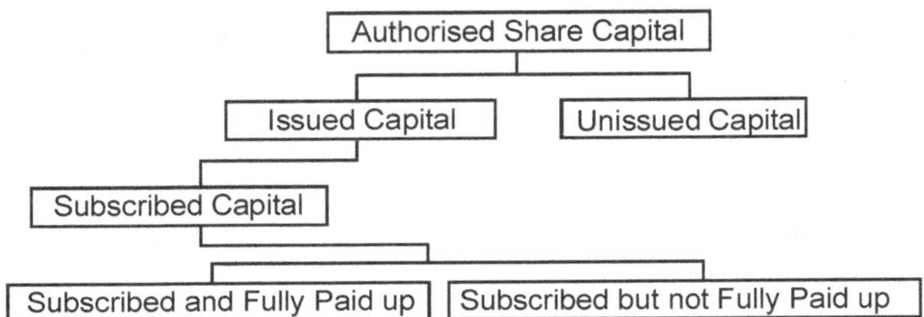

1. **Authorised Capital:** An Authorised Capital refers to that amount that is stated in the Memorandum of Association as the share capital of the company. It is the maximum amount with which the company is registered and which it is authorized to raise from the public by the issue of shares. The amount is also called the registered or nominal capital.
2. **Issued Capital:** It is that part of the authorised capital which is actually issued to the public for subscription including the shares allotted to vendors and the signatories to the company's memorandum. The authorised capital which is not offered for public subscription is known as 'unissued capital'. Unissued capital may be offered for public subscription at a later date.
3. **Subscribed Capital:** It is that part of the issued capital which has been actually subscribed by the public. When the shares offered for public subscription were subscribed fully by the public, in such a case the issued capital and subscribed capital would be the same.
4. **Called-up Capital:** It is that part of the subscribed share capital which the company actually demands from the share-holders. The company may decide to call the entire amount or part of the face value of the shares.
5. **Paid-up Capital:** It means the total amount paid up or credited as paid upon the subscribed capital. Some of the shareholders may fail to pay the amount due from them on account of a call which is termed as "call-in-arrears" or "unpaid capital".
6. **Uncalled Capital:** That portion of the subscribed capital that has not been called up is called uncalled capital. The company may collect this amount at any time when it needs further funds.
7. **Reserve Capital:** Sometimes a company, by means of a special resolution, decides that a certain portion of its uncalled capital shall not be called up during its existence and it would be available in the event of winding up of the company. Such a portion of uncalled capital is termed as 'reserve capital'.

Nature and Classes of Shares

Shares, refer to the units into which the total share capital of a company is divided. Thus, a share is a fractional part of the share capital and forms the basis of ownership interest in a company. The persons who contribute money through shares are called shareholders.

1. **Preference shares:** According to Section 43 of The Companies Act, 2013, a preference share is one, which fulfils the following conditions:

   (a) That it carries a preferential right to dividend to be paid either as a fixed amount payable to preference shareholders or an amount calculated by a fixed rate of the nominal value of each share before any dividend is paid to the equity shareholders.

   (b) That with respect to capital it carries or will carry, on the winding up of the company, the preferential right to the repayment of capital before anything is paid to equity shareholders.

2. **Equity Shares:** According to Section 43 of The Companies Act, 2013, shares which do not enjoy any preferential right in the payment of dividend or repayment of capital, are termed as equity/ordinary shares. The equity shareholders are entitled to share the distributable profits of the company after satisfying the dividend rights of the preference share holders.

   The equity share capital may be:

   (i) with voting rights; or

   (ii) with differential rights as to voting, dividend or otherwise in accordance with such rules and subject to such conditions as may be prescribed in the Articles of Association of the company.

Issue of shares:

The important steps in the procedure of share issue are:

1. **Issue of Prospectus:** The company first issues the prospectus to the public. Prospectus is an invitation to the public that a new company has come into existence and it needs funds for doing business. It contains complete information about the company and the manner in which the money is to be collected from the prospective investors.

2. **Receipt of Application:** When prospectus is issued to the public, prospective investors intending to subscribe the share capital of the company would make an application along with the application money. and deposit the same with a scheduled bank as specified in the prospectus. The company has to get minimum subscription within 120 days from the date of the issue of the prospectus. If the company fails to receive the same within the said period, the company cannot proceed for the allotment of shares and application money should be returned within 130 days of the date of issue of prospectus.

3. **Allotment of Shares:** If minimum subscription has been received, the company may proceed for the allotment of shares after fulfilling certain other legal formalities. Letters of allotment are sent to those whom the shares have been alloted, and letters of regret to those to whom no allotment has been made. When allotment is made, it results in a valid contract between the company and the applicants who now became the shareholders of the company.

NOTE: Shares of a company are issued either at par or at a premium. Shares are to be issued at par when their issue price is exactly equal to their nominal value according to the terms and conditions of issue. When the shares of a company are issued more than its nominal value (face value), the excess amount is called premium

Accounting Treatment:

1. **On Application:** The amount of money paid with various instalment represents the contribution to share capital and should ultimately be credited to share capital.

   Bank A/c Dr.

   To Share Application A/c

   (Amount received on application for — shares @ Rs. ______ per share)

2. **On Allotment:** When minimum subscription has been received and certain legal formalities on the allotment of shares have been duly compiled with, the directors of the company proceed to make the allotment of shares.

   The journal entries with regard to allotment of shares are as follows:

   1. For Transfer of Application Money

      Share Application A/c Dr.

      To Share Capital A/c

      (Application money on _____ Shares allotted/ transferred to Share Capital)

   2. For Money Refunded on Rejected Application

      Share Application A/c Dr.

      To Bank A/c

      (Application money returned on rejected application for ___shares)

   3. For Amount Due on Allotment

      Share Allotment A/c Dr.

      To Share Capital A/c

   4. For Adjustment of Excess Application Money

      Share Application A/c Dr.

      To Share Allotment A/c

      (Application Money on __Shares @ Rs__per shares adjusted to the amount due on allotment).

   5. For Receipt of Allotment Money Bank A/c Dr.

      To Share Allotment A/c

      (Allotment money received on ___Shares @ Rs. — per share Combined Account)

Combined Account: Sometimes a combined account for share application and share allotment is kept in the books of a company under the name Share Application and Allotment Account.

1. For Receipt of Application and Allotment

   Bank A/c Dr.

   To Share Application and Attotment A/c

   [Total Amount Received on Application]

   (Money received on applications for shares @ Rs.-per share)

2. Transfer of Application money and Allotment Amount Due

   Share App. and Allotment A/c Dr.

   To Share Capital [No. of share Allotted × (Application money per share + Allotment Amount per share)]

   (Transfer of application money to share capital for the amount due on allotment of shares @ Rs. – per share)

3. Money Refunded on Rejected Applications

   Share App. and Allotment A/c Dr.

   To Bank A/c [No. of share Rejected × App. money per share]

   (Application money returned on the rejected application for....share)

4. Receipt of Balance Allotment money

   Bank A/c Dr.

   To Share Application and Allotment A/c

   (Balance of Allotment money received)

1. Calls on Share: Two points are important regarding the Calls on shares.

1. The call amount should not exceed 25% of the face value of shares.
2. There must be an internal dynamics of keeping at least some months between the making of two calls unless otherwise provided by the Articles of Association of the company.

Accounting Treatment:

i. Call Amount Due

Share Call A/c Dr. [No. of shares × Call Amount per share]

To Share Capital A/c

(Call money due on – Shares @ Rs. – per share)

ii. Receipt of Call Amount

Bank A/c Dr.

To Share Call A/c

(Call money received)

2. Calls in Arrears: When any shareholder fails to pay the amount due on allotment or on any of the calls, such amount is known as 'Calls in Arrears'/'Unpaid Calls'.

Accounting Treatment:

Calls in Arrears A/c Dr.

To Share Allotment Account A/c

To Share Call Account A/c

(Calls in arrears brought into account)

3. Calls in Advance Sometimes shareholders pay a part or the whole of the amount of the calls not yet made. The amount so received from the shareholders is known as "Calls in Advance". The amount received in advance is a liability of the company and should be credited to 'Call in Advance Account.

Accounting Treatment:

Bank A/c Dr.

To Call-in-Advance A/c

(Amount received on Call-in-Advance)

On the due date of the calls, the amount of 'Calls in Advance' is adjusted by the following entry:

Calls in Advance A/c Dr.

To Particular Call A/c

(Calls in advance adjusted with the call money due)

As calls in advance are a liability to the company and it is under an obligation if provided by the Articles of Association, to pay interest on such amount. In case, the articles are silent then Table 'A' shall be applicable, according to which interest @ 6% p.a. may be paid.

1. Interest due

   Interest on Calls-in-Advance A/c Dr.

   To Sundry Shareholder's A/c [Amount of Interest due for payment]

   (Interest due on Calls-in-Advance)

2. Payment of Interest

   Sundry Shareholder's A/c Dr.

   To Bank A/c [Amount of Interest paid]

   (Interest paid on Calls-in-Advance)

Oversubscription:

When Shares are issued to the public for subscription through the prospectus by well-managed and financially strong companies, it may happen that applications for more shares are received than the number of shares offered to the public, such a situation is said to be a case of oversubscription.

In such a condition, three alternatives are available to the directors to deal with the situation:

(1) they can accept some applications in full and totally reject the others;

(2) they can make a pro-rata allotment to all; and

(3) they can adopt a combination of the above two alternatives which happens to be the most common course adopted in practice.

Accounting Treatment:

1. If the excess applicants are totally refused for allotment, the application money received on these shares refunded.

   (i) Bank A/c Dr. [No. of Application Received × Application money per Share]

   To Share Application A/c

   (Money received on application for – Share @ Rs. – per share)

   (ii) Share Application A/c Dr. [Application money Received]

   To Share Capital A/c [No. of Share Alloted × Application per share]

   To Bank A/c [No. of Share Rejected × Application Amount per Share]

2. If the applicants are made partial allotment (or pro-rata allotment):

   The directors can as well opt to make a proportionate distribution of shares available for allotment among the applicants of shares. The proportion is determined by the ratio which the number of shares to be allotted to bear to the number of shares applied for. This is called 'pro-rata allotment.

   Generally, excess application money received on these shares is adjusted towards the amount due on allotment or call.

(i) Bank A/c Dr. [No. of Application Received × Application amount per Share]

To Share Application A/c

(Application money received on – Shares @ Rs. – per share

(ii) Share Application A/c Dr. [Application money Received]

To Share Capital A/c [No. of Share Alloted × Application Amount per share]

To Share Allotment A/c [Excess Application money]

Transfer of application money to share capital and excess application money credited to share allotment.)

(iii) Bank A/c Dr. [No. of Share Allotted × Allotment Amount per Share]

To Share Capital A/c

(Amount due on the Attotment of – Share @ Rs. – Per Share)

(iv) Bank A/c Dr. [Amount per Share due – Excess Application Money]

To Share Allotment A/c

This is a combination of two alternatives described above as thus:

(a) Application for some shares are rejected outright, and

(b) pro-rata allotment is made to the applicants of a remaining number of shares.

Thus, money on the rejected applications is refunded and excess application money due to pro-rata distribution is adjusted towards the amount due on the allotment of shares allotted.

(i) Bank A/c Dr. [No. of Share Applied for × Application Amount per Share]

To Share Application A/c

(Money received on application for – Shares @ per share]

(ii) Share Application A/c Dr. [Application money Received]

To Share Capital A/c [No. of Share Alloted × Application Amount per share]

To Share Allotment A/c [Excess Application Money due to pro-rata Allotment]

To Bank A/c [No. of Share Rejected × Application Amount Per Share]

Transfer of application money to share capital, excess application amount credited to share allotment and money refunded on rejected application)

(iii) Share Allotment A/c Dr. [No. of Share Allotted × Allotment Amount per Share]

To Share Capital A/c

(Amount due on the Allotment of — Share @ Rs. — Per Share)

(iv) Bank A/c Dr. [Allotment Amount due – Excess Application Money]

Share Allotment A/c

(Allotment money received after adjusting the amount already received as excess application money)

Under Subscription: Under subscription is a situation where number of shares applied for is less than the number for which applications have been invited for subscription.

Issue of Shares at a Premium: When shares are issued at an amount more than the face value of a share, they are said to be issued at a premium. The difference between the issue price and the face value of the Share is called the premium.

It can be used only for the following five purposes:

(a) to issue fully paid bonus shares to the extent not exceeding unissued share capital of the company;

(b) to write-off preliminary expenses of the company;

(c) to write-off the expenses of, or commission paid, or discount allowed on any securities of the company; and

(d) to pay premium on the redemption of preference shares or debentures of the company.

(e) Purchase of its own shares (i.e., buy back of shares).

When Shares are issued at a premium, the journal entries are as follows:

(a) Premium Amount called with Application money

(i) Bank A/c Dr. [Total Application Money + Premium Amount]

Share Application A/c

(Money received on the application for— Shares @ Rs. — per share including premium)

(ii) Share Application A/c Dr. [Amount Received]

To Share Capital A/c [No. of Share Applicced for × Application Amount per Share]

To Securities Premium A/c [No. of share applied for × Premium Amount per share]

(Transfer of application money to share capital and premium accounts)

(b) Premium Amount called with Allotment money

(i) Share Allotment A/c Dr. [No. of Share Alloted × Allotment & Premium money per share]

To Share Capital A/c [No. of Share Alloted × Allotment Amount per share]

To Securities Premium A/c [No. of Share Alloted × Premium Amount per share]

(Amount due on allotment of shares @ Rs. – per share including premium)

(ii) Bank A/c Dr.

To Share Allotment A/c

(Allotment money received including premium)

Issue of Shares at a Discount: There are instances when the shares of a company are issued at a discount, i.e. at an amount less than the nominal or par value of shares, the difference between the nominal value and issue price representing discount on the issue of shares.

Issue of Shares for Consideration other than cash:

If a company purchases some assets from vendors, in exchange it can issue fully paid shares to them whereby the latter agrees to accepts it. Thus, no cash is received for the issue of shares. These shares can also be issued either at par, at a premium, or at a discount. The number of shares to be issued will depend on the price at which shares are issued and the amount payable to the vendor. To find out the number of shares to be issued to the vendor will be calculated as follows:

$$\text{No. of Shares to be issued} = \frac{\text{Amount Payable}}{\text{Issue Price}}$$

(a) On purchase of assets:

Assets A/c Dr.

To Vendor's A/c

(Assets Purchased)

(b) Shares can be issued to vendors in any manner out of the following:

1. At Par:

Vendor's A/c Dr.

To Share Capital A/c

2. At Premium:

Vendor's A/c Dr.

To Share Capital A/c

To Securities Premium A/c

3. At discount:

Vendor's A/c

Share Discount A/c

To Share Capital A/c

Forfeiture of Shares:

If a shareholder fails to pay allotment money or call money on his share as called upon by the company, his shares may be forfeited by giving due notice and following the procedure specified in the Articles of Association in this behalf. This is known as forfeiture of shares.

To forfeit a share means to cancel the allotment to the defaulting shareholders and to treat the amount already received thereon as forfeited to the company.

Accounting Treatment:

1. Forfeiture of Shares issued at par

Share Capital A/c Dr. [Amount Called-up]

To Share Forfeiture A/c [Amount paid]

To Share Allotment A/c

and/or [Amount unpaid]

To Share Call/calls

Note: In case'Calls-in-Arrears' A /c is maintained by a company, 'Call-in-Arrears' A/c would be credited in the above instead of 'Share Allotment' and/or 'Share Call or Calls' A/c.

The balance on the Share Forfeited A/c is shown in addition to the total paid capital of the company under the heading 'Share Capital' on the liabilities side of the Balance Sheet till the forfeited shares are reissued.

2. **Forfeiture of Shares issued at a Premium:**

(a) If Premium has not been paid by the Shareholders:

Share Capital A/c Dr. (Amount Called up Premium)

Securities Premium A/c Dr. (Premium amount)

To Share Allotment A/c (Amount unpaid)

To Share Call/Calls A/c (Amount unpaid)

To Share Forfeiture A/c (Amount paid)

(For Share forfeited)

(b) If Premium has been paid by the shareholder:

Share Capital A/c Dr. (Amount Called up Premium)

To Share Allotment A/c Dr. (Premium amount)

To Share Call/Calls A/c (Amount unpaid)

To Share Forfeiture A/c (Amount paid)

(For Share forfeited)

3. **Forfeiture of Shares issued at a discount:**

Share Capital A/c Dr. (Amount Calledup + Discount)

To Discount on Issue of Share A/c (Discount on forfeited share)

To Share Allotment A/c (Amount unpaid)

To Share Call/Calls A/c (Amount unpaid)

To Share Forfeiture A/c (Amount paid)

(Forfeiture of Shares and discount on issue adjusted)

Re-Tissue of Forfeited Share

The director of a company has the authority to re-issue the shares once forfeited. These forfeited shares are reissued at par, at a premium, or at a discount, the amount of the discount does not exceed the amount paid on such shares by the original shareholder but in case of shares originally issued at discount, the maximum permissible discount will be the amount paid on such shares by the original shareholder plus the amount of original discount.

Accounting Treatment:

1. For Forfeited Shares reissued at Par:

Bank A/c Dr.

To Share Capital A/c

2. For Forfeited Shares reissued at Premium:

Bank A/c Dr.

To Share Capital A/c

To Securities Premium A/c

3. For Forfeited Shares reissued at Discount:

Bank A/c Dr.

Share Forfeiture A/c Dr. (Discount Allowed)

To Share Capital A/c

Exercise

1. ______________ are the minimum number of members in a public company.
   (a) 5 (b) 6
   (c) 7 (d) 8
2. Arrange the following in proper sequence as types of share capital
   i. Issued capital
   ii. Paid up capital
   iii. Called up capital
   iv. Subscribed capital
   (a) i , iv, iii , ii (b) iv ,iii ,ii ,i
   (c) iii , ii, i, iv (d) ii , iv , i ,iii
3. ___________ interest is charged on calls
   (a) 5% (b) 6%
   (c) 7% (d) None of the above
4. Which of the following statement is true :-
   i. A company is formed according to the provisions of Law enforced from time to time
   ii. A company does not have a separate legal entity
   iii. The liability of the members of the company is unlimited
   iv. The shares of a public limited company are not freely transferable
   (a) i (b) ii
   (c) iii (d) iv
5. The portion of the authorised capital which can be called up only on the liquidation of the company is called
   (a) Called up capital (b) Issued capital
   (c) Reserve capital (d) None of the above
6. Axs Ltd. Forfeited 2000 shares of Rs. 10 each fully called up for non payment of final call of Rs. 2 per share. 1200 of these shares were reissued at Rs. 7 per share fully paid up. What is the amount of to be transferred to capital reserve account.
   (a) Rs. 6,000 (b) Rs. 7,200
   (c) Rs. 8,400 (d) Rs. 1,400
7. The following amounts were payable on the issue of shares by a company: Rs. 3 on application, Rs. 2 on the first call, and Rs. 2 on the final call. Sam holding 500 shares paid only application and allotment money whereas Tom holding 400 shares did not pay a final call. Amount of calls in arrear will be:
   (a) Rs. 1,800 (b) Rs. 2,800
   (c) Rs. 800 (d) Rs. 2,000
8. A shareholder holding 600 shares paid the amount of call @ Rs. 5 per share on 1st November 2019 whereas the call was due on 1st March 2020. Interest on calls in advance will be:
   (a) Rs. 100 (b) Rs. 120
   (c) Rs. 180 (d) Rs. 360
9. ABC LTD. invited applications for 1,00,000 shares and it received applications for 1,50,000 shares. Applications for 30,000 shares were rejected and the remaining were allotted shares on a pro-rata basis. How many shares on the applicant for 3,000 shares will be allotted?
   (a) Rs. 3,000 (b) Rs. 3,500
   (c) Rs. 2,500 (d) Rs. 1,500

10. Mr. Y applied for 80,000 shares and was allotted 60,000 shares on a pro-rata basis, the shareholder who was allotted 1,200 shares must have applied for:

(a) Rs. 1,600 (b) Rs. 2,400
(c) Rs. 1,800 (d) Rs. 1,000

11. The liability of members in a company is:

(a) Limited (b) Unlimited
(c) Stable (d) Fluctuating

12. When full amount is due on any call but it is not received, then the short fall is debited to :

(a) Calls-in-advance (b) Calls-in-arrear
(c) Share Capital (d) Joint Account

13. When a company issues fully paid shares to promoters for their services, the journal entry will be:

(a) Bank A/c Dr.
To Share Capital A/c

(b) Good will A/c Dr.
To Share Capital A/c

(c) Promoters Personal A/c Dr.
To Share Capital A/c

(d) Promotion Expenses A/c Dr.
To Share Capital A/c

14. When a company issues shares at a premium, amount of premium may be received by the company :

(a) Along with application money (b) Along with application money
(c) Along with calls (d) All of the above

15. If a share of Rs. 10 on which Rs. 8 has been called and Rs. 6 is paid is forfeited, the Share Capital Account should be debited with :

(a) Rs. 10 (b) Rs. 8
(c) Rs. 6 (d) Rs. 4

16. According to Companies Act, Minimum Subscription has been fixed at __________ of the issued amount.

(a) 25% (b) 50%
(c) 90% (d) 100%

17. **Assertion (A):** The liability of a shareholder is limited up to the nominal price of shares subscribed by one.

Reasoning (R): Paid-up Capital is the amount of nominal value of shares that have been called up by the company for payment by the subscriber towards the share.

Codes :

(a) Both Assertion (A) and Reason (R) are true and Reason (R) is the correct explanation of Assertion (A).

(b) Both Assertion (A) and Reason (R) are true and Reason (R) is not the correct explanation of Assertion (A).

(c) Assertion (A) is true but Reason (R) is False

(d) Assertion (A) is False but Reason (R) is true.

18. A Company issued 50,000 shares of Rs. 20 each at 5% premium. Rs. 10 were payable on application and balance on allotment. What will be the allotment amount?

(a) Rs. 5,50,000 (b) Rs. 4,5,000
(c) Rs. 5,00,000 (d) Rs. 5,25,000

19. Interest on calls in arrears is charged according to Table F at:

(a) 6% p.a. (b) 10% p.a.
(c) 5% p.a. (d) 12% p.a.

20. Pro-rata allotment of shares is made when there is :

(a) Under subscription (b) Oversubscription
(c) Equal subscription (d) None of the above

Topic Test – 1

1. Authorised capital of a Company is divided into 5,00,000 shares of Rs. 10 each. It issued 3,00,000 shares. Public applied for 3,60,000 shares. Amount of issued capital will be :

(a) Rs. 30,00,000 (b) Rs. 36,00,000

(c) Rs. 50,00,000 (d) Rs. 6,00,000

2. A Company offered 50,000 shares of Rs.10 each at par payable as to Rs.3 on applications, Rs. 5 on allotment and the balance on final call. Applications were received for 60,000 shares and the allotment was made pro-rata. The excess application money was to be adjusted on allotment and call. How much amount will be transferred from Share Application A/c to Share Allotment A/c?

(a) Rs. 1,50,000 (b) Rs. 30,000

(c) Rs. 1,80,000 (d) Rs. 40,000

3. **Assertion (A):** Forfeiture of a share refers to the cancellation or termination of membership of a shareholder by taking away the shares and rights of membership.

Reasoning (R): Forfeited shares can be reissued at a discount.

Codes:

(a) Both Assertion (A) and Reason (R) are true and Reason (R) is the correct explanation of Assertion (A).

(b) Both Assertion (A) and Reason (R) are true and Reason (R) is not the correct explanation of Assertion (A).

(c) Assertion (A) is true but Reason (R) is False.

(d) Assertion (A) is False but Reason (R) is true.

4. Loyd. Ltd. forfeited 500 equity shares of Rs. 10 each, fully called up, on which Rs. 6 per share (including premium of Rs. 1 per share) was received. It later reissued these shares at a discount. The maximum discount per share, which the company could have given on their reissue would be:

(a) Rs. 6 per share (b) Rs. 5 per share

(c) Rs. 4 per share (d) Rs. 3 per share

5. 10,000 equity shares of 10 Rs. each were issued to public at a premium of Rs. 2 per share payable on allotment. Applications were received for Rs. 12,000 shares. Amount of securities premium account will be :

(a) Rs. 20,000 (b) Rs. 24,000

(c) Rs. 4,000 (d) Rs. 1,600

6. Which of the following should be deducted from the called-up capital to find out paid-up capital:

(a) Calls-in-advance (b) Calls-in-arrear

(c) Share forfeiture (d) Discount on issue of shares

7. If a share of Rs.100 on which Rs. 60 has been paid up , is forfeited it can be reissued at the minimum price of

(a) Rs. 90 (b) Rs. 60

(c) Rs. 100 (d) Rs. 40

8. Which of the following statements is true?

(a) Authorised Capital = Issued Capital (b) Authorised Capital > Issued Capital

(c) Paid up Capital > Issued Capital (d) None of the above

9. A company Forfeited 2,000 shares of Rs 10 each issued at 20% premium to be paid at the time of allotment on which Rs 8 is called up, company not received Rs 4 on Allotment including premium and Rs. 2 in First call. What will be the amount Debited to share capital account:

(a) Rs. 20,000 (b) Rs. 16,000

(c) Rs. 24,000 (d) Rs. 18,000

10. The Interest on Calls-in-arrears Account is closed by:

(a) Crediting it to Statement of Profit & Loss

(b) Crediting it to Profit & Loss Account

(c) Debiting it to Profit & Loss Appropriation Account

(d) Debiting it to Statement of Profit & Loss

Topic Test – 2

For questions 1 to 4: Analyse the case given below and answer the questions that follows:

Akshay limited was incorporated on 1stApril 2019 with registered office in Delhi. The capital clause of memorandum of Association reflected a registered capital of 8,00,000 equity shares of Rs.10 each and 1,00,000 preference shares of Rs.50 each. Since some large investments were required for building and machinery the company in consultation with vendors, Ms.VPS Enterprises, issued 1,00,000 equity shares and 20,000 preference shares at par to them in full consideration of assets acquired. Besides this the company issued 2,00,000 equity shares for cash at par payable as Rs 3 on application, 2 on allotment, 3 on first call and 2 on second call. Till date second call has not yet been made and all the shareholders have paid except Mr. A who did not pay allotment and calls on his 300 shares and Mr. V who did not pay first call on his 200 shares. Shares of Mr. A were then forfeited and out of them 100 shares were reissued at Rs.12 per share. Based on above information you are required to answer the following questions.

1. Shares issue to vendors of building and machinery, Ms. VPS Enterprises, would be classified as:

(a) Preferential Allotment (b) Employee Stock Option Plan

(c) Issue for Consideration other than cash (d) Right Issue of Shares

2. How many equity shares of the company have been subscribed?

(a) 3,00,000 (b) 2,99,500

(c) 2,99,800 (d) None of these

3. What is the amount of security premium reflected in the balance sheet at the end of the year?

(a) Rs. 200 (b) Rs. 600

(c) Rs. 400 (d) Rs. 1,000

4. What amount of share forfeiture would be reflected in the balance sheet?

(a) Rs. 600 (b) Rs. 900

(c) Rs. 200 (d) Rs. 300

5. ABC Ltd. company issued 4,000 equity shares of Rs. 10 each at par payable as under: On application Rs. 3; on allotment Rs. 2; on first call Rs. 4 and on final call Rs. 1 per share. Applications were received for 10,000 shares Allotment was made pro-rata. How much amount will be received in cash on the allotment?

(a) Rs. 2,000 (b) Rs. 9,000

(c) Rs. 14,000 (d) Nil

6. When a company issues shares at a premium, amount of premium may be received by the company :

(a) Along with application money (b) Along with application money

(c) Along with calls (d) Along with any of the above

7. If a share of Rs. 10 on which Rs. 8 has been paid up is forfeited, it can be reissued at the minimum price of.......

(a) Rs. 8 per share (b) Rs. 6 per share

(c) Rs. 5 per share (d) Rs. 2 per share

8. Wills & Co. forfeited 100 shares of Rs. 10 each for non-payment of final call of Rs. 2 per share. All the forfeited shares were re-issued at Rs. 9 per share. What amount will be transferred to Capital Reserve A/c?

(a) Rs. 700 (b) Rs. 800

(c) Rs. 900 (d) Rs. 1,000

9. 10,000 equity shares of Rs. 10 each were issued to public at a premium of Rs. 2 per share payable on allotment. Applications were received for Rs. 12,000 shares. Amount of securities premium account will be :

(a) Rs. 20,000 (b) Rs. 24,000

(c) Rs. 4,000 (d) Rs. 1,600

10. Which of the following will define, when appropriation of a certain number of shares is made to an applicant in response to his application?

(a) Share allotment (b) Share forfeiture

(c) Share trading (d) Share Purchase

Answer Keys

Exercise

1. (c)	2. (a)	3. (b)	4. (a)	5. (c)	6. (a)	7. (b)	8. (b)	9. (c)	10. (a)
11. (a)	12. (b)	13. (b)	14. (d)	15. (b)	16. (c)	17. (c)	18. (a)	19. (b)	20. (b)

Topic Test – 1

1. (a)	2. (b)	3. (b)	4. (b)	5. (b)	6. (b)	7. (d)	8. (b)	9. (b)	10. (a)

Topic Test – 2

1. (a)	2. (b)	3. (c)	4. (d)	5. (c)	6. (c)	7. (c)	8. (d)	9. (c)	10. (a)

Solutions

Exercise

1. (c)
2. (a)
3. (b)
4. (a)
5. (c)
6. (a) 1200 × 7 = 8400
1200 × 2 = 2400 (8400 – 2400 = 6000)
7. (b) 500 × 4 = 2000
400 × 2 = 800 (2000 + 800 = 2800)
8. (b) (600 × 5 = 3000
3000 × 12/100 × 4 /12 = 120
9. (c) 1,50,000 – 30,000 = 1,20,000
Ratio = 5 : 6
3000 × 5/6 = 2500
10. (a) 80,000 / 60,000 = 4 : 3 = 1200 × 4/3 = 1600
11. (a)
12. (b)
13. (b)
14. (d)
15. (b)

16. (c)

17. (c) Paid up capital is the part of called up capital that actually has been paid by the subscriber.

18. (a) 20 × 5/100 = 1 50,000 × 11 = 5,50,000

19. (b)

20. (b)

Topic Test – 1

1. (a)

2. (b) 60,000 × 3 =1,80,000 – 50,000 × 3 = 1,50,000
Excess application = 1,80,000 – 1,50,000 = 30,000

3. (b) Both A and R are true but R does not explain why share are forfeited as per the law.

4. (b)

5. (b) 10,000 × 2 = 20,000

6. (b)

7. (d)

8. (b)

9. (b)

10. (a)

Topic Test – 2

1. (c)

2. (c)

3. (c)

4. (a)

5. (d)

6. (d)

7. (d)

8. (a)

9. (a)

10. (a)

CHAPTER 7

Issue and Redemption of Debentures

Section-I

Meaning Of Debentures

The word 'debenture' has been derived from a Latin word 'debere' which means to borrow. Debenture is a written instrument acknowledging a debt under the common seal of the company. It contains a contract for repayment of principal after a specified period or at intervals or at the option of the company and for payment of interest at a fixed rate payable usually either half-yearly or yearly on fixed dates.

Bond: Bond, like debenture, is an acknowledgment of debt issued under the seal of a company and signed by an authorized signatory.

Distinction between Shares and debentures:

Ownership: A 'share' represents ownership of the company whereas a debenture is only acknowledgement of Debt. A share is a part of the owned capital whereas a debenture is a part of borrowed capital.

Return: The return on shares is known as dividend while the return on debentures is called interest. The rate of return on shares may vary from year to year depending upon the profits of the company but the rate of interest on debentures is prefixed. The payment of dividend is an appropriation of profits, whereas the payment of interest is a charge on profits and is to be paid even if there is no profit.

Repayment: Normally, the amount of shares is not returned during the life of the company, whereas, generally, the debentures are issued for a specified period and repayable on the expiry of that period.

Voting Rights: Shareholders enjoy voting rights whereas debenture holders do not normally enjoy any voting right.

Security: Shares are not secured by any charge whereas the debentures are generally secured and carry a fixed or floating charge over the assets of the company.

Convertibility: Shares cannot be converted into debentures whereas debentures can be converted into shares if the terms of issue so provide, and in that case these are known as convertible debentures.

Types of Debentures

1. Security point of view

(a) **Secured/Mortgage Debentures:** Secured Debentures are those which are secured either on a particular asset or on all the assets of the company in general.

(b) **Unsecured/Naked Debentures:** Unsecured Debentures do not have a specific charge on the assets of the company.

2. Tenure point of view

(a) **Redeemable Debentures:** Redeemable debentures are those that will be repaid by the company at the end of a specified period during the existence of the company.

(b) **Irredeemable Debentures:** Irredeemable debentures are those that are not repayable during the lifetime of the company

3. Mode of Redemption point of view:

(a) **Convertible Debentures:** Convertible debentures are those the holder of which is given an option of exchanging the amount of their debenture for equity shares after a specified period.

These are of two types:

1. Fully Convertible Debentures (FCD) are those debentures where the whole amount is to be converted into equity shares.
2. Partly Convertible Debentures (PCD) are those debentures where only a part of the amount of debenture is convertible into equity shares.

(b) **Non-Convertible Debentures:** The debentures which cannot be converted into shares or in any other securities are called non-convertible debentures.

4. From Coupon Rate Point of view:

(a) **Specific Coupon Rate Debentures:** These debentures are issued with a specified rate of interest, which is called the coupon rate. The specified rate may either be fixed or floating. The floating interest rate is usually tagged with the bank rate.

(b) **Zero Coupon Rate Debentures:** These debentures do not carry a specific rate of interest. In order to compensate the investors, such debentures are issued at substantial discount and the difference between the nominal value and the issue price is treated as the amount of interest related to the duration of the debentures.

5. Registration point of view:

(a) **Registered Debentures:** Registered debentures are those which are payable to the persons whose name appears in the Register of Debenture holders. These can be transferred only by executing a transfer deed.

(b) **Bearer Debentures:** Bearer debentures are those which are payable to the bearer thereof. These can be transferred merely by delivery. Interest is paid to the persons who produced the interest coupon attached to such debenture.

Types of Debenture/Bond

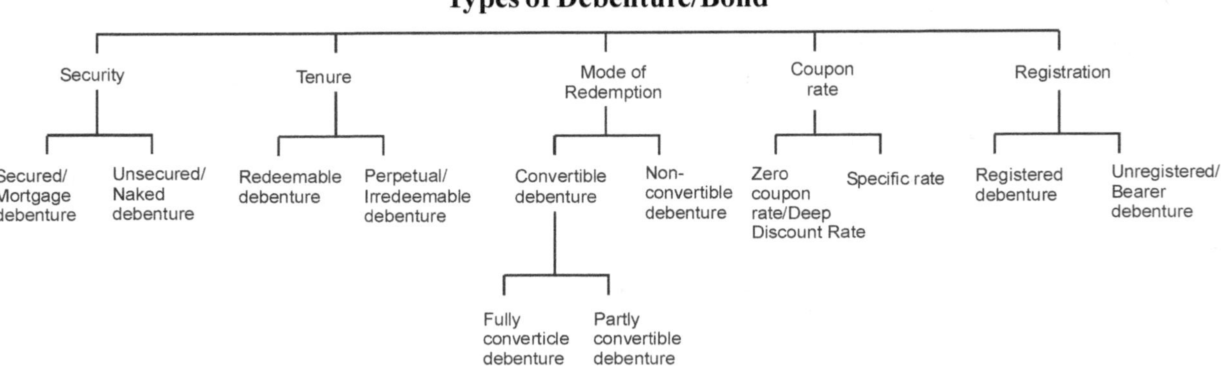

Issue of Debentures:

The procedure for the issue of debentures is the same as that for the issue of shares. The intending investors apply for debentures on the basis of the prospectus issued by the company. The company may either ask for the entire amount to be paid on application or by means of instalments on application, on allotment and on various calls. Debentures can be issued at par, at a premium or at a discount. They can also be issued for consideration other than cash or as a collateral security.

Issue of Debentures at Par: Debentures are said to have been issued at par when the issue price is equal to their face value.

1. If the debenture amount is received in one installment (lump sum).

a. On receipt of the money
Bank A/c Dr. [With the total money received on Application]
To Debenture Application & Allotment A/c

b. On making the allotment
Debenture Application & Allotment A/c Dr. [At the time of Allotment]
To Debenture A/c

ii. If the debenture amount is received in instalments

a. On receipt of Application money
Bank A/c Dr. [With the money received on application]
To Debenture Application A/c

b. On Acceptance of Applications
Debenture Application A/c Dr. [With Application money received on debenture alloted]
To Debenture A/c

c. On making Allotment money due
Debenture Allotment A/c Dr. [With allotment money due]
To Debenture A/c

d. On Receipt of Allotment money
Bank A/c Dr. [With allotment money received]
To Debenture Allotment A/c

e. On making the First Call
Debenture First Call A/c Dr. [With allotment money received]
To Debenture A/c

f. On Receipt of first Call money
Bank A/c Dr. [With the first Call money received]
To Debenture First Call A/c

Issue of Debentures at a Discount: When the debentures are issued at less than the face value, it is said to be issued at discount. Discount on issue of debenture is a capital loss and is shown on the assets side of the Balance Sheet under the head "Miscellaneous Expenditure" till it is written off.

Accounting Treatment:

On the issue of debentures at a discount
Debenture Allotment A/c Dr.
Discount of Issue of Debenture A/c Dr.
To Debenture A/c

Issue of Debentures at Premium: A debenture is said to have been issued at a premium when the price charged is more than the face value of debenture. Premium on Issue of Debenture represents a capital receipt and should be transferred to Securities Premium A/c. It can be used for writing off capital losses and fictitious assets. This account is shown on the liabilities side of the Balance Sheet under the head of 'Reserves & Surplus'.

Accounting Treatment:

On Issue of Debenture at Premium

Debenture Allotment A/c Dr.

To Debenture A/c To Securities Premium A/c

Over Subscription: When the number of debentures applied for is more than the number of debentures offered to the public, the issue is said to be oversubscribed. The excess money received on oversubscription may be retained for adjustment towards allotment and respective calls when the amount is payable in Instalments or excess money will be refunded.

Issue of Debentures for Consideration Other than Cash: When the company purchases some assets (including services) and instead of making the payment to the supplier in the form of cash, issues its fully paid debentures, such issue of debentures is called the Issue of Debentures for Consideration Other than Cash. Such debentures can be issued at par, a premium, or at a discount.

(a) On Purchase of Business

Sundry Assets A/c	Dr.	[With the agreed value of assets]
To Sundry Liabilities A/c		[With the agreed value of Liabilities]
To Vendor's A/c		[With Purchase consideration]

If the purchase consideration is greater than the value of the net assets acquired (i.e., the difference between the agreed value of the assets taken over and the agreed value of liabilities taken over), the difference is treated as a capital loss which should be debited to Goodwill A/c.

Sundry Assets A/c	Dr.	[Agreed value of assets taken over]
Goodwill A/c	Dr.	[Excess of purchase consideration over the value of net assets]
To Sundry Liabilities A/c		[Agreed value of liabilities]
To Vendors A/c		[Purchase consideration]

Or

If the amount of the purchase consideration is lower than the value of the net assets acquired, the difference is treated as a capital profit which should be credited to Capital Reserve A/c.

Sundry Assets A/c	Dr.	[Agreed value of assets taken over]
To Sundry Liabilities A/c		[Agreed value of liabilities]
To Vendor's A/c		[Purchase considerations]
To Capital Reserve A/c		[Excess of value of net assets over purchase considerations]

(b) On the issue of Debentures

1. At par

   Vendor's A/c Dr.

   To Debentures A/c

2. At Premium

   Vendor's A/c Dr.

   To Debentures A/c To Securities Premium A/c

3. At a Discount Vendor's A/c
   Discount on Issue of Debentures A/c
   To Debentures A/c
   No. of Debentures issued

Issue Price of a Debenture:

Issue of Debentures as Collateral Security: When a company takes a loan from a bank or any other party and gives some additional security in the shape of debentures, the debentures are said to be issued as collateral security. In such a case, the lender has the absolute right over the debentures unless and until the loan is repaid. On repayment of the loan, the lender is legally bond to release the debenture forthwith.

In case the loan is not repaid by the company on the cue date, the lender has the right to retain these debentures and realize them. The holder of such debentures is entitled to interest only on the amount of loan, but not on the debentures.

Debentures issued as collateral security can be dealt with in two ways in the books.

1. No accounting entry is required to be shown in the books at the time of issue of such debentures, but a footnote to the fact that the loan has been secured by the issue of debentures is appended.
2. If it is desired that such an issue of debentures is to be recorded in the books, the following entries are recorded:
   (a) On the issue of Debentures as Collateral Security
   Debentures Suspense A/c Dr.
   To Debentures A/c
   (b) On repayment of the loan
   Debentures A/c Dr.
   To Debentures Suspense A/c The net effect of the above two entries is nil.

Issue of Debentures From Condition of Redemption Point of View: Redemption of debentures means discharge of liability on account of debentures by repayment made to the debenture holders. Depending upon the terms and conditions of issue and redemption of debentures, there may be the following six cases:

Accounting Treatment:

Case 1: Issue at Par and Redemption at Par

Bank A/c	Dr. [With the nominal value of debenture]
To Debenture A/c	

Case 2: Issue at Discount and Redemption at Par

Bank A/c	Dr. [With actual amount received]
Discount on Issue of Debentures A/c	Dr. [With discount allowed]
To Debentures A/c	[With nominal value]

Case 3: Issue at Premium and Redemption at Par.

Bank A/c	Dr. [With Amount received]
To Debentures A/c	[With Nominal value of Deb.]
To Securities Premium A/c	[With the amount of premium]

Case 4: Issue at Par and Redemption at Premium

Bank A/c	Dr. [With amount received]
Loss on Issue of Debentures A/c	Dr. [With premium on redemption]
To Debentures A/c	[With nominal value]
To Premium on Redemption of Debenture A/c	[with premium on redemption]

Case 5: Issue at Discount and Redemption at Premium

Bank A/c	Dr. [With amount received]
Loss on Issue of Debentures A/c	Dr. [With discount allowed on issue and premium on redemption]
To Debentures A/c	[With nominal value of debenture]
To Premium on Redemption of Debentures A/c	[With Premium on redemption]

Case 6: Issued at Premium and Redemption at Premium

Bank A/c	Dr. [With amount received]
Loss on Issue of Debentures A/c	Dr. [With premium on redemption]
To Debentures A/c	[With nominal value of debentures]
To Securities Premeium A/c	[With premium on Issue]
To Premium on Redemption of of Debentures A/c	[With premium on redemption]

Interest on Debentures: Interest on debentures is a charge against the profits of the company and is payable irrespective of the fact whether there are profits or not. It is calculated on the face value of the debenture. According to Income-tax Act, 1961, the company must deduct income tax at the prescribed rate from the gross amount of interest payable on debenture before the annual amount is paid to debenture holders. Accounting Treatment:

1. For Interest due

Debentures Interest A/c	Dr. [With the amount of Gross Interest]
To Income Tax Payable A/c	[With the tax deducted at source]
To Debentureholder A/c	[With the interest payable to debentureholder]

2. For Payment of Interest

Debentureholder A/c	Dr.
To Bank A/c	

3. On Closing of Debenture Interest A/c

Profit and Loss A/c	Dr.
To Debenture Interest A/c	

4. For Payment of Income Tax to Government

Income Tax Payable A/c	Dr.
To Bank A/c	

Writing off Discount/Loss on Issue of Debentures: The discount/ loss on the issue of debentures is a capital loss and therefore must be written off during the lifetime of debentures. The discount/loss on the issue of debentures is shown under the head "Miscellaneous Expenditure" on the assets side of the Balance Sheet. Section 78 of the Companies Act, 1956 permits the utilization of Securities Premium for writing off the discount/loss on the issue of the debenture.

Entry is following:

Security Premium A/c Dr.

To Discount/Loss on

Issue of Debenture A/c

In case there are no capital profits or if the capital profits are not adequate, the amount of such discount/loss can be written off by utilizing the revenue profits.

There are two methods, which can be used to write off the Discount/Loss on the issue of debentures:

(a) **Fixed Installment Method:** When the debentures are redeemed at the end of a specified period, the total amount of discount should be written off in equal installments of a fixed amount over the period.

(b) **Fluctuating Installment Method:** When debentures are repaid by annual drawings or installments, the discount is written off in the ratio of debentures outstanding before redemption. The amount of discount, in this method, goes on reducing every year as a greater amount is used in the initial years than the later years. This method is also known as the Reducing Instalment Method.

Section-II

Redemption of Debentures: Redemption of debentures means repayment of the loan due on debentures to debenture holders. According to Section 117 C (3) of the Companies Act 1956, the debentures should be redeemed in accordance with the terms and conditions of their issue/ offer documents. The date, the terms, and the conditions are generally stated in the debenture certificate itself or in the trust deed.

On the due date or happening of the circumstances so specified, the company becomes liable to pay the principal amount to the debenture holder. A company may purchase its own debenture which then stands cancelled.

Methods of the Redemption of Debentures: The various methods of redemption of debentures are as under:

1. Payment in Lump-Sum
2. Payment in Instalments
3. Purchase in Open Market
4. Conversion of existing Debenture into Shares or New Debentures.

1. **Payment in Lump Sum:** It means debentures can be redeemed by paying the debenture holders in one lump sum at the expiry of the agreed time or earlier at the option of the company. In this case, the time of repayment is known in advance and thus the company can plan its financial resources accordingly.
2. **Payment in Instalments:** It means the redemption is made in annual installments. The amount of installment is worked out by dividing the total amount of debentures by the number of years it is to last. The number of debentures to be redeemed each year are selected by lottery. Thus, it is also known as drawing by lottery or draw of lots.
3. **Purchase in Open Market:** A company, if authorized by its Articles of Association, can purchase its own debenture in the open market. Debentures so purchased may be canceled and it means the debentures have been paid.

4. **Conversion of Existing Debentures into Shares or New Debentures:** It means the debenture holder can exchange their debenture either for shares or new debentures of the company and the debentures which carry such right are called convertible debentures.

Sources of funds for Redemption of Debentures: The redemption of debentures can be done either out of capital or out of profits.

(a) Redemption of Debenture out of Capital: In this case, profits of the company are not utilized for the redemption of debentures, so the assets of the company are reduced by the amount paid. Normally the profits are transferred to Debenture Redemption Reserve for redemption. In case no profits have been transferred to Debenture Redemption Reserve and debentures are redeemed on the due date, it is regarded as redemption out of the capital. It is, however, presumed that the company has adequate funds to redeem the debentures.

Accounting Treatment:

(a) If debentures are to be redeemed at par

1. On debentures becoming due
   Debentures A/c Dr.
   To Debenture- holder A/c
2. On Redemption Debentureholder A/c Dr.
   To Bank A/c

(b) If debentures are to be redeemed at a premium

1. On debentures becoming due
   Debentures A/c Dr.
   Premium on Redemption of
   Debenture A/c Dr.
   To Debentureholder A/c
2. On Redemption Debentureholder A/c Dr.
   To Bank A/c

(b) Redemption of Debentures out of Profits: Redemption of debentures out of profits means the amount equal to that utilized for repayment to debenture holders is transferred from Profit and Loss Appropriation A/c to a newly opened A/c called 'Debenture Redemption Reserve A/c' (DRR). The portion of the profits set aside may either be retained in the business or maybe invested.

Clarifications regarding Debenture Redemption Reserve:

The Department of Company Affairs, Government of India, vide their circular No. 9/2002, dates 18.04.2002 has issued the following clarifications regarding the creation of Debenture Redemption Reserve (DRR):

(a) No DRR is required for debentures issued by All India Financial Institutions, by RBI and, Banking Companies for both public as well as privately placed debentures.

(b) No DRR is required in case of privately placed debentures.

(c) Section 117c will apply to debentures issued and pending to be redeemed and, therefore, DRR will also be created for debentures issued prior to 13.12.2000 and pending redemption.

(d) Section 117c will apply to the non-convertible portion of debentures issued whether they are fully or partly paid.

Journal Entries:

1. Debenture A/c To Debentureholders A/c
2. Debenture holder A/c To Bank A/c
3. Profit and Loss Appropriation A/c To Debenture Redemption Reserve A/c

DRR A/c appears on the liability side of the Balance Sheet, under the head "Reserves and Surplus". The balance in DRR A/c increases with each redemption. When all the debentures are redeemed, the DRR A/c is closed by transferring its balance to General Reserve A/c.

Redemption by Purchase in the Open Market: A company, if authorized by its Articles of Association, can redeem its own debenture by purchasing them in the open market.

If a company purchases its own debenture for the purpose of immediate cancellation, the purchase and cancellation of such debenture are called, redemption by purchase in the open market.

Accounting Treatment:

(In case of Profits)

(a) On purchase of own debentures for immediate cancellation.
Debenture A/c Dr.
To Bank A/c
To Profit on Cancellation of Debenture A/c

(b) On transfer of Profit on Redemption
Profit on Cancellation of Debenture A/c Dr.
To Capital Reserve A/c

(In case of Loss)

(a) On purchase of own debenture for immediate cancellation.
Debenture A/c Dr.
Loss on Cancellation
of Debenture A/c Dr.
To Bank A/c

(b) On transfer of Loss on Redemption
Profit and Loss A/c Dr.
To Loss on Cancellation of Debenture A/c

Redemption by Conversion: Sometimes, at the time of issue of debentures, a company gives the convertible debenture holders the privilege that they can get their debentures converted into shares or new debentures after the expiry of a specified period. Whenever debenture is redeemed by conversion, the debenture holders have to.; apply for the same. The new shares or debentures may be issued at par, discount, or a premium.

No DRR is required in case of convertible debentures because no funds are required for redemption.

If debentures to be converted were issued at discount, the issue price of the share must be equal to the amount actually received from debentures. If this rule is not fol owed, it would be a violation of section 79 of the Companies Act, 1956.

Accounting Treatment:

(i) For the amount due to debenture holders

(a) If Redemption at par
Debentures A/c Dr.
To Debenture holder A/c

Or

If Redemption at a premium
Debentures A/c Dr.
Securities Premium A/c Dr.
To Debenture holder A/c

(b) For discharging obligation by issuing shares or debentures

Debenture holder A/c Dr.

To Equity Share Capital

Or

To Debentures A/c (New)

Sinking Fund Method: The amount required for the redemption of debentures is generally large and the date of redemption is known to the company. Thus, it is prudent for a company to make arrangements to ensure the availability of adequate funds for the redemption of debenture at the end of the stipulated period for which debentures are issued. Hence, it is better for the company to set aside every year a part of divisible profits and to invest the same outside the business in marketable securities.

Debenture Redemption Sinking Fund A/c will be created every year to provide means for the redemption of debentures. The company sets aside every year a certain sum of money out of its profits and invests the same along with the interest that may be earned on an investment. The investment is sold when debentures fall due for redemption. The amount available from the sale of investment is utilized for the redemption of debentures.

Accounting Treatment:

I. At the end of First Year

(a) For setting aside the amount out of Profit

Profit & Loss Dr. [With the amount of profit set aside]

Appropriation A/c

To Debenture Redemption

Fund A/c

(b) For Investing the amount set aside

Debenture Redemption Dr. [With the amount of investment made]

Fund

Investment A/c

To Bank A/c

II. At the end of the second year and subsequent years other than the last year.

(a) For Receiving the Interest on Investments made

Bank A/c Dr. [With the amount of Interest received]

To Interest on

Debentures

Redemption Fund

Inestment A/c

(b) For the transfer of Interest on Deb. Red. Fund Investment to DRF A/c

The interest of Deb. Red

Fund Investment A/c Dr.

To Debenture Redemption Fund A/c

(c) For Setting aside the number of profits

Profit and Loss Dr. [With the amount Appropriation A/c of Profit set aside]

To Debenture Redemption Fund A/c

(d) For Investing the amount set aside along with interest • received.

Deb. Red. Fund Investment A/c Dr.

To Bank A/c

III. At the end of last year

(a) For Receiving the Interest on Investment made

Bank A/c Dr.

To Interest on Deb. Red. Fund Investment A/c

(b) For the transfer of Interest on Deb. Red. Fund Investment to DRF A/c

Interest in Deb. Red.

Fund Investment A/c Dr.

To Deb. Red. Fund A/c

(c) For setting aside the number of profits

Profit & Loss

Appropriation A/c Dr.

To Deb. Red. Fund A/c

(d) For Realising the Investment made

Bank A/c Dr. [With the sale To Deb. Red. Fund proceeds]

Investment A / c

(e) For the transfer of profit/loss on realization of Deb. Red. Fund Investments

In case of profit

Deb. Red. Fund

Investment A/c Dr. [With the amount of profit]

To Deb. Red. Fund A/c

Or

In case of Loss

Deb. Red. Fund A/c Dr. [With the amount Loss]

To Deb. Red. Fund

Investment A/c

(f) For the amount due to debenture holders

Debenture A/c Dr.

To Debenture holders A/c

(g) For redemption

Debenture holders A/c

To Bank A/c

(h) For the transfer of the balance, if any, Discount on Issue of Debentures A/c/Loss on Issue of Debenture A/c

Deb. Red. Fund. A/c Dr.

To Discount on Issue of Debentures A/c,

To Loss on Issue of Debentures A/c

1. For the transfer of an amount from the Deb. Red. Fund A/c to General Reserve:

(a) If some of the Debentures are redeemed

Deb. Red. Fund A/c Dr. [With the nominal value of Debentures redeemed]

To Deb. Red. Reserve

(b) If all the Debentures are redeemed

Deb. Red. Fund A/c Dr. [With the balance left in Deb. Red. Fund A/c]

To General

Reserve A/c

Exercise

1. Redemption of debentures means ________.
   (a) Repayment of the due amount of debentures to the debenture holder
   (b) Repayment of the due amount of debentures to the Shareholders
   (c) Repayment of the due amount of debentures to the Employees
   (d) None of the options
2. Debenture holders are considered ___________ of the company
   (a) Owner (b) Creditors
   (c) Debtors (d) None of the above
3. The balance of 'Sinking Fund Account' after the redemption of debentures is transferred to :
   (a) Profit & Loss Account (b) Profit & Loss Appropriation Account
   (c) General Reserve Account (d) Sinking Fund Account
4. If debenture of Rs. 1,00,000 were issued for discount of Rs. 10,000, which are redeemable after four years. Then amount of discount to be written off from P. & L. Account each year is :
   (a) Rs. 2,000 (b) Rs. 5,000
   (c) Rs. 1,500 (d) Rs. 2,500
5. Debentures cannot be redeemed at:
   (a) Par (b) Premium
   (c) Discount (d) More than 10% premium
6. When debentures of Rs. 1,00,000 are issued as Collateral Security against a loan of Rs.1,50,000, the entry for issue of debentures will be :
   (a) Credit Debentures Rs. 1,50,000 and debit bank A/c Rs. 1,50,000
   (b) Debit Debenture suspense A/c Rs. 1,00,000 and Credit Bank A/c Rs. 1,00,000
   (c) Debit Debenture suspense A/c Rs. 1,00,000 and Credit Debentures A/c Rs. 1,00,000.
   (d) Debit Cash A/c Rs. 1,50,000 and Credit Bank A/c Rs. 1,50,000.
7. Which of the following statements is false?
   (a) Debenture is a form of public borrowing
   (b) It is customary to prefix debentures with the agreed rate of interest.
   (c) Debenture interest is a charge against profits
   (d) The issue price and redemption value of debentures can not differ.
8. ABC Ltd. Purchased building of XYZ Ltd. for Rs. 4,00,000. The consideration was paid by the issue of 10% Debentures of Rs. 100 each at a discount of Rs. 20. 10% Debentures Account is credited with
   (a) Rs. 5,10,000 (b) Rs. 5,00,000
   (c) Rs. 4,90,000 (d) Rs. 2,20,000
9. Which of the following statement is true in case of debentures?
   (a) They can be issued on credit
   (b) They can be issued for consideration other than cash
   (c) They can not be issued as collateral security
   (d) They can be issued partly on credit and partly in cash
10. W' Limited purchased the assets from 'V' Limited for Rs. 5,40,000. 'W' Limited issued 10% debentures of Rs. 100 each at 20% premium against the payment. The number of debentures received by 'V ' Limited will be:
   (a) Rs. 4,500 (b) Rs. 4,400
   (c) Rs. 40,000 (d) Rs. 7,000

11. On issue of debentures as a collateral security, which account is credited?

(a) Debentures Account

(b) Bank Loan Account

(c) Debenture Holdings Account

(d) Debenture Suspense Account

12. Atul Ltd. decides to redeem 1000, 10% Debentures of Rs. 100 each redeemable at 10% premium. The company will have to invest in specified securities at least:

(a) Rs. 25,000

(b) Rs. 30,000

(c) Rs. 10,000

(d) Rs. 15,000

13. When debentures are issued at par and redeemable at premium the loss on such an issue is debited to :

(a) Loss on debenture account (b) Loan account

(c) Discount on issue of debenture (d) None of the above

14. XYZ Ltd. Issued 20,000 , 8 % debenture of Rs. 10 each at par. The debentures are redeemable at a premium of 20% after 5 years. The amount of loss on redemption of debentures should be:

(a) Rs. 40,000 (b) Rs. 30,000

(c) Rs. 20,000 (d) Rs. 35,000

15. **Assertion (A):** Debenture holders are the creditors of the company carrying a fixed rate of interest.

Reasoning (R): Debentures are short-term loan taken from the public.

Codes :

(a) Both Assertion (A) and Reason (R) are true. and Reason (R) is the correct explanation of Assertion (A).

(b) Both Assertion (A) and Reason (R) are true, but Reason (R) is not the correct explanation of Assertion (A).

(c) Assertion (A) is true, but Reason (R) is false.

(d) Assertion (A) is false, but Reason (R) is true.

16. What amount of the money received in application is transferred to the securities premium reserve account:

(a) Rs. 4,00,000 (b) Rs. 30,000

(c) Rs. 50,000 (d) Rs. 2,00,000

17. Earth Ltd. Issued 4,000, 12 % debentures of Rs. 100 each at a premium of 4% redeemable at a premium of 10%. Loss on issue will be debited by

(a) Rs. 40,000 (b) Rs. 26,000

(c) Rs. 30,000 (d) Rs. 15,000

18. 'V' Ltd. Issued 1,000 10 % debentures of Rs. 100 each at a premium of 5%. What will be the total amount of interest in one year.

(a) Rs. 10,000 (b) Rs. 5000

(c) Rs. 15,000 (d) Rs. 7000

19. ____________ debentures can be converted nto equity shares of issuing company after a predetermined period.

(a) Secured (b) Unsecured

(c) Convertible (d) Non-convertible

20. A company should transfer to Debenture Redemption Reserve A/c at least what percent of the amount of debentures issued before the commencement of redemption of debentures-

(a) 50% (b) 25%

(c) 15% (d) 100%

Topic Test – 1

1. X Limited Issued 10,000, 12% debentures of Rs. 100 each payable Rs. 40 on application and Rs. 60 on allotment. The public applied for 14,000 debentures. Applications for 9,000 debentures were accepted in full; applications for 2,000 debentures were allotted 1,000 debentures and the remaining applications, were rejected. All money was duly received. Journal entry for allotment will be :-

(a) 12% Debenture Application A/c Dr. 5,60,000
To 12% Debentures A/c 4,00,000
To Debentures Allotment A/c 40,000
To Bank A/c 1,20,000

(b) 12% debenture A/c Dr. 5,60,000
To 12% debenture Application A/c 4,00,000
To Debenture allotment A/c 40,000
To Bank A/c 1,20,000

(c) Bank A/c Dr. 1,20,000
Debenture Allotment A/c Dr. 40,000
12% Debentures A/c Dr. 4,00,000
To 12 % Debenture Application A/c 5,60,000

(d) None of the above

For questions 2 to 4: Analyse the case given below and answer the questions that follows:

Sam Technologies Ltd. issued 5,000; 9% Debentures of Rs. 100 each at a premium of Rs. 20 payable as follows:

(i) Rs. 40 including premium of Rs. 10 on application
(ii) Rs. 40 including premium of Rs. 10 on allotment
(iii) Balance as first and final call.

Applications were received for 5,000 debentures and allotment was made to all the applicants. All the calls were made, and amounts received.

2. The amount of money received during application is:-

(a) Rs. 2,00,000 (b) Rs. 3,00,000
(c) Rs. 5,00,000 (d) Rs. 20,000

3. The amount of money received in application is transferred to the security premium reserve account

(a) Rs. 5,00,000 (b) Rs. 2,00,000
(c) Rs. 20,000 (d) Rs. 50,000

4. ___________ is the balance amount per debenture received at the first and final call.

(a) Rs. 20 (b) Rs. 10
(c) Rs. 40 (d) Rs. 30

5. 6,000 debentures of Rs. 10 each where discharged by issuing equity shares of Rs. 10 each at 20% premium. The number of shares issued will be :

(a) 50,000 (b) 60,000
(c) 5,000 (d) 6,000

6. 'Volvo' Ltd. issue 10,00,000, 7 % debentures of 100 Rs. each at a discount of 4%, redeemable after 5 years at a premium of 6%. Loss issue of debentures is :

(a) Rs. 10,00,000
(b) Rs. 16,00,000
(c) Rs. 6,00,000
(d) Rs. 14,00,000

7. If debentures of Rs. 4,50,000 are issued for the consideration of net assets of Rs. 5,00,000 balance Rs. 50,000 will be credited to:
   (a) Profit & Loss A/c
   (b) Goodwill A/c
   (c) General Reserve A/c
   (d) Capital Reserve A/c
8. ABC Ltd. Took over the assets of Rs. 7,60,0C0 and liabilities of Rs. 80,000 of Asha ltd. For a purchase consideration of Rs. 5,85,000 payable by the issue of 12% debentures of Rs. 100 each at a discount of 10%. The number of debentures issued is:
   (a) 6,600 (b) 7,500
   (c) 5,500 (d) 6,500
9. Sources of finance of the redemption of debentures are:
   (a) Redemption out of profits
   (b) Redemption out of capital
   (c) The proceeds from fresh issue of shares/debentures
   (d) All the above
10. If redemption of debentures is made by conversion method, the amount to be transferred to 'Debenture Redemption Reserve Account' will be equal to _____ percent of converted amounted.
   (a) 30 (b) 40
   (c) 60 (d) Not required

Topic Test – 2

1. When debentures are issued at par and are redeemable at a premium, the loss on such an issue is debited to:
   (a) Profit & Loss A/c
   (b) Debenture Application and Allotment A/c
   (c) Loss on Issue of Debentures A/c
   (d) Premium on Redemption A/c
2. CL Ltd. want to redeem its 900, 10% debentures at 105% by converting them into shares of Rs. 10 each at Rs. 9 each. The number of shares to be issued will be :
   (a) 10,000 Shares (b) 10,500 Shares
   (c) 11,000 Shares (d) 9,500 Shares
3. **Assertion (A):** Issue of debenture does not result in dilution of interest of equity shareholders.
   Reasoning (R): Debenture holders have voting rights.
   Codes:
   (a) Both Assertion (A) and Reason (R) are true and Reason (R) is the correct explanation of Assertion (A).
   (b) Both Assertion (A) and Reason (R) are true, but Reason (R) is not the correct explanation of Assertion (A).
   (c) Assertion (A) is true, but Reason (R) is false.
   (d) Assertion (A) is false, but Reason (R) is true.
4. When the company issues debentures to the lenders as an additional/secondary security, in addition to other assets already pledged/some primary security. What does such issue of debentures is called?
   (a) Issue of debentures as collateral security
   (b) Issue of Debentures for Cash
   (c) Debentures issued at Premium
   (d) Issue of Debentures for Consideration other than Cash

5. Banarsi Ltd. purchased machinery for a book value of Rs. 4,00,000. The consideration was paid by issue of 10% Debentures of Rs. 100 each at a discount of 20%. The Debenture Account will be credited by :

(a) Rs. 3,00,000
(b) Rs. 6,00,000
(c) Rs. 4,20,000
(d) Rs. 5,00,000

6. If debentures of Rs. 4,50,000 are issued for the consideration of net assets of Rs. 5,00,000 balance Rs. 50,000 will be credited to:

(a) Profit & Loss A/c
(b) Goodwill A/c
(c) General Reserve A/c
(d) Capital Reserve A/c

7. Which of the following statements is false?

(a) Debenture is a form of public borrowing.
(b) It is customary to prefix debentures with the agreed rate of interest.
(c) Debenture interest is a charge against profits.
(d) The issue price and redemption value of debentures cannot differ.

8. When debentures of Rs. 1,00,000 are issued as Collateral Security against a loan of Rs. 1,50,000, the entry for issue of debentures will be :

(a) Credit Debentures Rs. 1,50,000 and debit bank A/c Rs. 1,50,000
(b) Debit Debenture Suspense A/c Rs. 1,00,000 and Credit Bank A/c Rs. 1,00,000.
(c) Debit Debenture Suspense A/c Rs. 1,00,000 and Credit Debentures A/c Rs. 1,00,000.
(d) Debit Cash A/c Rs. 1,50,000 and Credit Bank A/c Rs. 1,50,000.

9. A Ltd. acquired assets of Rs. 20,00,000 and took over creditors of Rs. 20,000 from B Ltd. A Ltd. issued 8% debentures of Rs. 200 each at a discount of 10% as purchase consideration. Number of debentures issued will be :

(a) 10,000
(b) 11,000
(c) 11,500
(d) 10,500

10. Lions Ltd purchased a building for Rs. 5,00,000 payable as 15% in cash and balance by allotment of 9% debentures of Rs. 100 each at a premium of 25%. Number of debentures issued will be :

(a) 5,250
(b) 2,000
(c) 3,400
(d) 4,400

Answer Keys

Exercise

1. (a)	2. (b)	3. (c)	4. (d)	5. (c)	6. (c)	7. (d)	8. (b)	9. (b)	10. (a)
11. (a)	12. (d)	13. (a)	14. (a)	15. (a)	16. (b)	17. (a)	18. (a)	19. (c)	20. (b)

Topic Test – 1

1. (a)	2. (a)	3. (d)	4. (c)	5. (c)	6. (a)	7. (d)	8. (d)	9. (d)	10. (d)

Topic Test – 2

1. (c)	2. (b)	3. (c)	4. (a)	5. (d)	6. (d)	7. (d)	8. (c)	9. (b)	10. (c)

Solutions

Exercise

1. (a)
2. (b)
3. (c)
4. (d)
5. (c)
6. (c)
7. (d)
8. (b)
9. (b)
10. (a)
11. (a)
12. (d)
13. (a)
14. (a)
15. (a) If a company needs funds for extension and cevelopment purpose without increasing its share capital, it can borrow from the general public by issuing certificates called debentures for a fixed period of time and at a fixed rate of interest. Debenture is a long-term debt instruments.
16. (b) 5000 × 10 = 50,000
17. (a)
18. (a)
19. (c)
20. (b)

Topic Test – 1

1. (a)
2. (a) (5000 × 40)
3. (d) (5000 × 10)
4. (c)
5. (c)
6. (a)
7. (d)
8. (d)
9. (d)
10. (d)

Topic Test – 2

1. (c)
2. (b)
3. (c) Issue of debenture does not result in dilution of interest of equity shareholders as they do not have right either to vote or to take part in the management of the company.
4. (a)
5. (d)
6. (d)
7. (d)
8. (c)
9. (b)
10. (c)

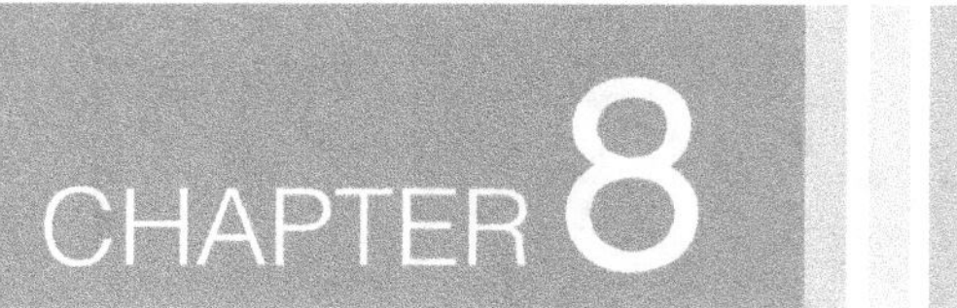

Financial Statements of A Company

Meaning of Financial Statements

Financial statements are the basic and formal annual reports through which the corporate management communicates financial information to its owners and various other external parties which include investors, tax authorities, government, employees, etc.

OR

The statements which are prepared to ascertain the profit earned or loss suffered and position of assets and liabilities at a particular date are known as financial statements. These are the final product of accounting process.

Nature of Financial Statement:

1. Recorded Facts
2. Accounting Conventions
3. Postulates

Objective of Financial Statement

(i) Financial statements provide the information about the earning capacity of the business.

(ii) Financial statements provide the information about the economic resources and obligation of an enterprise.

(iii) Financial statements also provide the information about the cash flows.

(iv) Financial statements supply the information useful for judging the management's ability to utilise the resources of business effectively.

(v) Financial statements have to report the activities of the business organisation affecting the society, which is important in its social environment.

Users of Financial Statements

(i) Owners including shareholders and investors

(ii) Debenture holders and financial institutions (bankers)

(iii) Creditors

(iv) Management

(v) Employees

(vi) Government, tax authorities and regulators

Limitations of financial Statements:

1. Qualitative elements are ignored
2. Historical records
3. Price level changes are ignored
4. Aggregate information
5. Different accounting practices
6. Historical records

Types of Financial Statements

The financial statements generally include two statements:

i. balance sheet and
ii. statement of profit and loss

Balance Sheet

It may be defined as a statement of assets and liabilities of the company, at a particular date. It must exhibit a true and fair view of the financial position at the close of the year. It is prepared and presented in the form prescribed in Schedule III Part I of the Companies Act, 2013, and is broadly divided into two parts, (i) Equity and liabilities (ii) Assets.

FORMAT OF BALANCE SHEET (AS PER SCHEDULE VI)

Balance Sheet as at 31 st March, 20.....

Particulars	Note No.	Figure as at the end of Current reporting period	Figure as at the end of Previous reporting period
I. Equity and Liabilities			
1) Shareholder's Funds			
(a) Share Capital			
(b) Reserves and Surplus			
(c) Money received against share warrnats			
2) Share Application money pending allotment			
3) Non-current Liabilities			
(a) Long term borrowings			
(b) Deferred tax liabilities (net)			
(c) Other long term liabilities			
(d) Long term provisions			
4) Current Liabilities			
(a) Short-term borrowings			
(b) Trade payables			
(c) Other current liabilities			
(d) Short-term provisions			
Total			

II. Assets			
1) Non-Current Assets			
(a) Fixed assets			
(i) Tangible assets			
(ii) Intangible assets			
(iii) Capital work-in-progress			
(iv) Intangible assets under development			
(b) Non-Current investments			
(c) Deferred tax assets (net)			
(d) Long-term loans and advances			
(e) Other non-current assets			
2) Current Assets			
(a) Current investments			
(b) Inventories			
(c) Trade receivable			
(d) Cash and cash equivalents			
(e) Short term loans and advances			
(f) Other current assets			
Total			

1. **Shareholders Fund:** The shareholders' funds are sub-classified on the face of the balance sheet.
   a) Share Capital
   b) Reserves and Surplus
   c) Money received against Share Warrants
2. **Share Capital:** Disclosures relating to share capital are to be given in notes to accounts
3. **Reserve and Surplus:** They can be classified as :-
   i) Capital Reserve
   ii) Capital Redemption Reserve
   iii) Securities Premium Reserve
   iv) Debenture Redemption Reserve
   v) Revaluation Reserve
   vi) Share Options Outstanding Account
   vii) Other Reserves (Specifying nature and purpose)
   viii) Surplus: Balance in statement of profit and loss; disclosing allocations and Appropriation such as dividend, bonus shares, transfer to/from reserve, etc.
4. **Money Received against share warrants:** It is the amount received by the company which are converted into shares at a specified date on a specified rate The instrument issued against the amount so received as share warrants. Money received against share warrants' to be disclosed as a separate line item under 'shareholder's fund'.
5. **Share application money pending allotment:** Share application money not exceeding the issued capital and to the extent non-refundable shall be classified as non-current. It will be shown on this face of balance sheet as share application money pending allotment.
6. **Borrowings :** Total borrowings are categorised into long-term borrowings, short-term borrowings and current maturities to long-term debt.

7. Deferred tax assets/liabilities are always non – current.
8. Trade payables Sundry creditors have been replaced with the term Trade payables and are classified as current and non-current. Trade payables to be settled beyond 12 months from the date of balance sheet or beyond the operating cycle are classified under "other long-term liabilities" with Note to Account.
9. **Proposed Dividend:** Board of Directors propose the dividend after the annual accounts for the year have been prepared. Annual General Meeting of the shareholders is held thereafter meaning it is held in the next financial year.
10. **Provisions:** The amount of provision settled within 12 months from balance sheet date or within operating cycle period from date of its recognition is classified as short term provisions and shown under current liabilities on the face of balance sheet.
11. **Fixed assets:** There is no change in the treatment of fixed assets. Both tangible and intangible assets are non-current
12. **Investments:** are also classified into current and non-current categories. Investments expected to realise within twelve months are considered as current investments under current assets
13. **Inventories:** are always treated as current
14. Trade receivables Trade receivables realised beyond twelve months from reporting date/ operating cycle starting from the date of their recognition are classified as "Other non-current assets" under the head non-current assets with Note to Accounts.
15. Cash and cash equivalent It is always current however, amounts which qualify as cash and cash equivalents as per AS-3 is shown here. The supremacy is accorded to AS over Schedule III, cash and cash equivalents are to the disclosed in accordance to the prescribed standard.

Profit and Loss Statement:

The title of 'profit and loss account' is charged to statement of profit and loss. If shows the net result of business operations. Its form is prescribed in Schedule III, Part II of the Companies Act, 2013.

FORMAT OF P/L STATEMENT

	Particulars	**Note No.**	**Figure as at the end of Current reporting period**	**Figure as at the end of Previous reporting period**
I	Revenue from operations			
II	Other income			
III	Total Revenue (I + II)			
IV	Expenses:			
	Cost of materials consumed			
	Purchases of stock-in-trade			
	Changes in inventories of finished goods			
	Work-in-progress and stock-in-trade			
	Employees benefits expense			
	Finance costs			
	Depreciation and amortisation expense			
	Finance costs			
	Depreciation and amortisation expense			
	Other expenses			
	Total expenses			
V	Profit before extraordinary items and tax (III-IV)			
VI	Exceptional itms			
VII	Profit before extraordinary items and tax (V-VI)			
VIII	Extraordinary items			
IX	Profit before tax (VII-VIII)			

X	Tax expense: (1) Current tax (2) Deferred tax			
XI	Profit/(Loss) for the period from continuing operations (IX-X)			
XII	Profit/(Loss) from discontinuing operations			
XIII	Tax expense of discontinuing operations			
XIV	Profit/(Loss) from discontinuing operations (after tax) (XII-XIII)			
XV	Profit/(Loss) for the period (XI + XIV)			
XVI	Earnings per equity share: (1) Basic (2) Diluted			

Exercise

1. Financial statements are summarised statements of accounting data that provide information of the business about
   (a) Current Assets and Quick Assets (b) Debt and Equity
   (c) Profitability and Financial Position (d) Operating and Non-operating Income
2. From the given items which is a part of current liabilities:
   (a) Inventories (b) Trade Payables
   (c) Cash and Cash Equivalents (d) Trade Receivables
3. Which of the following is not a subhead of Current Liabilities?
   (a) Short Term Provisions (b) Trade Payables
   (c) Deferred Tax Liabilities (d) Other Current Liabilities
4. Equity Rs. 90,000 Liabilities Rs. 60,000 Profit of the year Rs. 20,000. Then total assets will be :
   (a) Rs. 1,50,000 (b) Rs. 1,40,000
   (c) Rs. 1,70,000 (d) Rs. 50,000
5. The profit and loss disclosed by the accounts of a company is:
   (a) Transferred to share capital account
   (b) Shown under the head of 'Current liabilities' and provisions
   (c) Shown under the head 'Reserves and Surplus
   (d) None of these
6. Which of the following assets is not shown under the head 'Fixed Asset' in the Balance Sheet?
   (a) Goodwill (b) Bills Receivable
   (c) Buildings (d) Vehicle
7. Interest on loans given by a financial company is shown in the statement of profit and loss as :-
   (a) Other incomes (b) Expenses
   (c) Revenue from operations (d) All of the above
8. Dividend is paid on ____________
   (a) Authorised capital (b) Subscribed capital that is paid up
   (c) Capital not paid up (d) Issued capital

9. Capital reserve will be shown under ____________
   (a) Reserves and surplus
   (b) Current liabilities
   (c) Capital
   (d) Operations
10. Income statement is termed as:
   (a) Profit and loss
   (b) Balance sheet
   (c) Statement of profit and loss
   (d) Current asset
11. **Assertion (A):** Inventories may be shown as Non-current assets.
   Reasoning (R): Inventories are shown as current assets because they are held to be realized at the earliest.
   Codes :
   (a) Both Assertion (A) and Reason (R) are true and Reason (R) is the correct explanation of Assertion (A).
   (b) Both Assertion (A) and Reason (R) are true and Reason (R) is not the correct explanation of Assertion (A)
   (c) Assertion (A) is true but Reason (R) is False
   (d) Assertion (A) is false but Reason (R) is true.
12. Patents and copyrights fall under the category of :-
   (a) Intangible asset
   (b) Current assets
   (c) Current liabilities
   (d) Liquid assets
13. Current maturities of long-term debt are shown under:
   (a) Long term Provisions
   (b) Long term Borrowings
   (c) Short term Borrowings
   (d) Other Current liabilities
14. Indicate the item which appears as short-term provisions:
   (a) Provision for doubtful debts
   (b) Provision for gratuity
   (c) Employee's Provident fund
   (d) Securities premium reserve
15. Which of the following are the sub headings of Current Liabilities?
   i. Short term borrowings
   ii. Trade payables
   iii. Short term provisions
   iv. Short term Investment
   v. Other current liabilities
   vi. Short term loans and advances
   Select the correct code:
   (a) i, ii, iii, v
   (b) i, iv, v, vi
   (c) iii, iv, v, vi
   (d) ii, iv, v, vi
16. Match the following:
   1. Short term loan — (i) Other current liabilities
   2. Short term loans and advances — (ii) Short term borrowing
   3. Debentures — (iii) Long term borrowings
   4. Debentures redeemable during current year — (iv) Current investments
   Select the correct code:
   (a) 1 – iii, 2 – ii, 3 – iv, 4 – i
   (b) 1 – iii, 2 – iv, 3 – ii, 4 - i
   (c) 1 – ii, 2 – iv, 3 – iii, 4 – i
   (d) 1 – i, 2 – ii, 3 – iii, 4 – iv
17. Debit Balance of Profit & Loss Statement will be shown on:
   (a) Assets Side of Balance Sheet
   (b) Liabilities Side of Balance Sheet
   (c) Under the head Reserve & Surplus
   (d) Under the head Reserves and Surplus as a negative item

18. Bills Receivables appear in a Company's Balance Sheet under the Sub-head ____________.
(a) Current Investments
(b) Cash Equivalents
(c) Trade Receivables
(d) Short term Loans and Advances

19. Interest accrued but not due on loans appear in a Company's Balance Sheet under the Sub-head ____________.
(a) Short-term Borrowings
(b) Trade Payables
(c) Other Current Liabilities
(d) Short-term Provisions

20. Which of the following items is shown under the head 'Current Liabilities' while preparing the Balance Sheet of a company?
(a) Securities Premium Reserve
(b) Debentures
(c) Livestock
(d) None of the above

Topic Test – 1

1. Objectives of analysis and interpretation of financial statement are
(a) Prospect
(b) Position
(c) Progress
(d) All of the above

2. Gross profit is equal to ______________-
(a) Sale – expenses
(b) Sale – cost of sale
(c) Sale – profit
(d) None of the above

3. Bills receivable and debtors are
(a) Fixed assets
(b) Current assets
(c) Capital
(d) Tangible assets

4. Security premium is shown under ___________ major head
(a) Current assets
(b) Current labilities
(c) Shareholder funds
(d) All of these

5. **Assertion (A):** Surplus, i.e., Balance in Statement of Profit and Loss can be positive or negative and in both cases, it is shown in Note to Accounts on Reserves and Surplus.

Reasoning (R): Schedule III of the Companies Act, 2013 prescribes that whether the balance in Surplus, i.e., Balance in Statement of Profit and Loss is positive (Undistributed or Accumulated Profits) or negative (Accumulated Losses), it is to be shown under Reserves and Surplus.

Codes:
(a) Both Assertion (A) and Reason (R) are true and Reason (R) is the correct explanation of Assertion (A).
(b) Both Assertion (A) and Reason (R) are true and Reason (R) is not the correct explanation of Assertion (A)
(c) Assertion (A) is true but Reason (R) is False
(d) Assertion (A) is False but Reason (R) is True.

6. ___________ is a current liability
(a) Debtors
(b) Drawings
(c) Insurance
(d) Short term loans

7. The assets of a business can be classified as :
(a) Fixed and Non-fixed Assets
(b) Tangible and Intangible Assets
(c) Non-Current and Current Asset
(d) None of these

8. Financial statements disclose :
   (a) Monetary information
   (b) Qualitative information
   (c) Non-monetary information
   (d) All the above
9. The format of the financial statement of a company is prescribed in:
   (a) Section 129, Schedule III
   (b) Section 121, Schedule III
   (c) Section 130, Schedule III
   (d) Section 129, Schedule I
10. Financial statements are summarised statements of accounting data that provide information of the business about
    (a) Current Assets and Quick Assets
    (b) Debt and Equity
    (c) Profitability and Financial Position
    (d) Operating and Non-operating Income

Topic Test – 2

1. Under which of the following headings/subheadings, calls in Advance will be presented in the Balance Sheet of a company as per Schedule III part I of the Companies Act, 2013?
   (a) Current Liabilities
   (b) Share Capital
   (c) Share Application Money Pending Allotment
   (d) Reserves and Surplus
2. Which of the following is not shown as Non-Current Liabilities?
   (a) Trade Payables
   (b) Long term Borrowings
   (c) Deferred Tax Liabilities
   (d) Long term Provisions
3. Share capital is shown in Balance Sheet under. the head ?
   (a) Authorised Capital
   (b) Issued Capital
   (c) Paid-up Capital
   (d) Shareholders' Funds
4. Purchase of goods for reselling is shown in the statement of profit and loss under:-
   (a) Change in inventories
   (b) Purchase of stock in trade
   (c) Cost of materials consumed
   (d) None of these
5. Bills receivable and debtors are
   (a) Fixed assets
   (b) Long term assets
   (c) Current assets
   (d) Intangible assets
6. The unclaimed dividend appears in a company's balance sheet under the subhead
   (a) Short term Borrowings
   (b) Trade Payables
   (c) Other current liabilities
   (d) Short term provisions
7. **Assertion (A):** The Balance Sheet is a list of assets and liabilities of the company presented in the specified format for the year ended on that date.

   Reasoning (R): The Balance Sheet is a statement of assets and liabilities of the company as of that day.

   Codes:
   (a) Both Assertion (A) and Reason (R) are true and Reason (R) is the correct explanation of Assertion (A).
   (b) Both Assertion (A) and Reason (R) are true and Reason (R) is not the correct explanation of Assertion (A)
   (c) Assertion (A) is true but Reason (R) is False
   (d) Assertion (A) is False but Reason (R) is True.
8. The profit and loss statement is also known as
   (a) Income statement
   (b) Statement of earning
   (c) Statement of operation
   (d) All of these

9. Prepaid Expenses appear in a Company's Balance Sheet under the Sub-head ___________.

(a) Other Current Assets (b) Short-term Loans & Advances

(c) Intangible Assets (d) Other Non-Current Assets

10. Which one of the following items is shown under the heading 'current liabilities' in the Balance Sheet of a company?

(a) Investments (b) Reserve Fund

(c) Unclaimed Dividend (d) Livestock

Answer Keys

Exercise

1. (c)	2. (b)	3. (c)	4. (c)	5. (c)	6. (b)	7. (c)	8. (b)	9. (a)	10. (c)
11. (d)	12. (a)	13. (b)	14. (a)	15. (a)	16. (c)	17. (d)	18. (c)	19. (c)	20. (d)

Topic Test – 1

1. (d)	2. (b)	3. (b)	4. (c)	5. (a)	6. (d)	7. (c)	8. (a)	9. (a)	10. (c)

Topic Test – 2

1. (a)	2. (a)	3. (d)	4. (c)	5. (c)	6. (c)	7. (d)	8. (d)	9. (a)	10. (c)

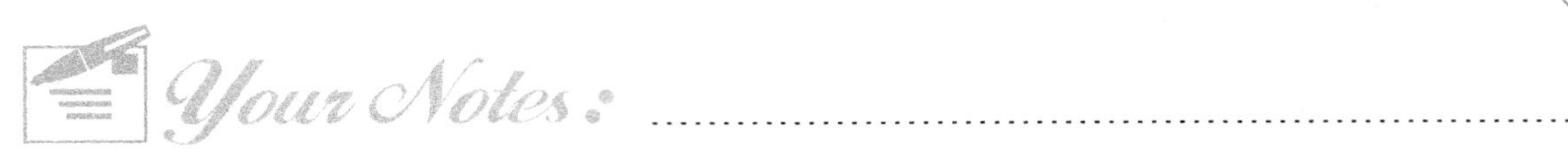
Your Notes :

CHAPTER 9

Analysis of Financial Statements

Meaning of Analysis of Financial Statements: It is the systematic numerical representation of the relationship of one financial fact with the other to measure the profitability, operational efficiency, solvency and the growth potential of the business. The term 'financial analysis' includes both 'analysis and interpretation'.

Significance of Analysis of Financial Statements: Financial analysis is the process of identifying the financial strengths and weaknesses of the firm by properly establishing relationships between the various items of the balance sheet and the statement of profit and loss.

Financial analysis is useful and significant to different users in the following ways:

1. Finance manager
2. Top management
3. Trade payables
4. Lenders
5. Investors
6. Labour unions

Objectives of Analysis of Financial Statements:

(i) Judging the operational efficiency of the business.
(ii) Measuring the profitability.
(iii) Measuring short-term and long-term financial position.
(iv) Indicating the trend of achievements.
(v) Assessing the growth potential of the business.
(vi) Inter-firm comparison

Limitations of Financial Analysis:

1. Financial analysis does not consider price level changes.
2. Financial analysis may be misleading without the knowledge of the changes in accounting procedure followed by a firm.
3. Financial analysis is just a study of reports of the company.
4. Monetary information alone is considered in financial analysis while non-monetary aspects are ignored.
5. The financial statements are prepared on the basis of accounting concept, as such, it does not reflect the current position

Tools of Analysis of Financial Statements:

1. Comparative Financial Statements:- Are used to compare the items of income statement i.e. profit and loss account and position statement i.e. balance sheet for ascertaining the trend of the performance and profitability of an enterprise are known as comparative financial statements. It usually applies to the two important financial statements, namely, balance sheet and statement of profit and loss prepared in a comparative form.

The following steps may be followed to prepare the comparative statements:

Step 1: List out absolute figures in rupees relating to two points of time

Step 2: Find out change in absolute figures by subtracting the first year (Col.2) from the second year (Col.3) and indicate the change as increase (+) or decrease (–) and put it in column 4.

Step 3: Preferably, also calculate the percentage change as follows and put it in column 5.
Absolute increase or Decrease (Col.4) / first year absolute figure (col 2) × 100

FORMAT OF COMAPRITIVE BALANCE SHEET

Comparative Balance Sheet

as at...

Particulars	**Previous Year (Rs.)**	**Current Year (Rs.)**	**Absolute Change (Increase or Decrease) (Rs.)**	**Percentage Change (Increase or Decreae) (%)**
I. Equity and Liabilities				
1. **Shareholders' Funds**				
(a) Share Capital				
(i) Equity Share Capital	...	...	...	...
(ii) Preference Share Capital	...	...	...	...
(b) Reserves and Surplus	...	...	...	...
2. **Non-current Liabilities**				
(a) Long-term Borrowings	...	...	...	...
(b) Long-term Provisions	...	...	...	...
3. **Current Liabilities**				
(a) Short-term Borrowings	...	...	...	...
(b) Trade-Payables	...	...	...	...
(c) Other Current Liabilities	...	...	...	...
(d) Short-term Provisions	...	...	...	...
Total	...	...	...	...
II. Assets				
1. **Non-current Assets**				
(a) Fixed Assets				
(i) Tangible Assets	...	...	...	...
(ii) Intangible Assets	...	...	...	...
(b) Non-current Investments	...	...	...	...
(c) Long-term Loans and Advances	...	...	...	...
2. **Current Assets**				
(a) Current Investments	...	...	...	...
(b) Inventories	...	...	...	...
(c) Trade Receivables	...	...	...	...
(d) Cash and Cash Equivalents	...	...	...	...
(e) Short-term Loans and Advances	...	...	...	...
(f) Other Current Assets	...	...	...	...
Total	...	...	...	...

2. **Common Size Statements:** These are the statements which indicate the relationship of different items of a financial statement with a common item by expressing each item as a percentage of that common item. Common size statements are useful, both, in intra-firm comparisons over different years and also in making inter-firm comparisons for the same year or for several years. This analysis is also known as 'Vertical analysis.

The following procedure may be adopted for preparing the common size statements.

1. List out absolute figures in rupees at two points of time, say year 1, and year 2 (Column 2 & 4).
2. Choose a common base (as 100)
3. For all items of Col. 2 and 3 work out the percentage of that total. Column 4 and 5 shows these percentage

COMMON SIZE BALANCE SHEET

as at...

Particulars	Absolute Amounts		Percentage of Balance Sheet Total	
	Previous Year (Rs.)	Current Year (Rs.)	Previous Year (%)	Current Year (%)
(1)	(2)	(3)	(4)	(5)
I. Equity and Liabilities				
1. **Shareholders' Funds**				
(a) Share Capital	...	...	...	...
(i) Equity Share Capital	...	...	...	...
(ii) Preference Share Capital	...	...	...	...
(b) Reserves and Surplus	...	...	...	...
2. **Non-current Liabilities**				
(a) Long-term Borrowings	...	...	...	...
(b) Long-term Provisions	...	...	...	...
3. **Current Liabilities**				
(a) Short-term Borrowings	...	...	...	...
(b) Trade-Payables	...	...	...	...
(c) Other Current Liabilities	...	...	...	...
(d) Short-term Provisions	...	...	...	...
Total	...	...	100	100
II. Assets				
1. **Non-current Assets**				
(a) Fixed Assets				
(i) Tangible Assets	...	...	...	...
(ii) Intangible Assets	...	...	...	...
(b) Non-current Investments	...	...	...	...
(c) Long-term Loans and Advances	...	...	...	...
2. **Current Assets**				
(a) Current Investments	...	...	...	...
(b) Inventories	...	...	...	...
(c) Trade Receivables	...	...	...	...
(d) Cash and Cash Equivalents	...	...	...	...
(e) Short-term Loans and Advances	...	...	...	...
(f) Other Current Assets	...	...	...	...
Total	...	...	100	100

3. Ratio Analysis The mathematical expression that shows the relationships between various groups of items contained in the financial statements is known as ratio analysis.
4. Cash Flow Statement It shows the inflows and outflows of cash and cash equivalents of an enterprise by classifying cash flows into operating, investing and financing activities during a particular period and analysing the reasons for changes in balance of cash between the two balance sheets dates.

Exercise

1. Which of the following are the tools of Vertical Analysis?

(i) Ratio Analysis.

(ii) Comparative Statements.

(iii) Common Size Statements.

Codes:

(a) Only (iii) (b) Both (i) and (iii)

(c) Both (i) and (ii) (d) Only (i)

2. Which of the following statements are false?

A. When all the comparative figures in a balance sheet are stated as percentage of the total, it is termed as horizontal analysis.

B. When financial statements of several years are analysed, it is termed as vertical analysis.

C. Vertical Analysis is also termed as time series analysis.

Choose from the following options:

(a) Both A and B (b) Both A and C

(c) Both B and C (d) All three A, B, C

3. Feature of financial analysis is to present the data combined in financial statement in

(a) Comparable form (b) Convenient groups

(c) Easy form (d) All of the above

4. Who among the following is not an external user of the financial statement analysis?

(a) Shareholders (b) Debenture holders

(c) Creditors (d) Management

5. Horizontal Analysis is also known as :

(a) Dynamic Analysis (b) Structural Analysis

(c) Static Analysis (d) None of these

6. Match the items given in Column I with the headings/subheadings (Balance sheet) as defined in Schedule III of Companies Act 2013.

Column I	Column II
(I) Loose Tools	(a) Intangible fixed assets
(II) Patents	(b) Other current assets
(III) Prepaid insurance	(c) Long term Borrowings
(IV) Debentures	(d) Inventories
(V) Machinery	(e) Tangible Fixed assets

Choose the correct option:

(a) (I)-(a), (II)-(b), (III)- (d), (IV)- (c), (V)-(e) (b) (I)-(d), (II)-(a), (III)-(b), (IV)-(c), (V)-(e)

(c) (I)-(d), (II)-(a), (III)-(b), (IV)-(e), (V)-(c) (d) (I)-(e), (II)-(d), (III)-(a), (IV)-(b), (V)-(b)

7. Trend ratios and trend percentage are used in :
   (a) Dynamic analysis (b) Static analysis
   (c) Horizontal analysis (d) Vertical Analysis
8. Company's current liabilities decreased from Rs. 4, 00,000 to Rs. 3, 00,000. What is the percentage change
   (a) 35 % (b) 25%
   (c) 50 % (d) 33.3 %
9. _________ is /are the limitation of financial statement:
   (a) Do not reflect changes in price level (b) Difficulty in forecasting
   (c) Just a study of reports of the company (d) All of the above
10. Revenue from operations Rs. 4, 00,000; cost of Revenue from operations 60% of Revenue from operations; operating expenses Rs. 30,000 and rate of income is 40%.what will be the amount of profit after tax.
   (a) Rs. 45,000 (b) Rs. 78,000
   (c) Rs. 68,000 (d) Rs. 75,000
11. Importance of Comparative Statement is
   (a) Indicate the trend with respect to the previous year
   (b) Make the data simple and more understandable
   (c) All of the options
   (d) compare the firm performance with the performance of other firm in the same business
12. A technique uses in comparative analysis of financial statement is
   (a) Graphical analysis (b) Common size analysis
   (c) Preference analysis (d) Returning analysis
13. Fixed Assets of a company increased from Rs. 3,00,000 to Rs. 4,00,000. What the percentage of change?
   (a) 25% (b) 33.3%
   (c) 20% (d) 40%
14. Which of the following is not a form of presenting financial analysis :
   (a) Absolute figure Comparison (b) Ratio Method
   (c) Cumulative figures and averages (d) Annual Report
15. For calculating trend percentages any year is selected as:
   (a) Current year (b) Previous year
   (c) Base year (d) None of these
16. Comparative financial analysis process shows the comparison between the items of which statement:
   (a) Balance Sheet (b) Profit & Loss Statement
   (c) Both (a) and (b) (d) None of these
17. Financial analysis is significant because it:
   (a) Ignores qualitative aspect
   (b) Judges operational efficiency
   (c) Suffers from the limitations of financial statements
   (d) It is affected by personal ability and bias of the analysis
18. For whom the analysis of financial statements is not significant?
   (a) Investor (b) Government
   (c) Ambassador of India (d) Company's Employee
19. A company's net sales are Rs. 15,00,000; cost of sales is Rs. 10,00,000 and indirect expenses are Rs. 3,00,000, the amount gross profit will be:
   (a) Rs. 13,00,000 (b) Rs. 5,00,000
   (c) Rs. 2,00,000 (d) Rs. 12,00,000

20. Common-size financial statements are mostly prepared:
(a) In proportion
(b) In percentage
(c) Both (a) and (b)
(d) None of these

Topic Test – 1

1. Which of the following is not true about vertical analysis
(a) Is also known as static analysis
(b) Is based on the basis of single set of financial statement
(c) Is made on the basis of financial statement for several years
(d) All of the above

2. When Financial Statements of two or more organisations are analysed, it is called :
(a) Intra-firm Analysis
(b) Inter-firm Analysis
(c) Vertical Analysis
(d) None of these

3. **Assertion (A):** Financial statement Analysis is undertaken by investors, lenders, and creditors for assessing the safety of the amount invested in the company.

Reasoning (R): Investors, lenders, and creditors undertake the analysis of the financial statements because they have invested their money in the company and have either indirect control or no control over the affairs of the company.

Codes:
(a) Both Assertion (A) and Reason (R) are true and Reason (R) is the correct explanation of Assertion (A).
(b) Both Assertion (A) and Reason (R) are true and Reason (R) is not the correct explanation of Assertion (A)
(c) Assertion (A) is true but Reason (R) is False
(d) Assertion (A) is False but Reason (R) is True

4. A company's working capital is Rs. 10 lakh (Negative balance) in the year 2019. It became Rs. 15 lakh (Positive balance) in the year 2020. What is the percentage of change?
(a) 150%
(b) 100%
(c) 250%
(d) 50%

5. Revenue from Operations Rs. 8,00,000; Gross Profit Ratio 32%; Indirect Exp. 10% of Gross Profit and income tax 40%. What will be the amount of profit after tax?
(a) Rs. 1,38,240
(b) Rs. 1,02,400
(c) Rs. 92,160
(d) Rs. 1,53,600

6. No profit no loss' point is called ____________
(a) Fund Flow Point
(b) Cash Flow Point
(c) Trend Analysis
(d) Break Even Point

7. Which Of the following is limitation of financial analysis?
(a) Window-dressing
(b) Basis of Valuation
(c) Lack of Accuracy
(d) All the above

8. A company's Revenue from Operations are Rs. 20,00,000; Cost of Revenue from Operations is Rs. 14,00,000 and indirect expenses are Rs. 2,00,000. What is the amount of Gross Profit?
(a) Rs. 10,00,000
(b) Rs. 6,00,000
(c) Rs. 18,00,000
(d) Rs. 8,00,000

9. Feature of financial analysis is to present the data contained in financial statement in
(a) Easy form
(b) Convenient and rational groups
(c) Comparable form
(d) All of the above

10. Financial analysis becomes useless because it:
    (a) Measures the profitability
    (b) Measures the Solvency
    (c) Lacks Qualitative Analysis
    (d) Makes a Comparative Study

Topic Test – 2

1. Why is a creditor interested in the analysis of financial statements?
    (a) To decide whether or not the borrower has the ability to repay interest and principal on borrowed funds.
    (b) To determine the concern's capital structure.
    (c) To determine the concern's future earnings stream.
    (d) To decide whether or not the concern has operated profitably in the past.
2. **Assertion (A):** Comparative Statement is an analytical tool to compare individual items of the Balance Sheet and/or Statement of Profit and Loss of the company for two or more years.

    Reasoning (R): Comparative Statement is prepared to compare individual items of Balance Sheet and/or statement of Profit and Loss and thus, the difference is ascertained both in amount and percent.

    Codes :
    (a) Both Assertion (A) and Reason (R) are true and Reason (R) is the correct explanation of Assertion (A).
    (b) Both Assertion (A) and Reason (R) are true and Reason (R) is not the correct explanation of Assertion (A).
    (c) Assertion (A) is true but Reason (R) is False.
    (d) Assertion (A) is False but Reason (R) is True.
3. Which of the following is untrue:
    (a) Common size balance sheet
    (b) Common size cash flow statement
    (c) Common size statement of profit and loss
    (d) All of the above
4. Revenue from Operations Rs. 8,00,000; Gross Profit Ratio 32%; Indirect Exp. 10% of Gross Profit and income tax 40%. What will be the amount of profit after tax?
    (a) Rs. 1,38,240 (b) Rs. 1,00,400
    (c) Rs. 82,160 (d) Rs. 2,53,600
5. Which objective is not fulfilled by comparative Statement of Profit & Loss :
    (a) To compare the items of Statement of Profit & Loss of two years
    (b) To know the absolute changes in items of Statement of Profit & Loss
    (c) To show the change in financial position
    (d) To know the percentage changes in items of Statement of Profit & Loss
6. Common-size financial statements are mostly prepared:
    (a) In proportion (b) In percentage
    (c) Both (a) and (b) (d) None of these
7. If total assets of a firm are Rs 10,00,000 and its non-current assets are Rs. 6,00,000, what will be the percentage of current assets on total assets ?
    (a) 20% (b) 50%
    (c) 40% (d) 10%

8. **Assertion (A):** Common Size statement is a statement in which individual items of financial statements of two or more years are converted into a percent of a common base for comparison.

   Reasoning (R): Common size Balance Sheet is prepared to place each item thereof and to convert them into percent of Total of Liabilities part or Assets Part.

   Codes:

   (a) Both Assertion (A) and Reason (R) are true and Reason (R) is the correct explanation of Assertion (A).

   (b) Both Assertion (A) and Reason (R) are true and Reason (R) is not the correct explanation of Assertion (A)

   (c) Assertion (A) is true but Reason (R) is False.

   (d) Assertion (A) is False but Reason (R) is True.

9. Which of the following statements are false?

   A. When all the comparative figures in a balance sheet are stated as percentage of the total, it is termed as horizontal analysis.

   B. When financial statements of several years are analysed, it is termed as vertical analysis.

   C. Vertical Analysis is also termed as time series analysis.

   Choose from the following options:

   (a) Both A and B (b) Both A and C

   (c) Both B and C (d) All three A, B, C

10. Tangible assets of company increased from Rs. 4,00,000 to Rs. 5,00,000. What is the percentage of change ?

    (a) 10% (b) 25%

    (c) 35% (d) 40%

Answer Keys

Exercise

1. (b)	2. (d)	3. (d)	4. (d)	5. (a)	6. (b)	7. (c)	8. (b)	9. (d)	10. (b)
11. (c)	12. (b)	13. (b)	14. (d)	15. (c)	16. (c)	17. (b)	18. (c)	19. (c)	20. (b)

Topic Test – 1

1. (c)	2. (b)	3. (a)	4. (c)	5. (a)	6. (d)	7. (d)	8. (b)	9. (d)	10. (c)

Topic Test – 2

1. (a)	2. (a)	3. (b)	4. (a)	5. (c)	6. (b)	7. (c)	8. (b)	9. (d)	10. (b)

Solutions

Exercise

1. (b)
2. (d)
3. (d)
4. (d)
5. (a)
6. (b)
7. (c)
8. (b)

   3,00,000 – 4,00,000 = (–1,00,000)

   Change in % = 1, 00,000 / 4, 00,000 x 100 = 25%
9. (d)
10. (b)

    Revenue from operations = 4,00,000

    Cost of revenue = 4,00,000 × 60/100 = 2,40,000

    Operating expense = 30,000

    Profit = 4, 00,000 – 2, 40,000 – 30,000 = 1,30,000

    1,30,000 × 40/100 = 52,000

    Profit after tax = 1,30,000 – 52.000 = 78,000
11. (c)
12. (b)
13. (b)
14. (d)
15. (c)
16. (c)
17. (b)
18. (c)
19. (c)
20. (b)

Topic Test – 1

1. (c)
2. (b)
3. (a)
4. (c)
5. (a)
6. (d)
7. (d)
8. (b)
9. (d)
10. (c)

Topic Test – 2

1. (a)
2. (a)
3. (b)
4. (a)
5. (c)
6. (b)
7. (c)
8. (b)
9. (d)
10. (b)

CHAPTER 10

Accounting Ratios

Summary

Meaning Of Accouinting Ratios

Ratio It is an arithmetical expression of relationship between two related or interdependent items. Accounting Ratios It is a mathematical expression that shows the relationship between various items or groups of items shown in financial statements. When ratios are calculated on the basis of accounting information, they are called accounting ratios.

Objectives Of Ratio Analyis

(i) To know the areas of an enterprise which need more attention.

(ii) To know about the potential areas which can be improved on.

(iii) Helpful in comparative analysis of the performance.

(iv) Helpful in budgeting and forecasting.

(v) To provide analysis of the liquidity, solvency, activity and profitability of an enterprise.

(vi) To provide information useful for making estimates and preparing the plans for future.

Advantages Of Ratio Analysis

(i) It is useful in analysis of financial statements.

(ii) Helps in simplifying accounting figures.

(iii) Useful in judging the operating efficiency of business.

(iv) Helps in identification of problem areas.

(v) Helpful in comparative analysis.

Limitations of Ratio Analysis

(i) Accounting ratios ignore qualitative factors.

(ii) Absence of universally accepted terminology.

(iii) Ratios are affected by window-dressing.

(iv) Effects of inherent limitations of accounting.

(v) Misleading results in the absence of absolute data.

(vi) Price level changes ignored.

(vii) Affected by personal bias and ability of the analyst.

Types Of Ratios

1. **Liquidity Ratios:** To meet its commitments, business needs liquid funds. The ability of the business to pay the amount due to stakeholders as and when it is due is known as liquidity, and the ratios calculated to measure it are known as 'Liquidity Ratios'. These are essentially short-term in nature.

They can be classfied as:

i. **Current ratio:** Current ratio is the proportion of current assets to current liabilities. It is expressed as follows: Current Ratio = Current Assets : Current Liabilities or Current Assets / Current Liabilities.

ii. **Liquid ratio/Quick ratio/Acid test ratio:** This ratio establishes relationship between liquid assets and current liabilities and is used to measure the firm's ability to pay the claims of creditors immediately. This ratio is a better indicator of liquidity and 1 : 1 is considered to be ideal.

Liquid Ratio/Quick Ratio/Acid Test Ratio = Liquid Assets or Quick Assets/Current Liabilities

2. **Solvency Ratios:** Solvency of business is determined by its ability to meet its contractual obligations towards stakeholders, particularly towards external stakeholders, and the ratios calculated to measure solvency position are known as 'Solvency Ratios'. These are essentially long-term in nature.

They can be classified as:

i. **Debt-Equity Ratio:** Debt-Equity Ratio measures the relationship between long-term debt and equity

Debt-Equity Ratio = Long – term Debts / Shareholders' Funds

where:

Shareholders' Funds (Equity) = Share capital + Reserves and Surplus + Money received against share warrants + Share application money pending allotment

Share Capital = Equity share capital + Preference share capital

Working Capital = Current Assets - Current Liabilities

ii. **Debt to Capital Employed Ratio:** The Debt to capital employed ratio refers to the ratio of long-term debt to the total of external and internal funds (capital employed or net assets).

Debt to Capital Employed Ratio = Long-term Debt/Capital Employed (or Net Assets)

iii. **Proprietary Ratio:** Proprietary ratio expresses relationship of proprietor's (shareholders) funds to net assets.

Proprietary Ratio = Shareholders', Funds/Capital employed (or net assets)

iv. **Total Assets to Debt Ratio:** This ratio measures the extent of the coverage of long-term debts by assets.

Total assets to Debt Ratio = Total assets/Long-term debts

v. **Interest Coverage Ratio:** This ratio expresses the relationship between net profit before interest and tax and interest payable on long-term debts. The ideal coverage ratio is 6 to 7 times.

Interest Coverage Ratio = Net Profit before Interest and Tax/Interest on Long-term Debts

3. **Activity (or Turnover) Ratios:** This refers to the ratios that are calculated for measuring the efficiency of operations of business based on effective utilisation of resources. Hence, these are also known as 'Efficiency Ratios'.

They can be classified as:

i. **Stock turnover ratio or Inventory turnover ratio:** The ratio indicates the number of times the stock is turned in sales during the accounting period, i.e. it measures how fast the stock is moving through the firm and generating sales.

Inventory Turnover Ratio = Cost of Revenue from Operations / Average Inventory

ii. **Trade Receivables or Debtors turnover ratio:** It indicates economy and efficiency in the collection of amount due from debtors.

Trade Receivable Turnover ratio = Net Credit Revenue from Operations/Average Trade Receivable

iii. **Trade payables or Creditors turnover ratio:** It indicates the speed with which the amount is being paid to creditors. The higher the ratio, the better it is.

Creditors/Payables Turnover Ratio = Net Credit Purchases/Average Payable

Net Credit Purchases = Credit Purchases – Purchase Return

iv. **Net Assets or Capital Employed Turnover Ratio:** It reflects relationship between revenue from operations and net assets (capital employed) in the business. Higher turnover means better activity and profitability.

Net Assets or Capital Employed Turnover ratio = Revenue from Operation Capital Employed

4. **Profitability Ratios:** It refers to the analysis of profits in relation to revenue from operations or funds (or assets) employed in the business and the ratios calculated to meet this objective are known as 'Profitability Ratios'.

They can be classified as:

i. **Gross Profit Ratio Gross profit ratio:** As a percentage of revenue from operations is computed to have an idea about gross margin.

Gross Profit Ratio = Gross Profit/Net Revenue of Operations × 100

ii. **Operating Ratio:** It is computed to analyse cost of operation in relation to revenue from operations.

Operating Ratio = (Cost of Revenue from Operations + Operating Expenses)/ Net Revenue from Operations ×100

iii. **Operating Profit Ratio:** It is calculated to reveal operating margin. It may be computed directly or as a residual of operating ratio.

Operating Profit Ratio = 100 - Operating Ratio

iv. **Net Profit Ratio Net:** Profit ratio is based on all inclusive concept of profit.

Net Profit Ratio = Net profit/Revenue from Operations × 100

v. **Return on investment/Capital employed:** It establishes the relationship between net profit before interest, tax and preference dividend and capital employed (equity + debts).

Return on Investment (or Capital Employed) = Profit before Interest and Tax/ Capital Employed × 100

vi. Return on Shareholders' Funds:- It helps the shareholder's in assessing whether their investment in the firm generates a reasonable return or not.

Return on Shareholders' Fund = Profit after Tax Shareholders' Funds × 100

vii. Earnings per Share The ratio is computed as:

EPS = Profit available for equity shareholders/Number of Equity Shares

viii. Book Value per Share This ratio is calculated as :

Book Value per share = Equity shareholders' funds/Number of Equity Shares

ix. Dividend Payout Ratio This refers to the proportion of earning that are distributed to the shareholders.

Dividend Payout Ratio = Dividend per share / Earnings per share

Exercise

1. Current Ratio is :
   (a) Solvency Ratio (b) Liquidity Ratio
   (c) Activity Ratio (d) Profitability Ratio
2. Current assets include only those assets which are expected to be realised within ....
   (a) 3 months (b) 6 months
   (c) 1 year (d) 2 years
3. Proprietory ratio is calculated by the following formula:
   (a) $\frac{\text{Total Assets}}{\text{Long-term Loans}}$ (b) $\frac{\text{Tangible Assets}}{\text{Long-term Loans}}$
   (c) $\frac{\text{Current Assets}}{\text{Total Liabilities}}$ (d) $\frac{\text{Total Assets}}{\text{Total Liabilities}}$
4. Equity share capital Rs. 15,00,000, Reserve and Surplus Rs. 7,50,000 . Total Assets Rs. 45,00,000. Calculate ProprietaryRatio ?
   (a) 40% (b) 33%
   (c) 100% (d) 50%
5. The gross profit ratio is the ratio of gross profit to :
   (a) Net Cash Sales (b) Net Credit Sales
   (c) Closing Stock (d) Net Total Sales
6. **Assertion (A):** The focus of calculation of working capital revolves around managing the operating cycle of the business.

   Reasoning (R): It is because the concept of operating cycle is required to ascertain the liquidity of assets and urgency of payments to liabilities.

   Codes:
   (a) Both (A) and (R) are true, but (R) is not the explanation of working capital management.
   (b) Both (A) and (R) are true and (R) is a correct explanation of (A).
   (c) Both (A) and (R) are false.
   (d) (A) is false, but (R) is true.
7. Which of the following are included in traditional classification of ratios?
   (i) Liquidity Ratios. (ii) Statement of Profit and loss Ratios.
   (iii) Balance Sheet Ratios. (iv) Profitability Ratios.
   (v) Composite Ratios. (vi) Solvency Ratios.

   Codes:
   (a) (ii), (iii) and (v) (b) (i), (iv) and (vi)
   (c) (i), (ii) and (vi) (d) All (i), (ii), (iii), (iv), (v), (vi)
8. The following groups of ratios primarily measure risk:
   (a) solvency, activity, and profitability (b) liquidity, efficiency, and solvency
   (c) liquidity, activity, and profitability (d) liquidity, solvency, and profitability
9. Which one of the following is correct?
   (i) A ratio is an arithmetical relationship of one number to another number.
   (ii) Liquid ratio is also known as acid test ratio.

(iii) Ideally accepted current ratio is 1: 1.

(iv) Debt equity ratio is the relationship between outsider's funds and shareholders' funds.

In the context of the above two statements, which of the following options is correct?

(a) All (i), (ii), (iii) and (iv) are correct.
(b) Only (i), (ii) and (iv) are correct.
(c) Only (ii), (iii) and (iv) are correct.
(d) Only (ii) and (iv) are correct.

10. If sales is Rs. 4,20,000 sales returns is Rs.20,000 and cost of goods sold Rs.3,20,000 gross profit ratio will be:

(a) 20%
(b) 15%
(c) 25%
(d) 10%

11. If opening stock is Rs. 1,20,000, cost of revenue from operations is Rs. 10,00,000 and inventory turnover ratio is 5 times, then closing stock will be :-

(a) Rs. 2,79,000
(b) Rs. 2,67,000
(c) Rs. 2,80,000
(d) Rs. 2,00,000

12. Working Capital is Rs. 7,20,000; Trade Payables Rs. 40,000; Other current Liabilities Rs. 2,00,000; Calculate Current Ratio.

(a) 3 : 1
(b) 2 : 3
(c) 3 : 2
(d) 4 : 1

13. Which of the following points out the significance of ratio analysis?

(a) It helps the business in identifying the problem areas.
(b) It ignores price level changes.
(c) It ignores qualitative aspects
(d) All of the above

14. __________ ratios are the measure of the speed with which various accounts are converted into revenue from operations

(a) Debt
(b) Profitability
(c) Activity
(d) Liquidity

15. Current ratio = 3 : 4. Current liabilities Rs. 24,000, the amount of current assets will be:

(a) Rs. 18,000
(b) Rs. 20,000
(c) Rs. 16,000
(d) Rs. 15,000

16. Sales ratio may also be called as ______________

(a) Working capital
(b) Turnover
(c) Both a and b
(d) Neither a nor b

17. Which ratio indicates the proportion of assets financed out of shareholders' funds?

(a) Debt equity ratio.
(b) Fixed assets turnover ratio.
(c) Proprietary ratio.
(d) Total assets to debt ratio.

18. A company's liquid assets are Rs. 5,00,000 and its current liabilities are 3,00,000. Therefore it paid Rs. 1,00,000 to its trade payables. Quick ratio will be:

(a) 1 : 33
(b) 2 : 1
(c) 5 : 3
(d) 4 : 1

19. Patents fall under the category of __________

(a) Intangible assets
(b) Current assets
(c) Liquid assets
(d) Tangible assets

20. ________ is not a solvency ratio

(a) Current ratio

(b) Total assets to debt ratio

(c) Debt to equity ratio

(d) Proprietary ratio

Topic Test – 1

For questions 1 to 4: Analyse the case given below and answer the questions that follows:

Astro Ltd., an manufacturing company wants to analyse its credit policy and see how much amount is usually blocked in Trade Receivables. For this, some details are given below:

Trade Receivables Turnover Ratio	4 times
Cost of Revenue from Operations	Rs. 6,40,000
Gross Profit Ratio	20%

Closing Trade Receivables were Rs. 20,000 more than at the beginning.

Cash Revenue from Operations being 33 and 1/3rd% of Credit Revenue from Operations.

From the information given above, answer the following questions:

1. State the amount of Revenue from operations.

(a) Rs. 5,00,000 (b) Rs. 8,00,000

(c) Rs. 16,00,000 (d) Rs. 14,00,000

2. State the amount of Gross Profit earned during the year.

(a) Rs. 1,60,000 (b) Rs. 2,00,000

(c) Rs. 90,000 (d) Rs. 1,10,000

3. State the amount of opening Trade Receivables.

(a) Rs. 1,00,000 (b) Rs. 1,30,000

(c) Rs. 1,40,000 (d) Rs. 1,20,000

4. State the amount of Closing Trade Receivables.

(a) Rs. 1,10,000 (b) Rs. 1,20,000

(c) Rs. 1,60,000 (d) Rs. 1,40,000

5. Current Ratio is :

(a) Liquid Assets/Current Assets (b) Fixed Assets/Current Assets

(c) Current Assets/Current Liabilities (d) Liquid Assets/Current Liabilities

6. Quick Assets do not include

(a) Cash in hand (b) Prepaid Expenses

(c) Marketable Securities (d) Trade Receivables

7. Total Assets Rs. 8,10,000

Total Liabilities Rs. 2,60,000

Current Liabilities Rs. 40,000

Debt-equity ratio is:

(a) 0.05 : 1 (b) 0.4 : 1

(c) 2.5 : 1 (d) 4 : 1

8. The ratios are primarily measures of earning capacity of the business.

(a) Liquidity (b) Activity

(c) Debt (d) Profitability

9. **Assertion (A):** Activity Ratios are the ratios that are calculated for measuring the efficiency of operations of business based on effective utilisation of resources.

   Reasoning (R): Current ratio and Quick Ratio are liquidity ratios

   (a) Both Assertion (A) and Reason (R) are true and Reason (R) is the correct explanationof Assertion (A).

   (b) Both Assertion (A) and Reason (R) are true and Reason (R) is not the correct explanationof Assertion (A).

   (c) Assertion (A) is true but Reason (R) is False

   (d) Assertion (A) is false but Reason (R) is true

10. When opening stock is Rs. 50,000 closing stock Rs. 60,000 and cost of goods sold is Rs. 2,20,000, then stock turn over ratio is:

    (a) 2 times (b) 3 times

    (c) 4 times (d) 5 times

Topic Test – 2

1. If Total sales is Rs.2,50,000 and credit sales is 25% of Cash sales. The amount of credit sales is:

   (a) Rs. 50,000 (b) Rs. 2,50,000

   (c) Rs. 16,000 (d) Rs. 3,00,000

2. What will be the amount of gross profit of a firm if its average inventory is Rs.80,000, Inventory turnover ratio is 6 times, and the Selling price is 25% above cost?

   (a) Rs.1,20,000. (b) Rs.1,60,000.

   (c) Rs.2,00,000. (d) None of the above.

3. Assertion (A): A high operating ratio indicates a favourable position.

   Reasoning (R): A high operating ratio leaves a high margin to meet non-operating expenses.

   In the context of the above two statements, which of the following is correct?

   Code:

   (a) (A) and (R) both are correct and (R) correctly explains (A).

   (b) Both (A) and (R) are correct but (R) does not explain (A).

   (c) Both (A) and (R) are incorrect.

   (d) (A) is correct but (R) is incorrect

4. Current ratio of Adaar Ltd. is 2.5 : 1. Accountant wants to maintain it at 2 : 1.

   Following options are available.

   (i) He can repay Bills Payable

   (ii) He can purchase goods on credit

   (iii) He can take short term loan

   Choose the correct option.

   (a) Only (i) is correct (b) Only (ii) is correct

   (c) Only (i) and (iii) are correct (d) Only (ii) and (iii) are correct

5. The term'CurrentAssets'include

   (a) Long-term Investment (b) Short-term Investment

   (c) Furniture (d) Preliminary Expenses

6. Cash Balance Rs.15,000; Trade Receivables Rs.35,000; Inventory Rs.40,000; Trade Payables Rs.24,000 and Bank Overdraft is Rs.6,000. Current Ratio will be :

   (a) 5 : 1 (b) 3 : 1

   (c) 1 : 3 (d) 1 : 5

7. Current Assets Rs.4,00,000; Current Liabilities Rs.2,00,000 and Inventory is Rs.50,000. Liquid Ratio will be :

(a) 3 : 1 (b) 2.5 : 1

(c) 4 : 7 (d) 1.75 : 1

8. If Credit Revenue from Operations is Rs. 7,00,000, Cash Revenue from Operations is Rs. 1,00,000. Cost of Revenue from Operations is Rs. 6,40,000, then Gross Profit Ratio will be

(a) 15% (b) 18%

(c) 25% (d) 20%

9. Ideal current ratio is

(a) 2 : 1 (b) 3 : 1

(c) 1 : 1 (d) 1 : 2

10. Cost of revenue from operations is the difference between

(a) Revenue from operations + Gross Profit

(b) Revenue from operations - Gross Profit

(c) Revenue from operations - Net profit

(d) Revenue from operations + Net Profit

Answer Keys

Exercise

1. (b)	2. (c)	3. (c)	4. (d)	5. (d)	6. (b)	7. (a)	8. (d)	9. (b)	10. (a)
11. (c)	12. (d)	13. (a)	14. (c)	15. (a)	16. (b)	17. (c)	18. (b)	19. (a)	20. (a)

Topic Test – 1

1. (b)	2. (a)	3. (c)	4. (c)	5. (c)	6. (b)	7. (c)	8. (b)	9. (b)	10. (a)

Topic Test – 2

1. (a)	2. (a)	3. (c)	4. (d)	5. (b)	6. (b)	7. (d)	8. (d)	9. (a)	10. (b)

CHAPTER 11

Cash Flow Statement

Summary

Cash Flow Statement Cash flow statement is a statement showing the changes in financial position of a business concern during different intervals of time in terms of cash and cash equivalents. The Revised Accounting Standard-3 has made it mandatory for all listed companies to prepare and present a cash flow statement along with other financial statements on annual basis.

Objectives of cash flow statement:

(i) Useful in short-term financial planning.
(ii) Useful inefficient cash management.
(iii) Helpful in formulation of business policies.
(iv) Assists in preparation of cash budget.
(v) Used for assessment of cash flow from various activities, viz operating, investing and financing activities.

Cash and cash equivalents: As per AS-3, 'Cash' comprises cash in hand and demand deposits with banks, and Cash equivalents means short-term highly liquid investments that are readily convertible into known amounts of cash and which are subject to an insignificant risk of changes in value.

Cash Flows: 'Cash Flows' implies movement of cash in and out due to some non-cash items. Receipt of cash from a non-cash item is termed as cash inflow while cash payment in respect of such items as cash outflow.

Classification of Business Activities Accounting Standard-3 (Revised) requires that the changes resulting in inflows and outflows of cash and cash equivalents will be classified into following three activities:
(i) Cash flow from operating activities.
(ii) Cash flow from investing activities.
(iii) Cash flow from financing activities.

1. **Cash flow from operating activities:** Operating activities are the activities that constitute the primary or main activities of an enterprise. Cash flows from operating activities are primarily derived from the main activities of the enterprise. They generally result from the transactions and other events that enter into the determination of net profit or loss.

Cash Inflows from operating activities	Cash Outflows from operating activities
I. Cash receipts from sale of goods and the rendering of services.	I. Cash payments to suppliers for goods and services.
II. Cash receipts from royalties, fees, commissions and other revenues	II. Cash payments to and on behalf of the employees
	III. Cash payments to an insurance enterprise for premiums and claims, annuities, and other policy benefits
	IV. Cash payments of income taxes unless they can be specifically identified with financing and investing activities

2. **Cash flow from investing activities:** Investing activities are the acquisition and disposal of long-term assets and other investments not included in cash equivalents. Investing activities relate to purchase and sale of long-term assets or fixed assets such as machinery, furniture, land and building, etc.

Cash Outflows from investing activities	Cash Inflows from Investing Activities
I. Cash payments to acquire fixed assets including intangibles and capitalised research and development	Cash receipt from disposal of fixed assets including intangibles
II. Cash payments to acquire shares, warrants or debt instruments of other enterprises other than the instruments those held for trading purposes.	Cash receipt from the repayment of advances or loans made to third parties (except in case of financial enterprise).
III. Cash advances and loans made to third party (other than advances and loans made by a financial enterprise wherein it is operating activities)	Cash receipt from disposal of shares, warrants or debt instruments of other enterprises except those held for trading purposes
	Interest received in cash from loans and advances.
	Dividend received from investments in other enterprises.

3. **Cash from financing activites:** Financing activities are activities that result in changes in the size and composition of the owners' capital (including preference share capital in case of a company) and borrowings of the enterprise.

Cash Inflows from financing activities	Cash Outflows from financing activities
Cash proceeds from issuing shares (equity or/and preference).	Cash repayments of amounts borrowed
Cash proceeds from issuing debentures, loans, bonds and other short/ long-term borrowings.	Interest paid on debentures and long-term loans and advances
	Dividends paid on equity and preference capital.

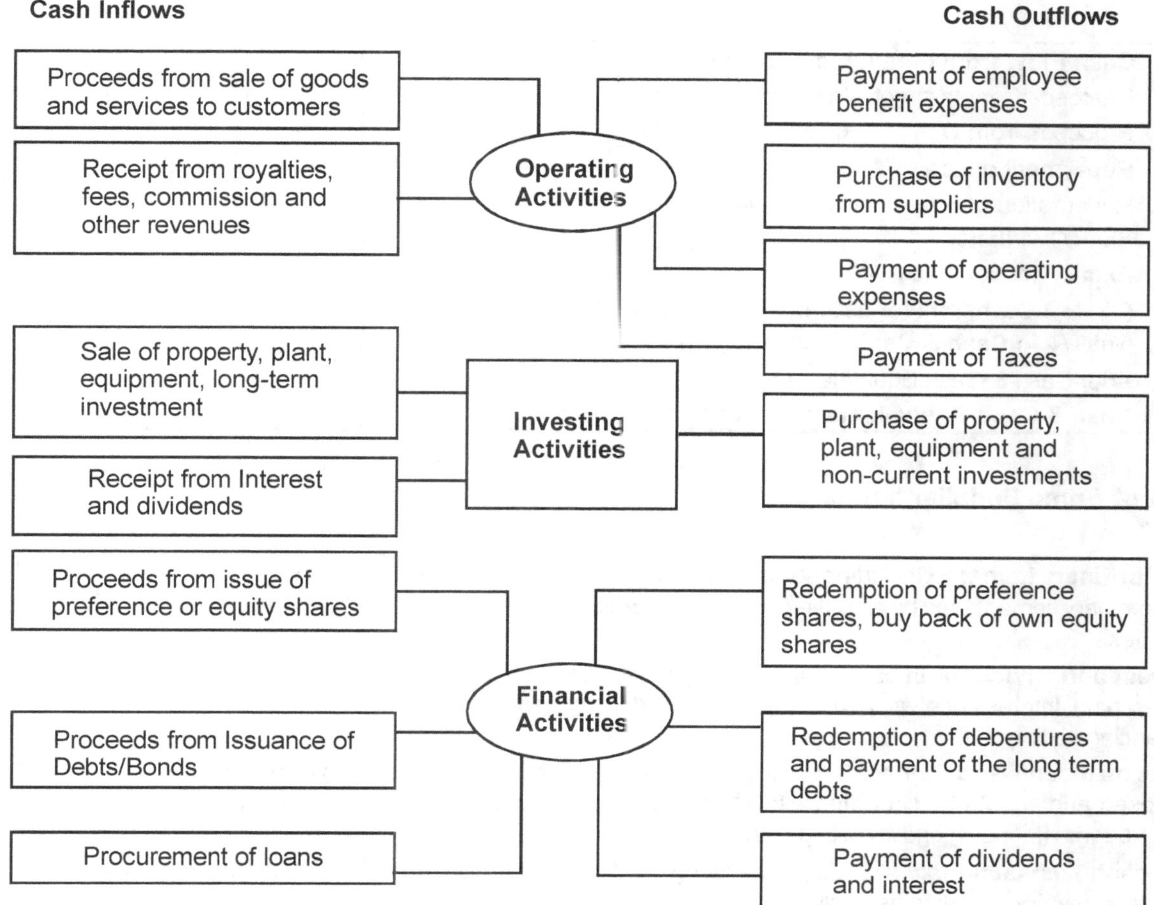

Format of cash flow statement:

Cash Flow Statement for the year ended xxxx

Particulars	Details	Amount
I. **Cash Flow from Operating Activities**		
(A) Net Profit before Taxation and Extraordinary Items		
Adjustment for Non-cash and Non-operating Items		
(B) Add: Items to be Added		
(C) Less: Items to be Deducted		
(D) Operating Profit before Working Capital Changes (A + B – C)		...
(E) Add: ↓ in CA and ↑ in CL		
(F) Less: ↑ in CA and ↓ in CL		
(G) Cash generated from Operations (D + E – F)		...
Less: Income Tax Paid (Net of Tax Refund received)		(...)
Cash Flow before Extraordinary Items		
Extraordinary Items (+/–)		...
(H) Net Cash from (or used in) Operating Activities		...
II. **Cash Flow from Investing Activities**		
Proceeds from Sale of Fixed Assets		...
Purchase of Fixed/Intangible Assets		(...)
Extraordinary Items (+/–)		...
(I) Net Cash from (or used in) Investing Activities		

III. Cash Flow from Financing Activities		
Proceeds from Issue of Shares or Debentures		...
Proceeds from Other Long-term Borrowings		...
Repayment of Loan		(...)
Redemption of Shares or Debentures		(...)
Bank Overdraft		...
Extraordinary Items (+/–)		...
(J) Net Cash from (or used in) Financing Activities		...
IV. Net ↑/↓ in Cash & Cash Equivalents (I + II + III)		...
Add: Cash & Cash Equivalents in the beginning of the year		...
V. Cash & Cash Equivalents at the end of the year		...

Treatment of Some Peculiar Items:

1. **Extraordinary items:** Extraordinary items are non-recurring in nature and hence cash flows associated with extraordinary items should be classified and disclosed separately as arising from operating, investing or financing activities.
2. **Interest and Dividend:** In case of a financial enterprise (whose main business is lending and borrowing), interest paid, interest received and dividend received are classified as operating activities while dividend paid is a financing activity.
3. **Taxes on Income and Gains:** AS-3 requires that cash flows arising from taxes on income should be separately disclosed and should be classified as cash flows from operating activities unless they can be specifically identified with financing and investing activities.
4. **Non-cash Transactions:** As per AS-3, investing and financing transactions that do not require the use of cash or cash equivalents should be excluded from a cash flow statement.

Cash flows from operating activities:

Operating activities are the main source of revenue and expenditure in an enterprise. Therefore, the ascertainment of cash flows from operating activities is of prime importance.

- i. **Direct Method:** The direct method provides information which is useful in estimating future cash flows.
- ii. **Indirect Method:** Indirect method of ascertaining cash flow from operating activities begins with the amount of net profit/loss.

1. As per AS-3, (Revised), under the indirect method, net cash flow from operating activities is determined by adjusting net profit or loss for the effects of:
   1. Non-cash items are to be added back. Non-cash items like
      (a) Depreciation
      (b) Goodwill has written off
      (c) Patents and Copyrights are written off
      (d) Appropriation to General Reserve
      (e) Interim dividend
      (f) Deferred taxes etc.

2. All other items for which the cash effects are investing or financing cash flows. The treatment of such items depends upon their nature. All investing and financing incomes are to be deducted from the number of net profits while all such expenses are to be added back.
3. Changes in current assets and liabilities during the period. An increase in current assets and a decrease in current liabilities are to be deducted while the increase in current liabilities and a decrease in current assets are to be added up.

Cash Flows from Operating Activities (Indirect Method)

	Rs.	Rs.
(A) Net Profit before Taxation and Extraordinary Items		×××
Adjustment For Non-cash and Non-operating Items		
(B) Add:		
– Depreciation	×××	
– Goodwill written off	×××	
– Preliminary Expenses written off	×××	
– Discount on Issue of Shares and Debentures written off	×××	
– Patents and Trademarks written off	×××	
– Interest on Borrowings and Debentures (For Finance Co.)	×××	
– Loss on Sale of Fixed Assets etc.	×××	×××
(C) Less:		×××
– Interest Income (For Finance (Co.)	×××	
– Dividend Income (For Finance Co.)	×××	
– Rental Income	×××	
– Profit on Sale of Fixed Assets etc.	×××	×××
(D) Operating Profit before Working Capital Changes (A + B – C)		×××
(E) Add:		
– Decrease in Current Assets	×××	
– Increase in Current Liabilities	×××	×××
		×××
(F) Less:		
– Increase in Current Assets	×××	
– Decrease in Current Liabilities	×××	×××
(G) Cash Flow from Operation (D + E – F)		×××
(H) Less: Income Tax Paid		×××
(I) Cash Flow from Operations before Extraordinary Items		×××
Add/Less: Extraordinary Items		×××
Net Cash Flow from Operating Activities		×××

Cash Flow from Investing Activities:

Investing activities are the acquisition and disposal of long terms assets and other investments not included in cash equivalent. Accordingly, cash inflow and outflow relating to fixed assets, shares, and debentures of other enterprises, advances, and loans to third parties and their repayments are shown separately under investing activities in the Cash Flow Statement.

Cash Flow from Investing Activities

– Sale of Fixed Assets	×××	
Add:		
– Sale of Investments	×××	
– Sale of Intangible Assets	×××	
– Interest and Dividend Received (Non finance Co.)	×××	
– Rent Income	×××	×××
Less:		
– Purchase of Fixed Assets/ Intangible Assets	×××	
– Purchase of Investments	×××	×××
		×××
Add/Less: Extraordinary Items		×××
		×××
Net Cash Flow from Investing Activities		×××

Cash Flows from Financing Activities:

The Financing Activities of an enterprise are those activities that result in a change in size and composition of owners capital and borrowing of the enterprise. It includes separate disclosure of proceeds from the issue of shares or other similar instruments, issue of debentures, loans, bonds, other short-term or long-term borrowings, and repayment of amounts borrowed. It is useful in predicting claims on future cash flows by providers of funds (both capital and borrowings to the enterprise.)

Cash Flow from Financing Activities

Issue of Shares		×××
Add:		
– Issue of Debentures	×××	
– Long Term Loan and Advances	×××	×××
		×××
Less:		
– Repayment of Loan etc.	×××	
– Dividend paid (Final, Interim)	×××	×××
– Redemption of Debenture, Preference Share	×××	
– Interest on Debenture and Loan	×××	×××
Add/Less:		
– Extraordinary Items		×××
		×××
– Net Cash Flow from Financing Activities		×××

Exercise

1. Issue of shares in consideration of purchase of plant and machinery results into __________
   (a) Inflow of Cash (b) Outflow of Cash
   (c) both (a) and (b) (d) Neither (a) nor (b)
2. If net profit is Rs. 50,000 after writing off goodwill Rs. 10,000 then the cash flow from operating activities will be:
   (a) Rs. 40,000 (b) Rs. 60,000
   (c) Rs. 35,000 (d) Rs. 70,000
3. From the following information, calculate cash flows from financing activities:

	April 1, 2019	March 31st 2020
Long-term Loans	2,00,000	2,50,000

   During the year, the company repaid a loan of Rs. 1, 00,000.
   (a) Rs. 40,000 (b) Rs. 48,000
   (c) Rs. 50,000 (d) Rs. 60,000
4. Cash from operating activities will decrease due to :
   (a) Increase in Current Assets (b) Decrease in Current Liabilities
   (c) Neither of the two (d) Both (a) and (b)
5. Which of the following transaction will result into 'flow of cash'
   (a) Deposited Rs. 20,000 into bank
   (b) Withdrew cash from bank Rs. 1400
   (c) Sale of machinery of the book value of Rs. 60,000 at a loss of Rs. 7000.
   (d) Converted 1,00,000 9% debentures into equity shares
6. If a machine whose original cost is Rs. 40,000 having accumulated depreciation Rs.12,000, were sold for Rs. 34,000 then while preparing Cash Flow Statement its effect on cash flow will be :
   (a) Cash flow from financing activities Rs. 34,000
   (b) Cash flow from financing activities Rs. 6,000
   (c) Cash flow from investing activities Rs. 34,000
   (d) Cash flow from investing activities Rs. 6,000
7. Calculate cash flows from operating activities from the following information.
   Statement of Profit and Loss for the year ended March 31, 2020

Particulars	Note No.	Amount (Rs.)
i) Revenue from Operations		60,000
ii) Other Income	1	5,000
iii) Total Revenue (i + ii)		**65,000**
iv) Expenses		
Cost of materials consumed		15,000
Employees benefits expenses		10,000
Depreciation and Amortisation expenses	2	7,000
Other expenses	3	13,000
		45,000
v) Profit before tax (iii-iv)		20,000
vi) Provision for taxation		8,000
vii) Profit after tax (v-vi)		**12,000**

Additional Information

	March 31, 2019	March 31, 2020
Provision for taxation	Rs. 10,000	Rs. 13,000
Rent payable	Rs. 2,000	Rs. 2,500
Trade payable	Rs. 21,000	Rs. 25,000
Trade receivables	Rs. 15,000	Rs. 21,000
Inventories	Rs. 25,000	Rs. 22,000

Choose the correct answer:

(a) Rs. 24,500 (b) Rs. 23,450

(c) Rs. 30,000 (d) Rs. 25,000

8. ABC Ltd. a financing company took deposits of Rs. 4, 00,000 during the year @ 12% p.a. It will be including which of the following activities while preparing the Cash Flow Statement?

(a) Investing Activities (b) Financing Activities

(c) Operating Activities (d) Both Investing and Financing Activities

9. Match the correct answer:

(A) Taxes Paid (i) Cash flow from investing activities

(B) Repayment of loans (ii) Cash flow from operating activities

(C) Sale of fixed assets (iii) Cash Flow from financing activities

(a) A-(ii), B-(iii), C-(i) (b) A-(i), B-(ii), C-(iii)

(c) A-(iii), B-(i), C-(ii) (d) B-(i), A – (ii), C–(iii)

10. For the calculation of cash flow from operating activities, payments and receipts shown in Profit & Loss account are converted into payments and receipts actually in cash by eliminating

(a) Non-cash revenue from the revenue earned (b) Non-cash expenses from expenses incurred

(c) Both (a) & (b) (d) None of the above

11. Given salary expenses Rs 40,000, Outstanding in the beginning of the year: Rs. 5,000 and outstanding at the end of the year Rs. 10,000. Cash outflow on salary will be:

(a) Rs. 45,000 (b) Rs. 35,000

(c) Rs. 40,000 (d) Rs. 15,000

12. **Assertion (A):** Sale of fixed assets is written under the Investing Activities.

Reasoning (R): Sale of fixed assets leads to inflow of cash.

Codes:

(a) Both Assertion (A) and Reason (R) are true, and Reason (R) is the correct explanation of Assertion (A).

(b) Both Assertion (A) and Reason (R) are true, but Reason (R) is not the correct explanation of Assertion (A).

(c) Assertion (A) is true, but Reason (R) is false.

(d) Assertion (A) is false, but Reason (R) is true.

13. Total sales Rs. 5,00,000 , credit sales Rs. 2,25,000, total purchases Rs. 2,48,000, credit purchases is Rs. 1,08,000, cash operating expenses is Rs. 40,000.

Cash flow from operation will be:

(a) Rs. 90,000 (b) Rs. 1,00,000

(c) Rs. 95,000 (d) Rs. 80,000

14. Which of the following is incorrect about the statement of cash flows?

(a) It provides information about the cash receipt and cash payments of an enterprise.

(b) It reconciles ending cash balance with the balance as per bank statement.

(c) It provides information about the operating, investing and financing activities.

(d) It explains the deviation of cash from Earnings.

15. Warehouse Ltd. has given you the following information:

	Rs.
Machinery as on April 01, 2019	50,000
Machinery as on March 31, 2020	60,000
Accumulated Depreciation on April 01, 2019	25,000
Accumulated Depreciation on March 31, 2020	15,000

During the year, a Machine costing Rs. 25,000 with Accumulated Depreciation of Rs. 15,000 was sold for Rs. 13,000.

Calculate cash flow from Investing Activities will be ____________

(a) Rs. 13,000 (b) Rs. 15,500

(c) Rs. 22,500 (d) Rs. 30,000

16. How will you treat payment of 'Interest of Debentures' while preparing a Cash Flow Statement ?

(a) Cash Flow from Operating Activities

(b) Cash Flow from Investing Activities

(c) Cash Flow from Financing Activities

(d) Cash Equivalents

17. Elf Ltd. has a balance in Provision for Tax Account of Rs. 50,000 and Rs. 75,000 as of 31st March, 2020 and 2021 respectively. It made a provision for tax during the year of Rs. 65,000. The amount of tax paid during the year was

(a) Rs. 70,000 (b) Rs. 30,000

(c) Rs. 40,000 (d) Rs. 55,000

18. Profit during the year Rs. 20,000. During the year there was increase in stock by Rs. 9,000 and decrease in debentures of Rs. 5,000. What is the amount of cash from operating activities?

(a) Rs. 16,000 (b) Rs. 10,000

(c) Rs. 20,000 (d) Rs. 14,000

19. If the amount of goodwill is Rs. 40,000 at the beginning of a year and Rs. 48,000 at the end of that year then while preparing cash flow statement its effect on cash flow will be :

(a) Cash used (Payment) in Investing Activities Rs. 8,000

(b) Cash received from operating activities Rs. 8,000

(c) Cash used (Payment) from Operating Activities Rs. 8,000

(d) Cash used (Payment) from Financial Activities Rs. 8,000

20. From the following information of Ibex ltd:

Particulars	31st march 2020	31st march 2021
Equity and liabilities 12% debentures	2,00,000	1,60,000

Additional Information:

Interest on Debentures is paid on a half-yearly basis on 30th September and 31st March each year. Debentures were redeemed on 30th September 2020.

How much amount (related to the above information) will be shown in the Financing Activity for Cash Flow Statement prepared on 31st March 2021?

(a) Outflow Rs. 50,000 (b) Inflow Rs. 32,600

(c) Outflow Rs. 61,600 (d) Outflow Rs. 44,000

Topic Test – 1

For questions 1 to 3: Analyse the case given below and answer the questions that follows:

Kaan initiated a startup Wani Ltd. In 2018. The profits of Wani ltd. in the year 2019-20 after all the appropriations was Rs. 31,25,000. This profit was arrived after taking all the consideration the following items:

Sl. No.	Particulars	Amount (Rs.)
1	Gain on sale of fixed tangible assets	12,50,000
2	Goodwill written off	7,80,000
3	Transfer to General Reserve	8,75,000
4	Provision for taxation	4,37,500

Additional Information:

Particulars	31-03-2020 Rs.	31-03-2020 Rs.
Prepaid Expenses	7,50,000	5,00,000
Inventory	10,50,000	8,20,000
Trade Payables	4,50,000	3,50,000
Trade Receivables	6,20,000	5,90,000

1. Net profit before tax will be __________
   (a) Rs. 44,37,500 (b) Rs. 33,56,000
   (c) Rs. 45, 38,750 (d) Rs. 50,00,000
2. Operating profit before working capital changes will be
   (a) Rs. 40,05,000 (b) Rs. 39,67,500
   (c) Rs. 39,00,000 (d) Rs. 35,98,000
3. Cash from operating activities before tax
   (a) Rs. 30,00,000 (b) Rs. 35,57,500
   (c) Rs. 37,78,000 (d) Rs. 33,57,600
4. Which of the following are added to net profit after tax and extraordinary items to reach to net profit before tax and extraordinary items?
   (A) Provision for tax made during the year (B) Proposed dividend made during the year
   (C) Interim dividend (D) Transfer to General reserves and other reserves
   (a) Both A and B (b) Both A and C
   (c) Both B and C (d) A, B, C and D
5. The statement of cash flows clarifies cash flows according to
   (a) Operating and non-operating flows (b) Investing and non-operating flows
   (c) Inflows and outflows (d) Operating, investing and financing activities
6. A Mutual Fund Company receives a dividend of Rs. 20 Lakhs on its investments in another company's shares. Where will it appear in a Cash Flow Statement?
   (a) Cash Flow from Operating Activities
   (b) Cash Flow from Investing Activities
   (c) Cash Flow from Financing Activities
   (d) No Cash Flow

7. While calculating operating profit which will be added to net profit:
   (a) Interest received (b) Profit on sale of Asset
   (c) Increase in General Reserve (d) Refund of Tax
8. Which of the following statements are false?
   (A) Cash Flow Statement is helpful in the formation of policies.
   (B) Cash Flow Statement is useful for external analysis
   (C) Cash Flow Statement is helpful in estimating future cash flow
   (a) Both A and B (b) Both A and C
   (c) Both B and C (d) None of the above
9. Which one of following is not a non-cash item ?
   (a) Cash sales (b) Goodwill written off
   (c) Depreciation (d) Provision of Bad Debts
10. Which of the following is not an example of cash outflows?
   (a) Repayment of loans (b) Decrease in creditors
   (c) Issue of debentures (d) None of these

Topic Test – 2

1. Assertion (A): Depreciation is added to the net profit before tax
   Reasoning (R): Depreciation is a non cash item which is an expense
   (a) Both Assertion (A) and Reason (R) are true, and Reason (R) is the correct explanation of Assertion (A).
   (b) Both Assertion (A) and Reason (R) are true, but Reason (R) is not the correct explanation of Assertion (A).
   (c) Assertion (A) is true, but Reason (R) is false.
   (d) Assertion (A) is false, but Reason (R) is true.
2. Net Profit during the year Rs. 1,00,000
   Debtors in the beginning the year of Rs.30,000
   Debtors at the end of the year Rs.36,000
   What is the amount of cash from operating activities ?
   (a) Rs. 40,000 (b) Rs. 84,000
   (c) Rs. 94,000 (d) Rs. 1,66,000
3. Refund of income tax is a __________ of cash
   (a) Inflow (b) Outflow
   (c) Both (a) and (b) (d) Neither (a) nor (b)
4. From the following information, calculate operating profit before working capital changes

Particulars	Amount
Net profit before working Tax and Extraordinary items	2,50,000
Depreciation	10,500
Interest on Loan	2,000
Goodwill written off	2,500
Loss on sale of plant	1,250
Premium on Redemption of Debenture	800
Interest and Dividend received on Investments	7,400
Profit on sale investment	1,500

   (a) Rs. 2,58,150 (b) Rs. 2,00,000
   (c) Rs. 3,15,890 (d) Rs. 2,08,785

5. From the following extract on Sano Ltd.

Particulars	2019	2020
Provision for tax	Rs. 26,000	Rs. 18,000

If tax paid during the year is Rs. 14,400. What is the provision of tax during the year?

(a) Rs. 20,700 (b) Rs. 22,400

(c) Rs. 30,000 (d) Rs. 45,678

6. If net profit is Rs. 35,000 after writing off good will Rs. 6,000 and loss on sale of furniture Rs. 1,000, cash flow from operating activities will be :

(a) Rs. 15,000 (b) Rs. 42,000

(c) Rs. 39,000 (d) Rs. 20,000

7. If the net profits earned during the year is Rs. 50,000 and the amount of debtors in the beginning and the end of the year is Rs. 10,000 and Rs. 20,000. Then the cash flow from operating activity will be ____________

(a) Rs. 30,000 (b) Rs. 40,000

(c) Rs. 50,000 (d) Rs. 80,000

8. Net Profit during the year Rs. 1,00,000

Debtors in the beginning the year of Rs. 30,000

Debtors at the end of the year Rs. 36,000

What is the amount of cash from operating activities ?

(a) Rs. 80,000 (b) Rs. 94,000

(c) Rs. 36,000 (d) Rs. 1,66,000

9. From the following extract of Aman ltd., calculate cash flow from investing activities:

Particulars	Purchases (Rs.)	Sales (Rs.)
Machinery	200,000	2,000,000
Building	400,000	
Investment	20,000	28,000
Goodwill	28,000	
Patent and Trademark	40,000	8,000

(a) Rs. 12,45,600 (b) Rs. 13,89,670

(c) Rs. 12,00,000 (d) Rs. 13,88,000

10. Given salary expenses Rs. 40,000. Outstanding in the beginning of the year Rs. 5,000 and the outstanding at the end of the year is Rs. 10,000. Cash out flow will be :

(a) Rs. 45,000 (b) Rs. 30,000

(c) Rs. 25,000 (d) Rs. 35,000

Answer Keys

Exercise

1. (d)	2. (b)	3. (c)	4. (d)	5. (c)	6. (c)	7. (a)	8. (c)	9. (a)	10. (c)
11. (b)	12. (b)	13. (c)	14. (b)	15. (c)	16. (c)	17. (c)	18. (a)	19. (a)	20. (c)

Topic Test – 1

1. (a)	2. (b)	3. (b)	4. (d)	5. (d)	6. (a)	7. (c)	8. (d)	9. (a)	10. (c)

Topic Test – 2

1. (a)	2. (c)	3. (a)	4. (a)	5. (b)	6. (b)	7. (b)	8. (b)	9. (d)	10. (d)

Solutions

Exercise

1. (d)

2. (b)

3. (c)

4. (d)

5. (c)

6. (c)

7. (a) Net profit + depreciation + goodwill amortized + loss on sale-profit on sale + decrease in inventories + decrease in rent payable + increase in trade payable – trade receivable – income tax paid + income tax refund

= 1,70,000 + 5000 + 2000 + 3000 – 2000 + 3000 + 500 + 4000 – 6000 – 5000 + 3000

= 24,500

8. (c)

9. (a)

10. (c)

11. (b)

12. (b)

13. (c)

14. (b)

15. (c) Cash inflow from investing activity

Sale of machinery = 13000

Purchase of machinery = (35,000) = (22000)

16. (c)

17. (c)

18. (a) Profit of the year = 20,000

(+) dec in debentures = 5000

(–) increase in stock = 9000 = 16000

19. (a) Goodwill at the end = 48,000

(–) G/w in the beginning = 40000 = 8000

20. (c)

Topic Test – 1

1. (a)

Particulars	Rs.
Net Profit after all appropriation	31,25,000
Add: Transfer to General Reserve	8,75,000
Add: Provision for Taxation	4,37,500
Net Profit Before Tax	44,37,500

2. (b)

Particulars	Rs.
Net Profit Before Tax	44,37,500
Add: Goodwill Written Off	7,80,000
Less: Gain on sale of fixed tangible assets	(12,50,000)
Operating profit before working capital changes	39,67,500

3. (b)

Particulars	Rs.
Net Proft Before Tax	44,37,500
Add: Goodwill Written Off	7,80,000
Less: Gain on Sale of fixed tangible assets	(12,50,000)
Operating profit before working capital changes	39,67,500
Add: Increase in Trade Payables	1,00,000
Less : Increase in Prepaid Expenses	(2,50,000)
Less : Increase in Inventory	(2,30,000)
Less : Increase in Trade Receivables	(30,000)
Net Proft Before Tax	35,57,500

4. (d)

5. (d)

6. (a)

7. (c)

8. (d)

9. (a)

10. (c)

Topic Test – 2

1. (a)
2. (c)
3. (a)
4. (a)
5. (b) Provision of tax during the year + closing provision for tax – opening provision for tax
   26,000 + 14,400 – 18,000 = 22,400
6. (b)
7. (b)
8. (b) Net profit + debtors in the beginning – debtors at the end of the year
   1,00,000 + 30,000 – 36,000 = 94,000
9. (d) Sale of machinery + sale of investment + sale of patent – purchase of machinery – purchase of building – purchase of investment – purchase of goodwi l
   = 20, 00,000 + 28,000 + 8000 – 2,00,000 – 4,00,000 – 20,000 – 28,000 = 13,88,000
10. (d)

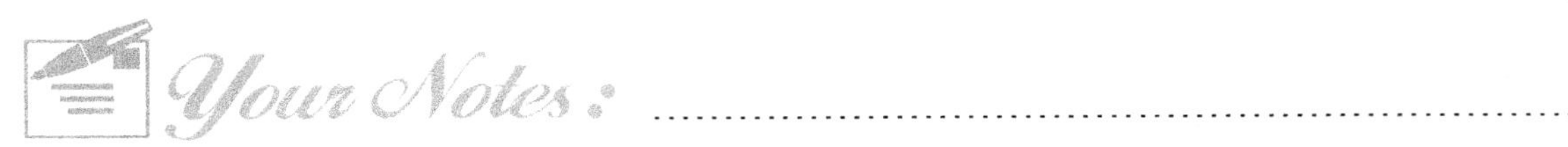
Your Notes :

CHAPTER 12

Computerised Accounting

Introduction:

The Computerised Accounting System (CAS) has the following components:

Procedure: A logical sequence of actions to perform a task.

Data: The raw fact (as input) for any business application.

People: Users.

Hardware: Computer, associated peripherals, and their network.

Software: System software and Application software

Computerised Accounting System Computerised Accounting System refers to the processing of accounting transaction through the use of hardware and software in order to produce accounting records and reports.

Basic flow of Accounting Transaction

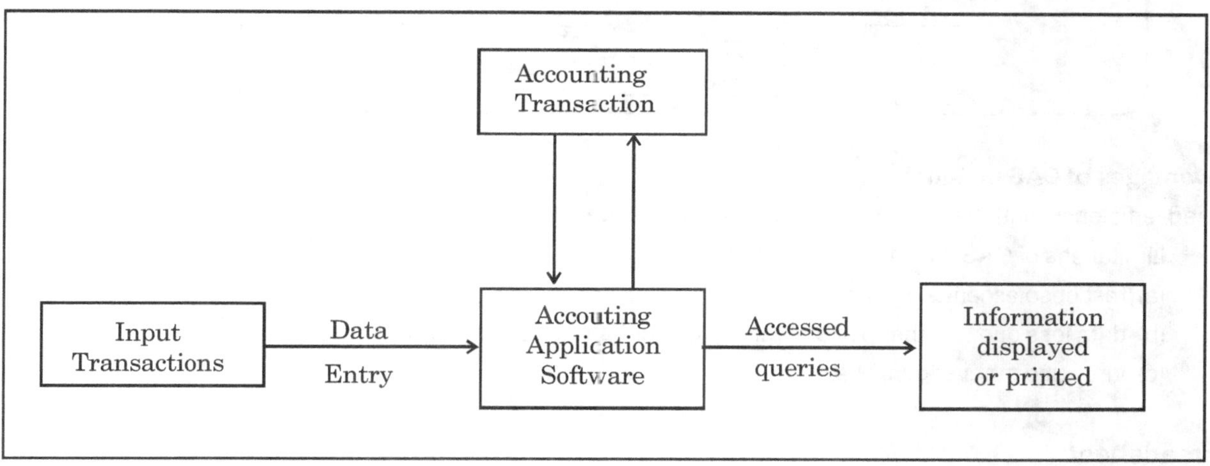

Codification of accounts:

1. **Sequential Codes:** In Sequential Code, numbers and/or letters are assigned in consecutive order. This process enables in either identification of missing codes (numbers) relating to a particular document or a relevant document can be traced on the basis of code.

   Example: Codes accounts

   CL001 GCERT LTD

2. **Block Codes:** In a block code, a range of numbers is partitioned into a desired number of sub-ranges and each sub-range is allotted to a specific group.

Example:	CODES	Dealer Type
	100-199	Small Pumps
	200-299	Medium Pumps

3. **Mnemonic Codes:** A mnemonic code consists of alphabets or abbreviations as symbols to codify a piece of information.

Accounting Information System (AIS):

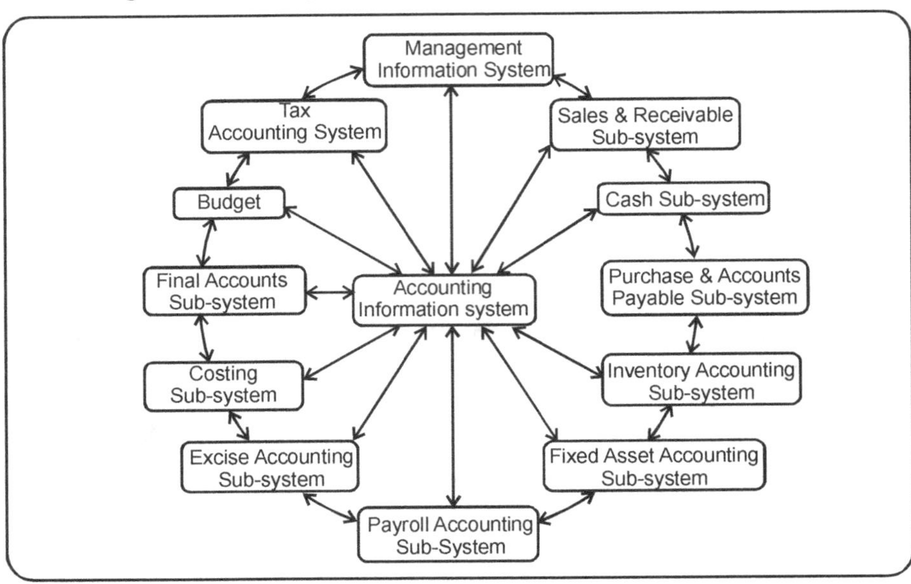

Advantages of CAS include:

Speed, efficiency, arithmetic accuracy, cost saving, confidentiality of data.

- Limitations of CAS include provision for;
  (a) fast obsolescence of technology,
  (b) data loss due to either power interruptions or damage to hard disk,
  (c) virus and other security hazards.

Spreadsheet:

A spreadsheet is a configuration of rows and columns. Rows are horizontal vectors while columns are vertical vectors. A spreadsheet is also known as a worksheet. Spreadsheet application (sometimes referred to simply as spreadsheet) is a computer program that allows us to add (i.e. enter) and process data. We shall understand spreadsheet with the help of MS-Excel (or simply, Excel), which is one of the Microsoft Office Suite of software.

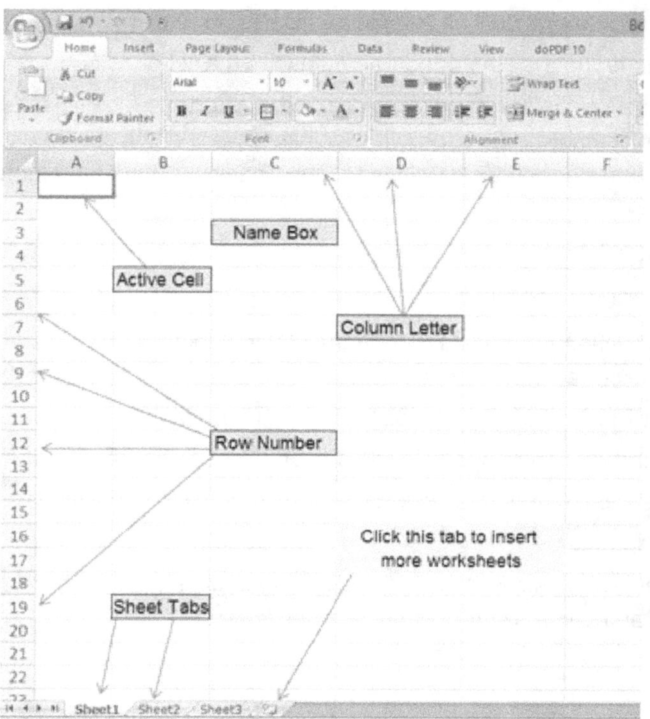

Rows are numbered numerically from top to bottom while Columns

Columns are referred by alpha characters from left to right.

In a spreadsheet, a value or function or an arithmetic expression is recorded in a cell.

The intersection of a row and a column is called a cell.

A cell is identified by a combination of a letter and a number corresponding to a particular location within the spreadsheet.

Movement	**Key Stroke (Press key)**
Top of Worksheet (Cell A1)	**CTRL + HOME** (i.e. Keep **CTRL** key pressed and then press **HOME** key
The cell at the intersection of the last row and last column containing data	**CTRL + END** keys
Moving consecutively to the first and the last filled cells of clusters of filled cells in a row by successive pressing of **CTRL + Right arrow key** (→) or else **END + Right arrow key** (→)	**CTRL + Right arrow key** (→) or else **END + Right arrow key** (→)
Moving consecutively to the first and the last filled cells of a clusters of filled cells in a column by successive pressing of **CTRL + Right arrow key** (↓) or else **END Down arrow key** (↓)	**CTRL + Down arrow key** (↓) or else **END + Down arrow key** (↓)
Beginning of the Row	**HOME key**
Beginning of the Column	

A reference to a range of cells is typically of the form (A1:A6) which specifies all the cells in the range A1 through to A6. A formula such as "=SUM (A1:A6)" would add all the cells specified and put the result in the cell containing the formula itself.

Labels: A text or especial character will be treated as labels for rows or columns or descriptive information.

Formulas: The formula means a mathematical calculation on a set of cells.

Functions: A function is a special key word which can be entered into a cell in order to perform and process the data which is appended within brackets. A function is a special key word which can be entered into a cell in order to perform and process the data which is appended within brackets. There is a function button on the formula toolbar (fx);

Date and Time Function:

1. Today () is the function for today's date in the blank worksheet. TODAY – Returns the serial number of the current date. The serial number is the date-time code used by Excel for date and time calculations.
2. Now () is similar function but it includes the current time also
3. Dday (serial_number) function returns the day of a date as an integer ranging from1 to 31
4. Datevalue (date_text) converts a date in the form of text to a serial number

Formatting of spreadsheets makes easier to read and understand the important information (e.g. conditional formatting, number formatting, text and general spreadsheet formatting etc.)

Mathematical Function:

1. **Sumif:** is the function which adds the cells
2. **Round:** is the function to rounds a number to specified number of digits
3. **Count:** This function counts the number of cells that contain numbers and counts numbers within the list of arguments
4. Counta function will be count logical values, text, or error values

Rows (array) the function returns the number of rows in a reference or array; where an Array is an array, an array formula or a reference to a range of cells for which we want the number of rows.

Columns (array) this function returns the number of columns in an array or named range reference; where an Array is an array or array formula or a reference to a range of cells for which we want the number of columns.

Countif (range, criteria): This function counts the number of cells within a range

Range is one or more cells to count, including numbers or names, arrays, or references that contain numbers.

Criteria are the form of a number, expression, cell reference, or text that defines which cells will be counted.

Text Manipulation Function:

1. Text This function converts a numeric value to text in a specific number format
2. Concatenate This function joins two or more text strings into one text string
3. A logical value (true or false) outcome is the comparison of data values or results of arithmetic expressions compared with another data values or results of another arithmetical expressions using logical operator.

Lookup and References Function

The Lookup function returns a value either from a one-row or one column range or from an array. The LOOKUP function has two syntax forms: vector and array.

1. **Lookup (Vector Form):** The syntax is Lookup (lookup_value, lookup_vector lookup_vector, result_vector)
2. **Lookup (Array Form):** The syntax is LOOKUP (lookup_value, array)
3. **Vlookup:** The Vlookup function, which stands for vertical lookup, helps us to find specific information in large data tables such as an inventory list of parts or a large employee contact list. The VLOOKUP function searches and matches first the required value from the column of a range of cells, and then returns a value from any cell on the same row of the range.
4. Hlookup The Hlookup function (short name of Horizontal Lookup), searches for a value in the first row of a table array and returns the corresponding value in the same column from another row of the same table array.

DATA FORMATTING:

Formatting of spreadsheets makes easier to read and understand he important information (e.g. conditional formatting, number formatting, text and general spreadsheet formatting etc.).

Formatting Tools:

1. **Number formatting:** Number formatting includes adding per cent symbols (%), commas (,), decimal places, and currency signs ($,Rs. etc), date, time, scientific values and as well as some special formats to a spreadsheet.
2. **Currency:** If we enter a financial value complete with the dollar/ currency sign and two decimal places, Excel assigns a Currency format to the cell along with the entry
3. **Percentages:** If we enter a value representing a percentage as a whole number followed by the per cent sign without any decimal places, Excel assigns to the cell the percentage format that follows this pattern along with the entry.
4. **Dates:** If we enter a date (dates are values, too) that follows one of the built-in Excel number formats, such as 16-04-2009 or 16-Apr-2009 the program assigns a Date format that follows the pattern of the date.

Preparation of reports using pivot table:

A Pivot Table is way to present information in a report format. A PivotTable report often provides enhanced layout, attractive and formatted report with improved readability.

One-Variable Data Table: Formula used in a one-variable data table must refer to an input cell. The input cell is a cell used by Excel in which each input value from a data table is substituted (column-oriented, i.e. input cell down one column or row-oriented, i.e. across one-row).

Two-variable data table: use only one formula with two lists of input values. The formula must refer two different input cells.

To print an entire spreadsheet choose Page Setup from the File Menu, Choose the appropriate options in terms of horizontal (landscape) or vertical (portrait) printing, Excel prints entire spreadsheet document, if the document is too wide to fit on a page, Excel will print the remaining columns on subsequent pages before continuing to print the remaining rows.

Uses of spreadsheet in business application:

PAYROLL COMPONENTS Every employee is under contractual relationship of service with an organisation, and is paid salary accordingly. The following elements are important for salary computation and its payment:

Current payroll period (Month and Year)

- Earnings
- **Basic Pay (BP):** It is the pay in the pay scale plus Grade Pay, but does not include Special Pay.
- **Grade Pay (GP):** It is the pay to be added to the Basic Pay according to the Designation of the employee and applicable pay band or scale of pay.
- **Dearness Pay (DP):** It is that portion of Dearness Allowance, which has been declared and deemed to have been merged with the Basic Pay.
- **Dearness Allowance (DA):** It is a compensation for erosion in the purchasing power of wage earner due to price rise. It is granted by the Government periodically as a percentage of (Basic Pay + Dearness Pay, if applicable).
- **House Rent Allowance (HRA):** It is an amount paid to facilitate employee in acquiring on lease of residential accommodation.
- **Transport Allowance (TRA):** It is an amount to facilitate commuting to the the place of work, i.e. Delhi, Bhopal, Haridwar, etc.
- **Any Other Earning:** It may include any other allowance not included above but declared from time to time, such as Education Allowance, Medical Allowance, Washing Allowance, etc.
- **Deductions:**
- **Professional Tax (Applicable in some states) (PT):** It is a statutory deduction according to the legislature of the State Government.
- **Provident Fund (PF):** It is a statutory deduction, as part of social security. It is decided by the Government under the Provident Fund Act and is computed as a percentage of (Basic Pay + Dearness Pay, if applicable).

§ Tax Deduction at Source (TDS) : It is a statutory deduction, which is deducted monthly towards Income Tax liability of an employee. It is essentially an apportionment of yearly Income Tax liability over 12 months.

Column	Column Heading	Abbrev Ref	First line shows Required Formula Second line refers the cell content
A	Employee No	Emp No	Value entered directly
B	Employee Name	Emp Name	Value entered directly
C	Employee Type	Emp Type	Value entered directly
D	Deduction Days	Ded Days	Value entered directly
E	Basic Pay	BP	Value entered directly
F	No. of Effective Days Present	NOEP	= NODM –[Ded Days] = I3 – D12
G	Baic pay Earned	BPE	BP * NOEP/NODM = E12 * F12 / I3
H	Dearness Allowance	DA	= BPE * DA Rate (in %) = G12 * I4
I	House Rent Allowance	HRA	= If (Emp Typ = "Sup" then 40% of BPE elese if (Emp type = "Nsup" then 30% of BPE else 0)) = IF(C12 = "Sup", G12 * I5, IF (C12 = "Nsup", G12*SI$6,0))
J	Transport Allowance	TRA	= If (Emp Typ = "Sup" then 1000 else if (Emp type = "Nsup" then 500 else 0)) = IF(C12 = "Sup", I7, IF(C12 = "Nsup", I8,0))
K	Gross Salary	TE	BPE + DA + HRA + TRA = G12 + H12 + I12 + J12

N	Provident Fund	PF	= BPE * PF Rate (in %) = G12 * I9
O	Tax Deduction at Source	TDS	Value entered directly
P	Loan Repayment Inst.	LOAN	Value entered directly
Q	Total Deductions	TD	= PF = TDS + Loan = N12 + O12 + P12
R	Net Salary	NS	= TE – TD = K12 – Q12

In these applications, some of the formulae use absolute address. The absolute address is used for those cells whose content should not change while the formula containing such cells is copied to other cells.

- If-function is also used in these applications. If-function is used to implement different action corresponding to different conditions.
- The Excel functions SLN and DB are used for computation of depreciation using Straight Line Method (SLM) and Written down Value Method (WDVM), respectively. WDV Method is also termed as declining balance (DB) method.

GRAPHS AND CHARTS FOR BUSINESS DATA

GRAPHS AND CHARTS:-

A graph is a pictorial representation of data, which has at least 2 dimensional relationship. Therefore, a graph has at least two axes, X and Y. X-axis is usually horizontal while Y-axis is vertical. A graph may either be a single line graph or a multiple line graph.

A pie chart represents multiple sub-groups of single variable. A bar diagram depicts two or more variables.

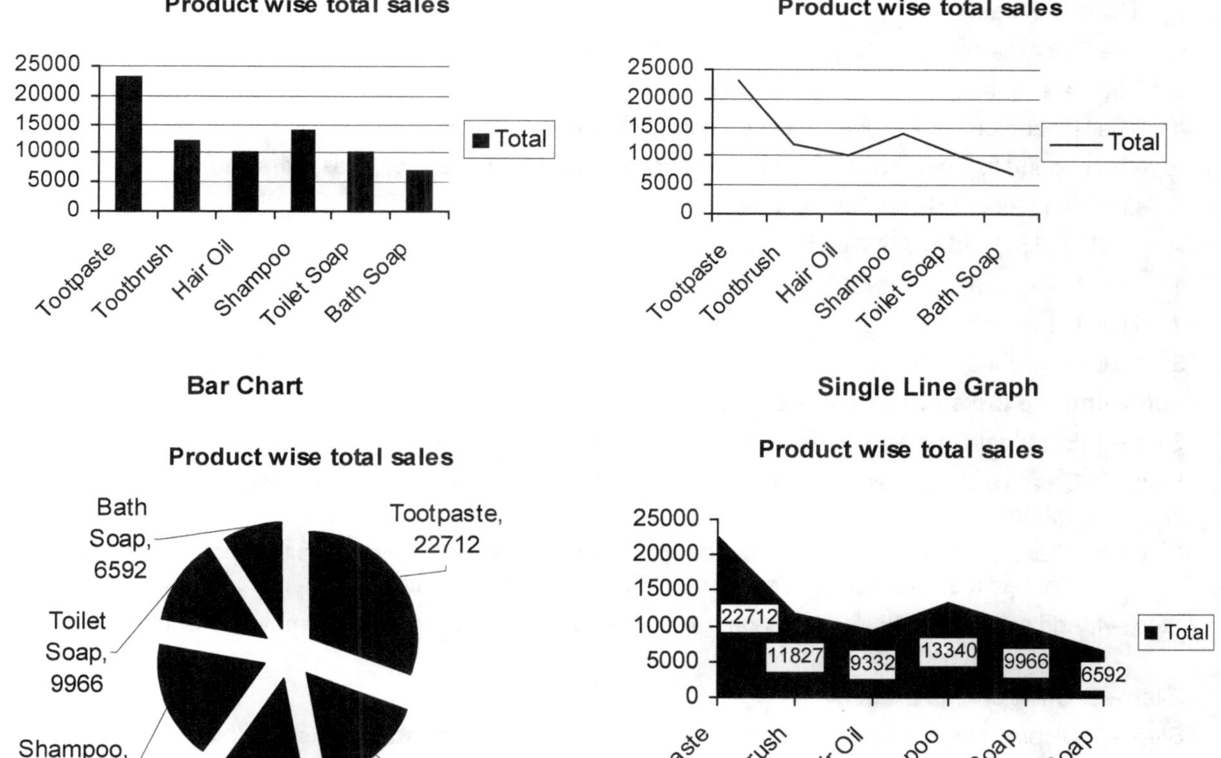

Bar Chart

Single Line Graph

Pie Chart

Area Chart

ELEMENTS OF A CHART/GRAPH:-

1. The chart area: The entire chart including all elements.
2. The plot area: In a 2-D chart, the area is bounded by the X and Y axes. In a 3-D chart, the area is bounded by the three (X, Y and Z) axes.
3. The data points: Individual values plotted in a chart and represented by bars, columns, lines, pie or various other shapes are called data markers.
4. The horizontal (category) and vertical (value) axis: The x-axis is usually the horizontal line which contains categories (independent values or categories) and y-axis is usually the verticals which contains data (dependent values).
5. The legend: It is an identifier of a piece of information shown in the chart/graph. The legends are assigned to the data series or different categories in a chart.
6. A chart and axes titles: Descriptive text for chart title (6-A) and axis title (6-B)
7. A data label: This provides additional information about a data marker to identify the details of data point in a data series.

A graph may be either a single line graph or a multi-line graph. Multi-line in a graph are distinguished either by using different shapes of line or different shapes and colors.

Doughnut: - Doughnut charts display data in rings, where each ring represents a data series.

Exploded Doughnut:- exploded doughnut charts display the contribution of each value to a total while emphasising individual values, but they can contain more than one data series

MS-Excel 2007 (or simply Excel) provides a convenient facility to draw graphs and charts. The nomenclature used in Excel for charts (charts include graphs) are as follows:

a. The Chart Area,
b. The Plot Area covering the plot of values in the selected type of chart,
c. The Data Points,
d. The Horizontal (Base Values, e.g. category) and Vertical (Derived Values) Axes,
e. The Legend to specify distinguishing criteria in case of multiple lines, pies, bars, etc.
f. Chart and Axes Titles g. Data Labels

ADVANTAGES IN USING GRAPH/CHART:-

1. Help to Explore
2. Help to Present
3. Help to Convince

Following are the steps prepare a chart:

Step – 1: Enter data in a worksheet with proper column and row titles.

Step – 2: Create a basic chart using the pattern from the panel available on top of worksheet in Chart groups' option.

Step – 3: Change the layout or style of chart. Apply a predefined chart layout. Apply a predefined chart style. Change the layout of chart elements. Change the format of chart elements.

Step – 4: Add or remove titles or data labels. Add (Remove) a chart title. Add (Remove) axis titles. Link a title to a worksheet cell. Add (Remove) data labels.

Step – 5: Show or hide a legend.

Step – 6: Display or hide chart axes or gridlines. Display (hide) primary axes Display (hide) secondary axes Display (hide) gridlines

Step – 7: Move (resize) a chart

Step – 8: Save a chart

DATABASE MANAGEMENT SYSTEM FOR ACCOUNTING:-

Database is a general term for any collection of related information stored in a logical way on a computer. A number of general purpose database programmes are available for PCs of which the best known is probably Microsoft's Access. Using such software one can define new databases enter information and process the information in various ways. One of the most important processing operations is to search for data that matches certain criteria. In the transactional database model, the database is divided into a number of tables. Each table consists of a number of records.

Types of Database

1. Relational Database: The most important type of database is the relational database. It is a tabular database in which data is defined so that it can be reorganized and accessed in a number of different ways.
2. Distributed Database: A distributed database is one that can be dispersed or replicated in a different point in a network.
3. Object Oriented Database: An object oriented database is one that is congruent with the data defined in object classes and sub-classes.

In Access, the term database refers to a single file that contains a collection of information. A database consists of the following objects

1. Tables: Tables store data in a row-and-column format similar to spreadsheets. Every table in a database focuses on one subject, for example, products, customers, students etc. Each row or record in the table is a unique instance of the subject of the table.
2. Queries: Queries extract data from a table on user-defined criteria. They enable us to view' fields from more than one table.
3. Forms: Forms display and print data from a table(s) or a query based on a user-defined custom format. Forms enable us to view, edit and print data.
4. Reports: Reports display and print data from a table(s) or query based on a user-defined custom format.
5. Pages: Pages can be posted on a website of an organisation using the internet or sent via email to someone on the organisation network.
6. Macros: Macros automate common database action based on user-specified commands and events.
7. Modules: Modules automate complex operations and give a programme more control than macros. Modules are procedures written in Visual Basic or Applicat on Programming Language.
8. Capabilities of MS Access: Access has certain capabilities, which bring it closer to an ideal Database Management System.

Exercise

1. To designate a primary key __________ click on a field to open a sub menu
   (a) Top (b) Right
   (c) Left (d) Bottom
2. A numeric data analysis tool that allows us to create a computerized ledger.
   (a) Spreadsheet package (b) Mathematical package
   (c) Word package (d) Graphical package
3. By default ,worksheets that are present in a computer excel workbook are
   (a) 4 (b) 10
   (c) 6 (d) 3
4. The data storage system which remains hidden from the user and responds to the requirement of the user to the extent the user is authorised to access is known as:
   (a) Back-end database (b) Front-end database
   (c) Data processing (d) Reporting system
5. Which bars have shortcut icon for frequent done tasks in spreadsheet?
   (a) Main toolbar (b) Object bar
   (c) Menu bar (d) None of the above
6. A spread sheet is also known as ____________
   (a) Work book (b) Work area
   (c) Work sheet (d) Spread book
7. Where is the address of the active cell displayed?
   (a) Row heading (b) Status Bar
   (c) Name Box (d) Formula Bar
8. A formula must starts with a ___________ sign
   (a) = (b) >
   (c) * (d) {}
9. Which function automatically totals a column or row of Values?
   (a) TOTAL (b) ADD
   (c) SUM (d) AVG
10. In column chart, the X-axis shows
    (a) Value of each category (b) Different categories
    (c) Height of the chart (d) Depth of the value
11. ________ Chart is similar to the column chart, with the difference being that the data series are displayed horizontally
    (a) Line chart (b) Pie chart
    (c) Bar chart (d) Area chart
12. In 3D chart X, Y & Z axes are used to show
    (a) Category, Value, Total (b) Depth, Vertical, Horizontal
    (c) Length, Breadth, Depth (d) Category, Value, Series.

13. The full form of DDL is
    (a) Dynamic Data Language
    (b) Detailed data Language
    (c) Data Definition Language
    (d) Data Derivation Language
14. ____________ command is used to remove a relation from an SQL
    (a) Delete
    (b) Remove
    (c) Purge
    (d) Drop table
15. In which of the following formats data is stored in the database management system?
    (a) Image
    (b) Graph
    (c) Table
    (d) None of the above
16. MS Access is a:
    (a) Word processing Software
    (b) Presentation Software
    (c) Spread sheet Software
    (d) Data Base Management Software
17. 'Join line' in the context of Access Tables means:
    (a) Graphical representation of relationship between tables
    (b) Lines bonding the data within table
    (c) Line connecting two fields of a table
    (d) Line connecting two record of a table
18. The 2D graph using _______, _________ axes and in 3D graph ______ axis is also used.
    (a) Category, value, vertical.
    (b) Horizontal, vertical, depth.
    (c) Category, value, series.
    (d) b and c both.
19. What do you see if you move over the mouse over a chart object?
    (a) Key Tip.
    (b) ScreenTip
    (c) Chart Tip.
    (d) Chart Key.
20. When Extend Selection is active, what is the keyboard shortcut for selecting all data up to and including the last row?
    (a) [Ctrl]+[Down Arrow].
    (b) [Ctrl]+[Home].
    (c) [Ctrl]+[Shift].
    (d) [Ctrl]+[Up Arrow].
21. Which of these is not an argument of the IF function?
    (a) Logical_test.
    (b) Value_if_false.
    (c) Value_when_false.
    (d) Value_if_true.
22. Which key combination collapses the ribbon?
    (a) [Ctrl]+[F1]
    (b) [Ctrl]+[F3]
    (c) [Ctrl]+[F5]
    (d) [Ctrl]+[F7]
23. When navigating in a workbook, which command is used to move to the beginning of the current row?
    (a) [Ctrl] + [Home]
    (b) [Page Up]
    (c) [Home]
    (d) [Ctrl] + [Backspace]
24. Which function results can be displayed in Auto Calculate?
    (a) SUM and AVERAGE
    (b) MAX and LOOK
    (c) LABEL and AVERAGE
    (d) MIN and BLANK
25. How many blank worksheets are shown when a new workbook is created?
    (a) One
    (b) Two
    (c) Three
    (d) Four

26. The CAS should be

(a) Simple and integrated, transparent, accurate, scalability, reliability;

(b) Complex, Accurate, Transparent, Faster to work;

(c) Able to transform the manual accounting system to computerised accounting system;

(d) None of the above.

27. What is the activity sequence of the basic information processing model?

(a) Organise data, process data, and collect data

(b) Collect data, organise and process data, and communicate information

(c) Process data, organise data, and collect data

(d) Organise data, collect data, and communicate information

28. Where are amounts owed by customers for credit purchases found?

(a) Accounts receivable journal
(b) General ledger
(c) Sales journal
(d) Accounts receivable subsidiary ledger

29. Which of the following is a function of DBMS

(a) Storing data
(b) Data integrity
(c) Providing multi –users access control
(d) All of the above

30. Faster way to change horizontal alignment in a computer document is

(a) Alight left
(b) Center
(c) Align right
(d) All of these

Topic Test – 1

1. What is the activity sequence of the basic information processing model?

(a) Organise data, process data, and collect data

(b) Collect data, organise and process data, and communicate information

(c) Process data, organise data, and collect data

(d) Organise data, collect data, and communicate information

2. Codification of Accounts required for the purpose of:

(a) Hierarchical relationship between groups and components

(b) Data processing faster and preparing of final accounts

(c) Keeping data and information secured

(d) None of the above

3. Which mathematical operator is represented by an asterisk (*)?

(a) Exponentiation
(b) Addition
(c) Subtraction
(d) Multiplication

4. What category of functions is used in this formula: = PMT (C10/12, C8, C9,1)

(a) Logical
(b) Financial
(c) Payment
(d) Statistical

5. When Extend Selection is active, what is the keyboard shortcut for selecting all data up to and including the last row?

(a) [Ctrl]+[Down-arrow]
(b) [Ctrl]+[Home]
(c) [Ctrl]+[Shift]
(d) [Ctrl]+[Up Arrow]

6. Which formulae would result in TRUE if C4 is less than 10 and D4 is less than 100?

(a) =AND(C4>10, D4>10)
(b) =AND(C4>10, C4<100)
(c) =AND(C4>10, D4<10)
(d) =AND(C4<10, D4, 100)

7. Where is the address of the active cell displayed?
   (a) Row heading (b) Status bar
   (c) Name Box (d) Formula bar
8. Which of the following arguments in a financial function represents the total number of payments?
   (a) FV (b) PV
   (c) Nper (d) Rate
9. Which function results can be displayed in Auto Calculate?
   (a) SUM and AVERAGE (b) MAX and LOOK
   (c) LABEL and AVERAGE (d) MIN and BLANK
10. When navigating in a workbook, which command is used to move to the beginning of the current row?
   (a) [Ctrl]+[Home] (b) [Page Up]
   (c) [Home] (d) [Ctrl]+[Backspace]
11. The DBMS acts as an interface between __________ and __________ of an enterprise class system
   (a) Database application and the database (b) The user and the software
   (c) Application and SQL (d) Data and the DBMS
12. Vertical dimension of a computer spreadsheet is called a __________
   (a) Row (b) Field
   (c) Column (d) Block
13. The Computerised Accounting System refers to
   (a) Printing of Balance Sheet and Profit and Loss Accounts using computer;
   (b) Processing of accounting transaction through computer and produce records and reports;
   (c) Processing of accounting related data and printing reports;
   (d) None of the above.
14. The components of Computerised Accounting System refers to :
   (a) Business transactions are analysed, transactions recorded, prepare trial balance, preparation of balance sheet and profit and loss account;
   (b) From data entry to preparation of final statements;
   (c) Transformation of manual accounting system to CAS;
   (d) None of the above.
15. What are internal controls designed to do?
   (a) Safeguard assets and optimise the use of resource
   (b) Only achieve maximum revenue
   (c) Only safeguard assets
   (d) Only ensure accurate accounting records
16. **Match with the correct option :-**

1. Rows	a. intersection of a row and a column
2. Columns	b. numerical numbers from top to bottom
3. Cell	c. unique identification code of a cell
4. Cell address	d. alpha characters from left to right

   (a) 1- b , 2-d , 3-a , 4-c (b) 2-b , 3-c , 1-a , 4-d
   (c) 1-d , 2-a, 3-b , 4-c (d) 1-b , 2-a , 3-c , 4- d

17. Which of the following is correct according to the technology deployed by DBMS?
(a) Pointers are used to maintain transactional integrity and consistency
(b) Cursors are used to maintain transactional integrity and consistency
(c) Locks are used to maintain transactional integrity and consistency
(d) Triggers are used to maintain transactional integrity and consistency

18. In a computer spreadsheet absolute cell reference can be represented as
(a) B3 (b) B3
(c) B$3 (d) None of the above

19. Title bar in MS-excel displays name of the
(a) Formula (b) Workbook
(c) Worksheet (d) All of the above

20. Graphical representation of data is known as ___________
(a) chart (b) graphics
(c) Pictures (d) Figures

21. In a computer spreadsheet, SUM, AVG, MIN and MAX are the examples of
(a) Formulas (b) Calculation
(c) Relations (d) Functions

22. Address of first cell in the worksheet is ___________
(a) A (b) A1
(c) A0 (d) None of the above

23. The common fields used in a relationship between tables are called:
(a) Joint fields (b) Main fields
(c) Key fields (d) Table fields.

24. Which two files are used during operation of the DBMS?
(a) Query language and utilities (b) Data manipulation language and query language
(c) Data dictionary and transaction log (d) Data dictionary and query language

25. The intersection of rows and columns creates
(a) Worksheets (b) Spreadsheets
(c) Cells (d) None of these

Topic Test – 2

1. Give a suitable name to the diagram

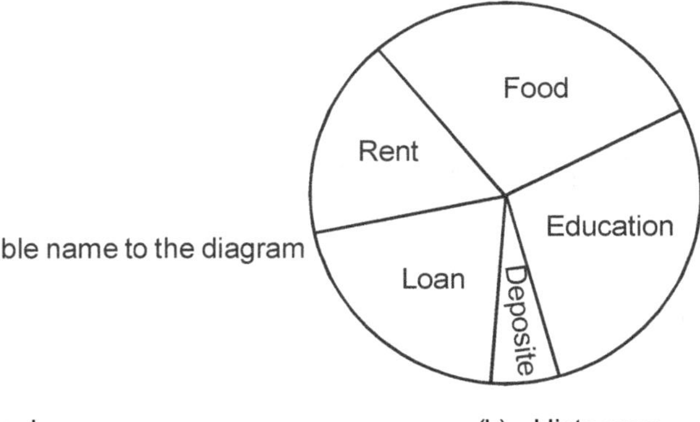

(a) Bar Graph (b) Histogram
(c) Pie chart (d) Single line graph

2. The Grouping of Accounts means the classification of data from :
   (a) Asset, liabilities and capital
   (b) Asset, capital, liabilities, revenue and expenses
   (c) Asset, owners' equity, revenue and expenses
   (d) None of the above.
3. The need of Codification is :
   (a) The Encryption of data
   (b) The Generation of mnemonic code
   (c) To secure the accounts, reports, etc.
   (d) Easy to process data, keeping proper records
4. Which view shows margins and the rulers?
   (a) Normal (b) Page Layout
   (c) Page Setup (d) Review
5. When navigating in a workbook, which command is used to move to the beginning of the current row?
   (a) [Ctrl]+[Home] (b) [Page Up]
   (c) [Home] (d) [Ctrl]+[Backspace]
6. Which cell alignment is assigned to most values by default?
   (a) Right (b) Left
   (c) Centre (d) Decimal
7. Which step completes an entry and moves the pointer to the cell to the right?
   (a) Pressing [Enter] (b) Pressing [Tab]
   (c) Pressing [Shift]+[Tab] (d) Pressing [Shift]+[Enter]
8. What category of functions is used in this formula: =PMT(C10/12, C8, C9,1)
   (a) Logical. (b) Financial.
   (c) Payment. (d) Statistical.
9. In what cell is the Rate for PMT function where =PMT (C8, C9, C10, C11, C12)?
   (a) C8. (b) C9.
   (c) C10. (d) C12
10. The Ribbon allows us to:
   (a) Create either an embedded chart or a chart sheet chart:
   (b) Create only an embedded chart.
   (c) Create only a chart sheet chart.
   (d) Change the data values used to create the chart.
11. Excel automatically redraws the chart ___________:
   (a) If any change is made in data. (b) If any change is made in the range data.
   (c) a and b both. (d) None of the above.
12. Which chart element details the data values and categories below the chart?
   (a) Data point. (b) Data labels.
   (c) Data marker. (d) Data table
13. SQL stands for:
   (a) Simple Questions Language (b) Simple Que line up
   (c) Singular Quantity Loading (d) Structured Que Language

14. The default extension of MS Access (2007) file is :
(a) .accbd (b) .exl
(c) .doc (d) .exe

15. In a computer spread sheet, which is true if current or active cell is B4 and you pressed enter key?
(a) You will be in the cell in A1 (b) You will be in the cell in A5
(c) You will be in the cell in B1 (d) You will be in the cell in B5

16. Which among the following is the special feature of 3D chart
(a) Chart area (b) X & Y axes
(c) Chart wall (d) Legend

17. __________ is a relational database management system
(a) Office (b) Ms excel
(c) Base (d) None of the above

18. Text {VARCHAR} data type accepts ____________ data.
(a) Binary (b) Calendar
(c) Numeric (d) Alpha numeric

19. Database in Libre Office Base is called ________
(a) Data group (b) Mass Data
(c) Rows and columns (d) Data Source

20. _________are used to store the data in the database
(a) Reports (b) Forms
(c) Tables (d) Queries

21. Which among the following is not a DBMS?
(a) Base (b) Access
(c) Oracle (d) None of these

22. The placement of information within a cell at the left edge, right edge or centered is
(a) Identification (b) Placement
(c) Alignment (d) All of the above

23. The cell that is in use is referred as ___________
(a) Formula cell (b) Highlighted cell
(c) Active cell (d) Main cell

24. In 3D chart X, Y & Z axes are used to show
(a) Category, Value, Total (b) Depth, Vertical, Horizontal
(c) Length, Breadth, Depth (d) Category, Value, Series.

25. Data is :
(a) Information (b) Collection of facts
(c) Both (a) and (b) (d) None of these

Answer Keys

Exercise

1. (b)	2. (a)	3. (d)	4. (a)	5. (b)	6. (c)	7. (c)	8. (a)	9. (c)	10. (b)
11. (c)	12. (d)	13. (c)	14. (d)	15. (c)	16. (d)	17. (a)	18. (c)	19. (c)	20. (c)
21. (c)	22. (a)	23. (c)	24. (a)	25. (c)	26. (a)	27. (b)	28. (d)	29. (d)	30. (d)

Topic Test – 1

1. (b)	2. (a)	3. (d)	4. (b)	5. (c)	6. (d)	7. (c)	8. (c)	9. (a)	10. (c)
11. (a)	12. (b)	13. (b)	14. (a)	15. (a)	16. (a)	17. (c)	18. (b)	19. (b)	20. (a)
21. (d)	22. (b)	23. (c)	24. (c)	25. (c)					

Topic Test – 2

1. (c)	2. (b)	3. (a)	4. (b)	5. (c)	6. (b)	7. (b)	8. (b)	9. (a)	10. (d)
11. (c)	12. (b)	13. (d)	14. (a)	15. (d)	16. (c)	17. (c)	18. (d)	19. (d)	20. (c)
21. (d)	22. (c)	23. (c)	24. (d)	25. (b)					

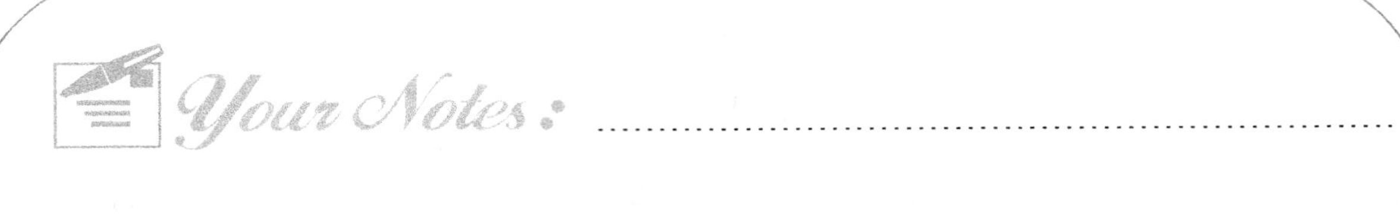
Your Notes :

www.ingramcontent.com/pod-product-compliance
Lightning Source LLC
LaVergne TN
LVHW080819170826
845678LV00011B/2083